THE SUPREME CONTROL AT THE
PARIS PEACE CONFERENCE 1919

LORD HANKEY

THE SUPREME CONTROL

AT THE PARIS PEACE CONFERENCE 1919

A Commentary

London
GEORGE ALLEN AND UNWIN LIMITED

FIRST PUBLISHED IN 1963

PRINTED IN GREAT BRITAIN
in 12 on 13 point Fournier type
BY UNWIN BROTHERS LIMITED
WOKING AND LONDON

CONTENTS

I From War to Peace   *page* 9

II President Wilson's Visit to London   15

III The Build-up of the Conference Organization   21

IV The Conference and the Dominions   32

V The First Plenary Meetings   42

VI The Conference and Russia   49

VII German Colonies and Dominions Mandates   55

VIII The Churchill Intervention   67

IX The Foreign Ministers Speed up the Conference   74

X Accumulating Difficulties   82

XI Military Terms of Peace   87

XII Origin of the Council of Four   97

XIII Summit Reorganization   107

XIV Italy's Claims: Orlando's Dilemma   120

XV Completion of the Draft Treaty with Germany 134

XVI The Presentation of the Treaty   150

XVII Mandates and the Austrian Treaty   156

XVIII The Greek Episode and Italian Claims   162

XIX Changes in Procedure   167

XX Will the Germans Sign?   172

XXI The Signing   182

EPILOGUE   194

INDEX   199

CHAPTER I

FROM WAR TO PEACE

'Daddy, what is it like in time of peace?' A question in
1918 from a child born in 1914.

AT the eleventh hour of the eleventh day of the eleventh month of the
year 1918, when the German Armistice was signed, I was bedridden
in my home at Limpsfield, Surrey, stricken down by that deadly type
of influenza that was sweeping over the world, and which is said to
have caused more deaths than the war itself. I had contracted the
disease on arrival from the Armistice discussions in Paris. Adeline, my
wife, also became desperately ill, and every member of my household
caught the infection, but all recovered eventually, except a daily
woman who, to our great distress, died.

Before I was out of the convalescent stage, I had to take a difficult
decision, for on November 17th Lloyd George sent his famous Rolls-
Royce car, which had once belonged to Kitchener, with a peremptory
demand that I should return in it to his home at Walton Heath. Defying
the doctor and my wife, I obeyed, and lunched alone with Mr and Mrs
Lloyd George and their two daughters. After thanking me again and
again for my help in the war, Lloyd George asked if I would like to go
into political life, and offered me a ministerial appointment in the
Reconstruction Cabinet he was hoping to form if he won the General
Election. I declined at once, as I had no liking for party politics. I did
not conceal my hope that, in the interests of efficiency, he would
project the system of a War Cabinet Secretary into his peace Cabinet,
and that I should be appointed to the post. I thought that Lloyd George
looked relieved. I never regretted my decision, and believe that my
instinct was right, and that I was able to serve my country better in
the pivotal official posts that I was destined to hold than in politics.

About this time I received enough congratulations to turn anyone's
head. They began with the following resolution taken on November
5th by the War Cabinet, which reached me during my illness:

The War Cabinet decided:
To record upon their minutes their warm appreciation of the remarkable

work done by their Secretary, Sir M. Hankey, KCB, in producing for their information, within so short a time and in the midst of such heavy labours, the notes which he had circulated of the Versailles deliberations and conversations.

On November 12th I received, *in absentia*, as I was not fit to travel, an honorary LL D from Birmingham University, of which Lord Robert Cecil was Chancellor. I learned also that I had been accorded the order of Commendatore of the Crown of Italy.

A day or two later, out of the blue, came the following letter from Asquith in his own hand:

My dear Hankey,

I was lunching *en famille* at the Palace today, and the question was propounded as to whom we owed the most for the success of the war. I replied without any hesitation; to yourself and Cowans.[1] And I am glad to say that the King heartily assented to my opinion.

No one knows as well as I how much we owe to you for our (ignorantly derided) pre-war preparations; nor the extent and value of your daily, and almost hourly contribution, during the first two and a half years, to every measure, in all spheres, that was thought out and done. I know that you have continued to the end, under a constant strain which cannot be measured, to render the same invaluable service.

I should like you to know that, in my judgment, you have been in a true sense (what Carnot was called) 'the organizer of victory'.[2]

Yours always sincerely,

(Sgd.) H. H. ASQUITH.

A week later, still rather feeble after my influenza, I was in my office grumbling at having to come to Town on a fine and sunny Saturday morning to clear up some War Cabinet Minutes, when, about noon, I received a command for an audience with King George V at such short notice that I had to go to Buckingham Palace in my rubbly old office uniform. In the most gracious manner imaginable, His Majesty thanked me for my war work.

I also had wonderful letters from Milner, Curzon, Esher, F. S. Oliver of the *Round Table* (a strong critic of Asquith), and many other distinguished people—but self-glorification has already gone too far, and I refrain from quoting them.

[1] Lieut.-Gen. Sir John Cowans, GCMG, KCB, MVO, Quartermaster-General of the Forces throughout the war.
[2] The last sentence was printed in the cover to *The Supreme Command, 1914–1918*.

Very soon it became clear that Lloyd George intended that I should fill some important rôle at the Peace Conference, but he had not yet cleared his mind on the subject in detail. I was very anxious not to tread on the toes of my old friend Viscount Hardinge of Penshurst, who, as Permanent Under-Secretary at the Foreign Office, and responsible for the elaborate plans and preparations for the Conference, was entitled to a first-rate post. As early as November 22nd I had a long talk with him at the Foreign Office, and we agreed that the best plan would be that I should look after the collective secretarial needs of the British and Dominion delegates, while he should be in charge of all Conference arrangements. Although I worked hard for that, it was not to be. It was a very delicate matter, because Lloyd George insisted on reversing the arrangement,[1] with the result that I became the British Secretary of the Paris Peace Conference, and Hardinge became the head of the British Official Delegation.

In his speech (March 22, 1775) on conciliation with the Colonies Edmund Burke said:

The proposition is peace. Not peace through the medium of war; not peace to be hunted through the labyrinth of intricate and endless negotiations; not peace to arise out of universal discord . . .; not peace to depend on the juridical determination of perplexing boundaries of a complex government. It is simple peace, sought in its natural course, and in its ordinary haunts—it is peace sought in the spirit of peace, and laid in principles purely pacific.

It is rare that a peace such as Burke demanded can be achieved in the atmosphere of bitterness, hate, revenge and acute nationalism that follows a great war like that of 1914–18, especially when a large number of nations is concerned in the peace-making. During World War I there had never been anything approaching the 'unconditional surrender' of World War II. The national leaders of the victorious Powers had sought in their war aims to provide for a peace of justice rather than retribution. But in the weeks that elapsed between the Armistice and the first Plenary meeting of the Paris Peace Conference (January 18, 1919), the tendency was to stiffen up their terms. Criticism has sometimes been directed against the length of the interval. It was due to a number of circumstances. The collapse of our enemies had come more suddenly than anyone had expected. In Britain Lloyd

[1] *Vide infra*, chap. iii.

George had decided that a general election was necessary to give him a constitutional authority which he lacked owing to the fact that the existing Parliament had been elected in 1911 and had been led by Asquith until December 1916; he wanted his own and not Asquith's Parliament. Owing to the delay in bringing home the soldiers' votes from distant theatres of war, the results of the election were not due until December 28th, and after that the new government would have to be formed, a process which always takes time, especially in the case of a coalition. In the United States, President Wilson's desire to attend the Peace Conference in person involved delay. In France and Britain, the first reaction in responsible circles to that desire was unfavourable, owing to the fact that the President was not only the head of the Government, but also the Head of the State, and his coming might encourage a wish among other heads of states to be present. In addition it would involve difficulties about precedence, even in the presidency of the Conference. These difficulties were overcome by Wilson's decision to attend, not as President of the United States, but as head of the American Government, and by his acceptance of Clemenceau as President of the Conference. But it was not until November 18th that the President finally announced his intention to make the trip. In Paris there was a very serious outbreak of influenza in November, which laid many people low, including Colonel House, Grew, the Secretary of the United States Commission to Negotiate Peace, and others. On December 9, 1918, Clemenceau said that 'the English elections, the French celebrations, and the official visits to Paris have made it absolutely impossible to begin these formal conferences before January 3rd or 4th'.[1]

On the whole the delay suited most of the nations. They needed time for choosing their delegates, organizing their delegations, arranging the conduct of affairs at home during the absence of political leaders, and in completing their cases for the Conference. In London the first step was to reassemble the Imperial War Cabinet in order to overhaul the war aims that had been agreed at earlier sessions. The first meeting was held on November 20th, but it is rather difficult to give a clear account of events because the continuity of the meetings was interrupted by meetings of the British War Cabinet which had important decisions to take, by an Inter-Allied Conference which was held in London between November 30th and December 2nd, and by President Wilson's visit to London just after Christmas, to say nothing

[1] *The Foreign Relations of the United States: The Paris Peace Conference, 1919*, vol. i, p. 144.

of the preoccupation of the Prime Minister and his colleagues with the general election.

One problem, however, in which Lloyd George was much interested, had to be taken up at once, namely, what was to be done about the Kaiser, who had taken refuge in Holland. The subject was first raised on November 20th by Curzon on his return from a visit to Paris, where he had discussed it with Clemenceau, though not in a very vindictive spirit. But Lloyd George, who felt strongly on the subject, took it up with great vigour. In his memoirs he deals with it at great length, but it is sufficient here to say that it was discussed at the War Cabinet, the Imperial War Cabinet and with Clemenceau and the Italian Ministers (Orlando and Sonnino), who were in London in connexion with the presentation of a Sword of Honour by the King to Foch on the latter's becoming a British Field-Marshal. At one point the subject was referred to the law officers of the Crown, on whose behalf Lloyd George's newly appointed Attorney-General, F. E. Smith (afterwards Lord Birkenhead), persuaded the War Cabinet and the Imperial War Cabinet to decide in favour of a trial. On December 2nd, Clemenceau and Orlando authorized him to send a telegram to President Wilson asking his assent to a telegram to the Government of Holland asking them to hand over the Kaiser for trial by an Allied court. The President agreed to co-operate and sent a similar telegram to Holland.

This episode, however, though popular at the moment, elicited criticism from Balfour, Sonnino, Borden, Botha and others. The sequel can be left until later.

After about December 15th meetings of the Cabinet and Imperial War Cabinet became fewer, and on December 17th I learned from Borden that the representatives of the Dominions were getting rather restive. He suggested that I should arrange for some meetings with British ministers. I had to tell him that at the moment it was very difficult as the Prime Minister and his colleagues were preoccupied with their constituents and general problems but I promised to do my best. Of course I reported at once to the Prime Minister and the Secretary of State for the Colonies (Walter Long), who on that very same day saw Borden separately; and that same afternoon Borden saw me again, after a talk with the Prime Minister, and expressed his warm thanks for what I had done.

About this time Lloyd George and most of his colleagues became completely engrossed in election business; Bonar Law, who was to have replaced him, fell ill and so I was able to slip off for a few days with my wife to Torquay, where I had relations, for a much needed rest.

CHAPTER II

PRESIDENT WILSON'S VISIT TO LONDON

'I was anxious that President Wilson should visit our island. Had he passed Britain on his way to the Peace Congress it might have seemed an unfriendly act. I have never been quite certain of his real attitude towards this country.' (D. LLOYD GEORGE, *The Truth about the Peace Treaties*, vol. 1, p. 156.)

ON our return from our holiday I found that there was still a good deal of dissatisfaction among the Dominions representatives, and Borden asked me again if I could not arrange for further meetings of the Imperial War Cabinet, but they accepted my explanation that business was still badly blocked by the heavy calls of the election campaign on the time of British ministers. However, I succeeded in arranging for a meeting next day, and as the result I was instructed to draft some conclusions on the subject of the German Colonies as a basis for discussion. This I did, and after I had spent the whole of December 21st in lobbying in succession Botha, Borden, Balfour, Massey and Hughes (who was tackled by Leo Amery), a concordat was reached on the basis of the nomination by the eventual League of Nations of mandatories for these territories with the exclusion of German South West Africa which would be taken over by the Union of South Africa, and the Pacific Islands which would be reserved for Australia and New Zealand. On the following day (Sunday, December 22nd) however, my hopes were dashed to the ground, when Lloyd George held my conclusions up until after his coming conversations with the American President. Still, they came in useful later.

By the time of Wilson's arrival in London on Boxing Day, 1918, the Imperial War Cabinet had covered most of the outstanding matters on which Lloyd George desired to have the views of his colleagues before his conversations. In his book Lloyd George reproduces the text of the account he gave to the Imperial War Cabinet a few days later of the talks that he with Balfour, and sometimes other colleagues, had with the President, as well as my notes of the discussion that ensued.[1] They are too long to repeat here, and only the briefest summary and a few extracts are given.

[1] *The Truth about the Peace Treaties*, vol. 1, pp. 185–202.

The President had given the impression that the League of Nations was the only thing he really cared much about. There was nothing in what he said which would in the least make it difficult for us to come to some arrangement with him. His mind was apparently travelling in very much the direction of the proposals advocated by Robert Cecil and Smuts. . . . What he was anxious about was that the League of Nations should be the first subject discussed at the Peace Conference.

On the freedom of the seas, the President, as we had expected, 'was very vague'. There was none of the missionary zeal that House had displayed at the armistice discussions. The President did not oppose Lloyd George's suggestion 'that the matter could be left for further consideration after the League of Nations had been established and proved its capacity in actual working'. It was a great relief to me to feel Lloyd George had been as successful as had Castlereagh before the Conference of Vienna in virtually excluding this thorny question from the Conference.

Lloyd George and the President 'agreed that the Conference should not separate before a definite provisional limitation of arma-ments had been imposed on Germany and her allies, a limitation which would enable them to maintain order in the troubled conditions of their territories but no more. Subsequently, Germany might raise at the League of Nations the question of revising the provisional limitation'. The President also suggested the abolition of conscription in Germany, except for the concession that, in the event of failure to raise by voluntary means the small army assigned to her, 'she might be allowed to make good the deficit by ballot'. As the result of dis-cussion by the Imperial War Cabinet, the CIGS (General Sir Henry Wilson) was asked to make a provisional recommendation for the strength of the military forces required by enemy countries to maintain order, and as to the manner in which they should be raised. The First Sea Lord (Admiral Sir Rosslyn Wemyss) was to do the same for enemy fleets.

The President 'was very much opposed to armed intervention' in Russia. 'He disliked the Archangel and Murmansk expeditions and would no doubt withdraw his troops from there.' Information was too defective to enable the western frontiers of Russia to be worked out. 'The President should be represented at the Conference', but favoured ascertaining what the Russian proposals were. On Turkey 'President Wilson had expressed himself in favour of the Turks being cleared out of Europe altogether, and of their place at Constantinople being taken by some small Power acting as a mandatory of the League of Nations.' The idea of the United States accepting a mandate in Turkey made no appeal to him.

'The President agreed that the German Colonies should not be returned to Germany, and that they should be put under some Power acting as a mandatory.' He did not contest that German South West Africa could not be separated from the Union of South Africa, but held that the position of Australia (and presumably New Zealand) in relation to the German Pacific Colonies was not quite the same. He was by no means prepared to accept the Japanese Treaty promising the German islands in the North Pacific to Japan, 'and was doubtful whether Japan could be admitted there even in the capacity of a mandatory Power'. Lloyd George and Balfour 'had not succeeded in moving him from that position'. The upshot of the discussion was thus summarized by Lloyd George: 'With regard to the colonies, he had left the matter by telling the President that the question would have to be fought out at the Conference, when the Dominions would be able to present their own case.'

On indemnities 'Lloyd George reported that he had found the President on the whole stiffer than on any other question. The utmost concession he seemed inclined to make was that the claims for pure reparation should be tabled first, and that then other claims might possibly be considered afterwards.' Lloyd George's argument that that practically ruled out the British Empire in spite of the enormous burdens it had borne, 'failed to make any impression on the President'. The President had shown no inclination to raise the question (opened in the third of his fourteen points) of the removal of economic barriers.

Lloyd George had 'found President Wilson distinctly anti-Italian, as the consequence of conversations he had had with Sonnino . . . in any case it was clear that the President would strongly support the Jugoslavs against Italy'. Nor did Lloyd George 'think the President was prepared to tolerate schemes for the control of the west bank of the Rhine, though he might be prepared to accept the French annexation of the Saar valley'.

Regarding the proposed Inter-Allied Conference, Lloyd George reported that 'they had found the President entirely opposed to holding such a conference, at any rate formally. He considered that the general Peace Conference would be a sham if definite conclusions were simply arrived at beforehand, and these presented to Germany.

B

He was quite prepared to hold inter-Allied discussions in Paris between the Four Powers informally, and agreed that definite decisions would have to be arrived at then and presented to Germany at the Peace Conference. It really came to the same thing, but the President insisted definitely on his point of view.'

The President (to my own relief) supported the attitude already taken up by House in Paris that 'English and French should both be the official languages, and that the reports of the Conference should be published in both languages'.

Lloyd George observes in his memoirs that 'the account of the Buckingham Palace conversations with the President produced a worse impression on the minds of the (Imperial War) Cabinet than the actual interview had on mine'.[1] By far the most powerful criticism came from Hughes, the Prime Minister of Australia, the official report of whose remarks (which was only a summary) is reproduced in Lloyd George's account.[2] Much of it is devoted to a caustic warning 'that if we were not very careful we should find ourselves dragged quite unnecessarily behind the wheels of President Wilson's chariot'. 'Speaking for Australia, he wanted to know what Australia was to get for the sacrifices she had made. When he had secured what he wanted, the freedom of the seas as we knew it and meant to have it, and necessary guarantees for the security and development of the Empire and reparation and indemnities,[3] then he would have no objection to handing over other matters to a League of Nations. . . .' As for the German Colonies 'President Wilson was talking of a problem he did not really understand. New Guinea was only eighty miles from Australia. . . . The people of Australia were united on the retention of these islands.'

Many of those present agreed with much of what Hughes said. Austen Chamberlain wanted 'a British Monroe Doctrine for the South Pacific'. Curzon and Walter Long strongly supported the Australian Prime Minister. Churchill wanted America to let us off our debt and return the bullion and scrip we had handed over, on condition that we did the same to our allies. If that were done we might go some way

---

[1] *The Truth about the Peace Treaties*, vol. 1, p. 201.   [2] *Ibid.*, pp. 194-7.'

[3] It must be mentioned at this point that at about this time the question of reparation (indemnities) was referred by Lloyd George to a committee composed of Hughes (chairman), Walter Long, Sir G. E. Foster (Canadian Minister of Finance), W. A. S. Hewins, the economist, Lord Cunliffe, Governor of the Bank of England and Herbert Gibbs of the firm of Antony Gibbs and Son.

to meet the President's views on indemnity. Borden brought the Imperial War Cabinet back to the importance of good relations with the United States which were 'the best asset we could bring home from the war'. A policy of co-operation with some European nation against the United States would not have the support of Canada, where it was held that 'as an Empire we should keep clear, as far as possible, of European complications and alliances'. That view was supported by Robert Cecil, who pointed out that we could not achieve a good understanding with the United States without adherence to the idea of a League of Nations.

At the last meeting of the Imperial War Cabinet held during Wilson's visit to discuss these matters, the following decisions were taken on the representation of the Dominions at the Peace Conference:

(a) Representatives of the British Dominions and India ought to be present at the opening session and at any other session of the Peace Conference or the Allied Preliminary Conference (should it be held) at which Belgium and other smaller Allied states were represented.

(b) The British Dominions and India should in all respects have the same powers as, and be on equal footing at the Conference with Belgium and other smaller Allied states.

(c) Lord Robert Cecil should recast the telegram to Paris on these principles.

(d) The Prime Ministers of the Dominions and the representatives of India should be placed on a panel from which part of the personnel of the British Delegation could be filled, according to the subject for discussion.[1]

These conclusions gave great satisfaction especially as we were deeply committed to them by the telegram to Paris, and as we shall see anon, they were faithfully observed.

No apology is offered for the length at which these matters have been treated. It is necessary in order to refute the allegation made twenty-seven years later that we were caught unprepared at the Peace Conference, and to show the beginnings of the realization and achievement of full nationhood by the British Dominions, a theme which will be found to run like a thread through this story.

The Royal Banquet to President Wilson at Buckingham Palace on December 27th is described in a note I made that night as a 'superb function, most beautiful and impressive'. At the reception of the guests

---

[1] *The Truth about the Peace Treaties*, vol. 1, p. 208.

I record that 'as I came up, the King said, "This is a very important person, the Secretary of the War Cabinet"; the President said "I am very pleased to meet you", and the Queen said "I am delighted to meet you at last, Sir Maurice" '. Little did I realize that that was the starting point of two of the most highly-prized memories of my life, and at the time 'I found myself absurdly tongue-tied. . . . After dinner I got myself put on the list to talk to the President, but, just as I was coming up, Curzon pressed in before me, and remained talking for the rest of the evening. I was sorry to miss my talk with the President, as I wanted to give my experience as Secretary of two Leagues of Nations, the Allied Conferences and the Imperial War Cabinet.' As a matter of fact I had a premonition (as all my life I have often had in the case of first meetings with distinguished people) that we were destined some time or another to close association, and I wanted an opportunity to size the President up. But I did not succeed in getting access to him either at the Palace or at the Guildhall, or the dinner at 10, Downing Street, next evening.

All day on December 28th the election results were coming in. According to my diary, Lloyd George

was almost stunned by his overwhelming victory and seemed really upset by Asquith's defeat. . . . Bonar Law admitted that he was not elated, but greatly sobered by the overwhelming success. . . . Balfour tried to persuade me to go with him to the Riviera on Monday. I told him I was tied to the Prime Minister. After the other guests had gone, he and I and Reading remained behind, and Balfour tried to persuade the P.M. to come to the Riviera, and he practically agreed, and said, 'I have requisitioned Hankey to go with me, wherever I go'.

December 29th. Drove home in the morning and packed for the Riviera, sending my bags back in the car to Town.

However, I never got to the Riviera, for the next entry is as follows:

December 31, 1918–January 5, 1919. At Criccieth with the Prime Minister and Philip Kerr. Long walks and scrambles; long talks about the membership of the new Cabinet; many drives about the constituency, interlarded with speeches in Welsh, cheers, and interminable conversations about local Welsh politics. On the whole a very delightful interlude, the Prime Minister being always gay and cheery in spite of his terrible task.

But I never really enjoyed a holiday without my wife, who needed a rest even more than I.

CHAPTER III

THE BUILD-UP OF THE CONFERENCE ORGANIZATION

'We had a bad passage, but I got a bunk and was all
right, and we had a desperately slow journey. I am
frightfully busy.' (Extract from a private letter dated
January 13, 1919.)

THAT laconic account of our journey to Paris on January 11th for
the opening of the Peace Conference was to prove prophetic of the
Conference itself and of my own part therein. The Conference had a
rough passage; I secured a good berth, and we had what seemed at
the time a desperately slow journey. Throughout the Conference I
was frightfully busy.

In Paris our material circumstances were agreeable, and are briefly
described in the following extract from a private letter home dated
January 18, 1919:

And now a word as to our life here. We have two vast hotels, the
Astoria, where most of the offices of the various departmental missions are,
and the Majestic, where they live—fine, modern hotels in every respect.
The Majestic has an annexe called the Villa Majestic. Here I live and have
my offices, though I have lunch and dinner in the hotel—for which we
get free coupons. I have a very fine bedroom and bathroom with lots of
hot water[1] and nice but rather dark offices.

The Hotel Majestic is a very lively place, all the most beautiful and
well-dressed society ladies appear to have been brought over by the various
departments. I do not know how they do their work, but in the evening
they dance and sing and play bridge! As a matter of fact I have been there
very little as I am in tremendous demand for lunch and dinner for business
purposes, and this hour before dinner today is the first leisure hour I have
had. I am off to dine at the Embassy—quietly.

Lloyd George and Balfour had flats in the Rue Nitot, five minutes'
walk from the Hotel Majestic, just opposite to Wilson's house in the
Place des États-Unis. The Foreign Office, who were responsible for
these arrangements, had done their work extremely well. There were
plenty of translators, interpreters, stenographers, typists, messengers,

---

[1] In England we were as short of coal as we were after the war of 1939–45, and hot water
was scarce.

motor cars and a security service that was efficient without being too obtrusive. There was even a confidential printing press tucked away somewhere in the Bois de Boulogne, of which I made great use. So on the evening of January 11th I settled down comfortably in the Villa Majestic with my wonderful private secretary, Sylvester, my trusted superintending clerk, Major (afterwards Lieut.-Col.) Rawlins, a few clerks and lady typists, and a small detachment of my own corps, the Royal Marines, responsible 'old soldiers' to act as messengers and to look after our security. Although my responsibilities soon increased, until a large part of the secretarial work of the Conference passed through my hands and necessitated larger staff, I remained to the end of the Peace Conference in the Villa Majestic, living above my office.

At the time of our arrival in Paris, the rôle for which I was to be cast was still undecided. Of course I had my own views. It was obvious that the representatives of the Dominions, who had devoted much time to consideration of terms of peace ever since the Imperial War Cabinet meetings of 1917, and especially since the Armistice, would be represented at the Conference in some shape or form, although details were not yet settled. I was equally certain that their deliberations were bound to continue during the Conference. The British Empire interested me more than the peace settlement, and it seemed to me appropriate, therefore, that I should continue the secretarial services to the Imperial War Cabinet for which I had been responsible for the previous two years; Hardinge had agreed as early as November 22nd.[1] The Dominions representatives, whom I consulted individually, gave me every encouragement, and Lloyd George authorized me to base my arrangements on that assumption, but beyond that he was enigmatic. I fancy he anticipated that my experience at the war-time international conferences and at the Supreme War Council would inevitably involve me in even greater responsibilities, and so it turned out from the very first day, Sunday, January 12, 1919. Strictly speaking, the Peace Conference was not yet in existence on that date. The leading statesmen of the Inviting Powers (France, Great Britain, Italy, Japan and the United States) had assembled a week or two in advance to put the final touches on the arrangements which had been started at the December meetings in London, and pursued through diplomatic channels. But these discussions had been mainly concerned with

[1] *Vide supra*, p. 11.

policy, and nothing had been settled about the organization or procedure of the Conference.

The Foreign Office Librarian, it is true, had prepared an ingenious diagram, rather resembling a spider's web, with the Supreme Council in the centre, and vast numbers of committees and sub-committees branching out. The Quai d'Orsay had also prepared a plan containing many practical suggestions, some of which took shape in the eventual organization. It reached me just in time to study on the journey to Paris, and, like the Foreign Office plan, it struck me as over-elaborate. My own views, formed long before, were to build up the organization on the pattern of the Supreme War Council, which had been modelled largely on our own War Council and Imperial War Cabinet. Part of it could be, and indeed was, adopted from the outset. I had hoped, however, that we should be given a day or two's grace in which to establish contact between the delegation staffs on a comparatively low level, in order to cement an orderly scheme before the heads came together formally, and we were plunged into the welter of the Conference.

To some extent it did work out that way, for, on arrival in Paris late on the evening of Saturday (January 11th), we learned that urgent decisions were required by Foch on certain military questions arising out of the Armistice and not directly connected with the Peace Conference, which would have to be disposed of before arrangements for the Peace Conference could be tackled.

I saw at once that this was the moment to spring my own plan of bringing into play the machinery of the Supreme War Council. It would be waste of time to drag the delegates of the five Powers, with the necessary experts, to their council chamber at Versailles to settle Foch's points, but it should not be difficult to bring the famous and highly efficient secretariat from Versailles to Paris. They would first take notes of the meeting of the Supreme War Council, and when that ended, they could, if the Quai d'Orsay agreed, be kept on to take the notes for a second meeting for the opening discussions pre-liminary to the Peace Conference. Lloyd George agreed at once. But was the time sufficient to arrange it? Our arrival on the Saturday was too late for effective action, and Sunday morning was not an auspicious opportunity. All I had time to do that Sunday morning, was to arrange with the Quai d'Orsay that Foch's business should be taken first, and to ensure that Henry Wilson would be there, and would do his best to collect the military representatives of the Supreme War Council and the four secretaries. In the event, at 2.30 p.m. Foch and Weygand, Henry Wilson and the American General Bliss were present, but there was no Italian military representative. Of the Council's secretariat, neither of the British secretaries (Major Caccia and Major Abraham) turned up, but the French Captain Portier, the American Mr Frazier, and the Italian Maggiore Jones—all first-class secretaries—were present. They were looked at rather askance, I thought, by Dutasta, the Secretary-General designate, and his French colleagues, and no wonder, for I had not had time to explain. Clemenceau, with whom I had a few words before the meeting, was quick to see the importance of keeping the two classes of business separate. He conducted the first part of the meeting as the Supreme War Council, and, when that was concluded, got the military representatives to retire, and after a short adjournment, started the Peace Conference discussions.

When the second meeting was over, in order to ensure that the records were kept as two separate meetings, I decided, late as it was, to dictate and circulate the minutes that evening. My little office was on its metal, and played up splendidly. Then Rawlins raised the point what title they should carry. Nothing had been decided on the subject, so I replied at random, 'The Council of Ten'. The name was never criticized and remained for years. My records of the two meetings, namely of the Supreme War Council and of the Council of Ten, were completed and circulated to all who had attended them soon after midnight, i.e. before anyone else had begun to work on them. Nothing remained to be done except to produce a French version, which was child's play for the Versailles secretariat. On January 13th I wrote home as follows:

I was too busy to write yesterday, as I was doing *all* the work of the Conference. I had to take single-handed first a Supreme War Council and then a 'hush-frocks' conference[1]—five hours on end. I was working until past midnight, dictating thirty pages of minutes.

A pardonable exaggeration perhaps, but it illustrates the state of my mind at the time.

On the next day, feeling rather guilty of an unwarranted intrusion on the responsibilities of the Secretariat-General, I was relieved to receive from Dutasta and his staff a warm welcome to my *fait accompli*; but I never learned whether they knew I had done the whole job

---

[1] A term coined by Henry Wilson for a secret meeting of ministers.

myself, or whether they attributed it to the three representatives of the Versailles secretariat, who had been present at both meetings. That day, January 13th, there was again urgent military business to be disposed of before the affairs of the Conference could begin. The Versailles team turned up, and the same procedure as on the previous day was adopted, except that the Supreme War Council team took charge unobtrusively from start to finish and I was able to drop out.

It was not until the morning meeting of January 15th, by which time the system was working satisfactorily, that it received the formal approval of the Council of Ten during a discussion on the rules of procedure for the Conference, which had been drafted by the Secretariat-General when 'Lloyd George observed the interpretation to be given to this clause was that the Secretariat should be organized on exactly the same lines as had been followed in the case of the Supreme War Council. The same organization should be continued. That organization had always worked very well.' (This was agreed to.)[1]

That decision gave official sanction to the plan and the Versailles team, with the addition of a secretary from the Japanese Delegation who only attended when Japanese delegates were present, kept the records of the Council of Ten throughout its existence. The Secretary-General, however, whose accommodation at the Quai d'Orsay was barely sufficient for his needs, could not find either a room or the clerical staff for this joint secretariat. With Lloyd George's approval, therefore, I offered the hospitality of the Villa Majestic. Thus from start to finish, the Villa Majestic served the needs of both the British Empire Delegation and the Council of Ten—and, eventually, of the Council of Four and the Council of Five (Foreign Ministers). In this latter respect it could almost be described as an outlier to the Secretariat-General.

Before leaving the subject, a tribute must be paid to the brilliant young officers and officials who constituted the group of secretaries. Major Anthony Caccia was originally a member of the Indian Forest Service, in which he reached high rank. Both before and after the war he was Director of Forest Studies in Oxford. He was proficient in French and Italian, a tremendous worker and a perfect 'mixer'—an ideal man for the job. Major Edgar Abraham, his colleague, was a distinguised Indian Civil Servant. Hailing from the Channel Islands, he had a perfect mastery of the English and French languages. Both of them, I am glad to say, were rewarded at the end of the Conference

[1] *The Foreign Relations of the United States: The Paris Peace Conference 1919*, vol. iii, p. 418.

by the CB. The French Secretary, Captain Portier, was a most likeable man of great tact and with a complete knowledge of English. He was an indefatigable worker. Maggiore Jones, as typically Italian as Major Caccia was British, was also a first-rate team worker, as were the American secretaries, Frazier, Mr L. Harrison and Colonel Grant. Mr Saburi, who joined up for Japan was destined to become one of my greatest friends. I cannot imagine a more perfect international group. Their comradeship was a joy to witness, their work flawless.

Although after the first day I had got rid of the drudgery of keeping the minutes of the Council of Ten, I was still responsible for the secretarial work for the British Empire Delegation, the title adopted for the prolongation into the Peace Conference of the Imperial War Cabinet meetings in London. During this preliminary week, the representation at the coming Peace Conference of the different states (including the Dominions and India) was one of the most contro- versial questions before the Council of Ten. The Dominions and India were fighting the battle of their future status, and the Empire Dele- gation was meeting daily. I was able, of course, to attend its meetings, but I soon realized that I could not possibly continue indefinitely to keep its records and to organize its work, because Lloyd George and Balfour insisted that I should accompany them (as I had done during the war) to the two daily meetings of the Council of Ten. I had also to marshal for them the experts for each meeting according to the subjects for discussion and to see that they were properly briefed. Where was I to get the help I needed for the British Empire Delega- tion? The answer is contained in the following letter home dated January 14, 1919:

My mind is chock full of a great scheme of Imperial development which I have actually carried out: that is to say, I have got approved that I shall have an assistant secretary from each Dominion for the work of the British Empire Delegation. As this is, for all practical purposes, the Imperial War Cabinet, it means that when I return home I shall continue the same procedure with the Imperial War Cabinet. In short—I have actually started a great Imperial Office. It is at this moment in existence. I have tried to do this for six years but circumstances have always blocked it. But I know that Milner favours it. I got the P.M. to agree on the plea that I was over- worked! The Canadians and Australians absolutely jumped at it, and at our meeting yesterday I had a Canadian assistant secretary. I am firing them with my own enthusiasm and shall just make things hum.

The next thing to be done was to depute some dependable person who shared my views to take charge of and organize this improvised Empire secretariat under my general direction. The officials nominated by the Dominions Prime Ministers were all busy men, namely, for Canada, Loring Christie (Legal Adviser to the Department of External Affairs); for Australia, Sir Robert Garran, Solicitor-General, and Lieut.-Com. J. Latham (afterwards Chief Justice for the Commonwealth and Deputy Prime Minister and much else); for New Zealand, F. D. Thomson, Massey's private secretary; for South Africa, Brebner and Captain E. F. C. Lane, private secretaries to Botha and Smuts respectively; for Newfoundland, W. J. Carew; and for India, C. H. Kisch of the India Office. None of them could have been spared whole-time, and my plan was that each Dominion should have one day a week 'on duty', during which its representative should perform all the secretarial duties of the Empire Delegation. A British secretary was, therefore, necessary to act as a permanent nucleus and chief organizer. For this purpose I was fortunate in obtaining the services of Clement Jones (afterwards Sir Clement Jones, KCB), who arrived in Paris from the War Cabinet secretariat on January 21, 1919, and at once took charge with the greatest enthusiasm and success. The responsibility was now in safe keeping, and I left him a free hand to work up the organization in consultation with his fine team of Dominions colleagues, which he did with the utmost efficiency. We allotted to this Dominions secretariat a charming, well-dressed and well-mannered young lady stenographer in the Villa Majestic, who, as she was also very expert in her job, contributed appreciably to the success of the experiment.

During this preliminary phase of the Peace Conference, an event occurred which was destined to exercise a great influence on my career. The rules of procedure drawn up at the Quai d'Orsay, and approved by the Supreme Council on January 15th, and by the Plenary Conference at the opening meeting on the 18th, provided, *inter alia*, for the nomination of a secretary from each of the delegations of the principal Powers to assist the French Secretary-General on the Bureau of the Conference. Lloyd George asked me to undertake the job for Great Britain. I asked to be excused on the ground of my arrangement with Hardinge, of which he was aware. He was adamant. So was I. I insisted that I would rather return to London than let down Hardinge. By the evening of Saturday (January 18th) the situation was difficult, and in spite of the success of the formal opening on that afternoon, I was deeply depressed.

Philip Kerr (the later Marquis of Lothian) brought me a peremptory order from Lloyd George that I must accept, and on his own account he begged me to find a way out of the difficulty. All that night I tried to worry it out, but I had to tear up all my drafts, and by Sunday morning (January 19th) I was thoroughly befogged. After a further failure I decided, in order to clear my mind, to take some exercise, and in the rain tramped to an *octroi* at the outskirts of Paris. At that dingy spot I saw in a flash the solution. A shabby old taxi soon brought me to the Villa Majestic. Sylvester, my private secretary and stenographer, by some happy chance had not gone out, and there and then I dictated at full speed a brief instruction, occupying no more than a single sheet of foolscap, to be issued by the Prime Minister on the organization of the British Delegation.

It began by designating Hardinge as 'Organizing Ambassador' and placing him in control of the elaborate organization at the Hotel Astoria, and ended with a laconic reference to myself as 'British Secretary to the Peace Conference'. That did the trick. That afternoon, Hardinge agreed, subject to minor modifications, if Balfour and the Prime Minister approved, and it was printed and circulated to the whole British Empire Delegation over Lloyd George's initials. The only trouble I had was with my close friend Lord Derby, the British Ambassador in Paris, who protested that there could not be two ambassadors in one capital and that the plan would undermine his own authority with the French. I explained that Hardinge's title as organizing ambassador would of course operate only within the zone of the Peace Conference, which might easily shift its location elsewhere (as afterwards it did to London, San Remo, etc.), and I guaranteed that he should not be interfered with as the channel of communication with the French Government. I said that he was in much greater danger from me, as British Secretary at the Conference, because I was already up to the neck in discussions at the Quai d'Orsay, but that he could rely on me not to pass outside Conference business. Eventually he agreed to give the new system a trial, and in practice no difficulty ever arose. Only in 1934, during a tour of the British Dominions, did I learn that the Prime Ministers of Canada, Australia, New Zealand and South Africa (particularly Botha) had insisted to Lloyd George on his nominating me as British secretary.

In order to strengthen my liaison with Hardinge and his organization, and to keep him fully informed of all that I was doing in my new and delicate rôle, I asked him to nominate three or four Foreign

Office officials to my staff. He nominated H. Norman, Eric Phipps who remained an intimate friend until the end of his life, Sir Percy Loraine, Bart., and the Hon. T. A. Spring-Rice, a most likeable person and brilliant pianist, who unfortunately died young. They soon became a tower of strength to my organization.

After the opening plenary meeting in the afternoon of January 18th the Preliminary Peace Conference as it was termed (for as yet it was only a Conference of Allies and Associated Powers), began to get into its stride. As already mentioned, and as I had always anticipated, the informal Conference of the Inviting Powers, known as the Council of Ten, which had spent the previous week in arranging preliminaries, automatically assumed to themselves the leadership and conduct of the Conference, without any resolution by the Plenary Conference. For the next two months it thus provided a 'steering committee' to the whole Conference, controlling and supervising the business, taking important decisions for approval, when necessary, to the Plenary Conference, giving preliminary hearing to the territorial and other claims of the various states; setting up expert commissions to report on those claims in detail; and examining the reports of those commissions, which, only too often, were unable to submit agreed solutions. Actually, like the British Cabinet, it had no constitutional or statutory basis. It was in effect a continuation of the system of conference that had gradually grown up during the war, and had culminated in the Supreme War Council.

On January 22nd I wrote home:

I am getting a most terrific hustle on, both in the Conference itself, and in the organization. . . . I found the whole place in a state of considerable chaos and inefficiency. I had a very delicate task to perform, as I had to reorganize it all without treading on the toes of Lord Hardinge. . . .

My methods were summarized in the following extract from a letter written on the next day (January 23rd):

- At 9.45 a.m. I have all my staff to my room, and I give them a whole mass of instructions on all the innumerable points of organization which have occurred to me, and which I have been jotting down in the little black note book that Robin[1] gave me for a Christmas present, with the pencil that Christopher[1] gave me. . . .

With Norman of the Foreign Office as deputy for this work, I also

---

[1] Two of my sons.

attended meetings with the French Secretary-General and his staff and with my 'opposite numbers' in the American, Italian and Japanese delegations who, with myself, formed the Secretariat-General. Although the meetings were nominally concerned with drafting the press communiqués, they provided an excellent opportunity to concert detailed arrangements on organizational matters.

My relations with my foreign colleagues were admirable, except on one point, namely, the language of the Conference. Lloyd George had instructed me to insist from the outset on English becoming at this Conference in all respects equal with French. Quite naturally, the French officials objected strongly to the displacement of French from the privileged position it had occupied so long as the language of diplomacy. They never ceased to urge its advantages in precision and nuance, and, quite rightly from their point of view, they fought tooth and nail to secure it as the sole official text for the proceedings of the Conference. But at the Peace Conference the case for the English language was overwhelming. The English-speaking countries—Great Britain, the Dominions and the United States of America—played a great part in the victory, and were, as was clear from the outset, going to play an equally important rôle in the making of peace. In Europe, the French language might still predominate, but in some countries outside Europe, where there were many problems awaiting settlement, English had a big lead. Between Chinese and Japanese, for example, English was commonly used as the language for diplomatic communication, and among French and other European peoples it was both a grievance and an acid jest that in China they found themselves compelled to acquire the barbarous 'pidgin English' in order to converse with their own domestics.

In the preparatory week preceding the opening of the Conference, after preliminary skirmishes in the Secretariat-General, where in co-operation with Grew I opposed the adoption of French as the sole official language, the matter was brought before the Council of Ten and discussed on January 19th for the greater part of the day. Unfortunately, Sonnino complicated the issue by insisting that, if there was to be more than one official language, Italian must be added. He could accept French as the sole official language in case of dispute, but not two official languages, which might give rise to difficulties of interpretation. Lloyd George and Wilson countered this by pointing out that Italian could not be accepted as a third official language without admitting Japanese as a fourth. Moreover, they said, Italian was not spoken widely outside Italy. British experience in Canada and South Africa, Lloyd George pointed out, did not support the argument of liability to disputes in interpretation, and Wilson reinforced him by quoting the experience of Switzerland with its three official languages.

Neither side would give way, and when the Conference opened on January 18th the subject remained undecided, and all mention of it had to be deleted from the draft regulations submitted to and approved by the Conference. But the question could not long remain dormant, as appears from the following extract from one of my letters home dated one week later (January 25th):

I spent the morning fighting the Secretary-General, who had issued the *procès-verbal* of the last Conference in French only, though he had formally promised me to send with it the English versions which I had all ready. I told him that, if it happened again, I should start my own distribution department, in which case I can always beat him by two days at least, because of the superiority of my 'machine'.

Actually, I carried out that threat by circulating the English version to the whole Conference on the morning of the 25th. But a much sharper rebuff was administered the same afternoon when Clemenceau announced that at the request of the delegation of the United States approval of the Protocol of the First Session was postponed until the next Session, as that delegation had not yet received the English text of Protocol No. 1, which it reserved the right to present to the Conference, and as a result it was not approved until February 4th. That proved decisive, and thereafter all the proceedings of the Conference were circulated simultaneously in French and English, and, by a process of *solvitur ambulando*, the French and English languages achieved an equal status throughout the whole series of the Peace Treaties. That status was eventually passed on to the League of Nations, and inherited by the United Nations. The struggle was not in vain.

CHAPTER IV

THE CONFERENCE AND THE DOMINIONS

'In all negotiations of difficulty a man may not look to
sow and reap at once, but must prepare business, and
so open it by degrees.' (BACON, *Essay xlviii—Of
Negotiation.*)

WITH great wisdom an understanding had been reached earlier that
Clemenceau, the President of the Council in France, should be the
President of the Conference. He took effective charge from the first
moment, and his position was never challenged. That was a most
admirable decision, for Clemenceau was one of the best chairmen I
have ever known—firm to the point of 'tigerishness' when necessary,
understanding, conciliatory, witty and a tremendous driver. His
leadership never failed from first to last, and was never questioned.
The value of a *permanent* chairman was the first great lesson that I
learned from the Paris Peace Conference, and, at all the other international conferences I attended in the next twenty years, either as a
secretary or secretary-general, I did my utmost to establish the principle—though not always successfully.

The secretary-general and the international secretariat of a great
conference have, necessarily, to take the initiative in fixing much of
the business, drawing up the agendas, securing an adequate documen-
tation for the Conference and its committees. If the 'big guns' try to
do this themselves, they usually make a mess of it. That work is
immensely strengthened if the secretary-general has behind him the
authority of a permanent whole-time chairman. The League of Nations,
the United Nations, and nearly all the post-World War II conferences
suffered from the insensate system of the changing president, which
can only be defended as providing for the *amour-propre* of second-
rate nations and statesmen. Lloyd George, Wilson and Orlando lost
nothing of their great prestige by accepting without question the
chairmanship of Clemenceau, and no one should hesitate to follow
their example!

As foreshadowed at the outset of the rather belated French Government note of January 5th, which had only reached me in the train en
route to Paris on January 11th, the early meetings dealt with in this
chapter were not part of the Peace Conference, but merely preparatory

meetings of the members of the Supreme Council of Versailles, to settle certain questions of form and substance such as:

1. Representation of belligerent and neutral states at the different stages of the negotiations.
2. Leading principles, and the order in which questions should be examined.
3. Organization of the work, including the Rules of Procedure, of which a sensible draft was attached. In the official record, they are described as 'conversations' and not as minutes, as in the case of those relating to the Supreme War Council.

Moreover, the French note suggested that there would be no question of enemy Powers being represented before the Allied and Associated Powers had agreed on the terms of peace, for we did not yet know who could validly negotiate on behalf of Germany, Austria-Hungary, Bulgaria and Turkey. All that was accepted from the first, though there were occasional misgivings how far the Inviting Powers ought to go at this stage in giving a lead to the Conference before the first meeting, which Clemenceau was anxious to hold at the earliest possible date.

The first question to be taken at the meeting on the afternoon of Sunday (January 12th) was the list of countries to be represented and how many delegates each should have. The French note had proposed:

Five each for each Great Power, Great Britain, United States, France Italy and Japan.

Two for each small belligerent Power (Belgium, Greece, Portugal, Roumania, Serbia, Siam), or Powers with a special interest (China, Brazil).

Two for each recognized new State (Poland, the Czechoslovakian Republic).

One for each small Power theoretically belligerent (Cuba, Panama, Liberia, Guatemala, Nicaragua, Costa Rica, Haiti, Honduras), or having simply broken off diplomatic relations (Bolivia, Peru, Uruguay, Ecuador).

One for each neutral State.

One for each State in process of formation.

The note recalled that, for the representation of the British Dominions, it had been decided in London on December 3rd, that their delegations should be admitted as additional members on the conditions in respect of members and participation adopted for small belligerent Powers.

C

There was a good deal of discussion on this list. The allotment in the draft of three representatives for Brazil, for example, was criticized on the ground that Brazil had not done much in the war, and had suffered little. Why, it was asked, should Brazil have more representatives than Belgium, which had fought hard throughout the war, and suffered cruelly, and which at the time was only to have two? Then Balfour, solicitous for the claims of our oldest ally, asked why Brazil should have more representatives than Portugal, her parent nation which had sent two divisions to the Western Front in Europe, and in addition had taken part in the fighting in Africa. But Wilson put up a hard fight for Brazil because of its size and power. Next, claims were raised for Serbia, which had suffered worse than Belgium, and, even after the German occupation, had raised new divisions that played a decisive part in the final campaign in Macedonia. But what about Greece, asked Lloyd George? She too had played a great part under Venizelos, throwing off the yoke of the pro-German Constantine. Roumania also had its champions, to say nothing of Poland and Czechoslovakia, which were in course of coming into existence before the end of the war.

All the time, from the very outset, Lloyd George was steadily keeping up the end of the Dominions—Canada, who had lost more men than Belgium; Australia, who had lost more men than the United States; New Zealand, with her wonderful fighting record; and South Africa, who 'had conquered their enemy', and fought many campaigns. India, too, he would not allow to be overlooked. Her armies had fought in every theatre of war, and the Native States alone had raised 180,000 men. They too must be represented.

That raised questions. Were not the five representatives allotted to the British Empire sufficient for the Dominions on the panel system? If, in addition, Canada was to have two, Australia two, South Africa two, New Zealand one or two and India two, as Lloyd George was demanding, the British Empire would, in effect, have fourteen or fifteen plenipotentiaries, against the five apiece for the United States, France, Italy, and Japan. The whole Conference would be thrown out of balance. As Wilson put it:

This question of representation was largely one of sentiment and psychology. If the Dominions were given this additional representation, the impression amongst those who did not know the full facts would be that they were merely additional British representatives. This impression would be especially strong among the small Powers. The Great Powers, to put the matter brutally, would appear to be running the Peace Conference.[1]

To all this, Lloyd George replied:

If five of the Dominions representatives were included in the British Delegation, Great Britain would have no representation at all. In his opinion, the smaller Powers ought to be satisfied with one representation apiece. In this case, he asked for the same representation for the Dominions and India. Take Australia for example. They had sent more men to the war than Belgium, Serbia or Roumania.

Later in this first meeting, he raised his claim to two for each Dominion and India, with one for Newfoundland. At his request the discussion was suspended in order to enable him to discuss it with the Imperial War Cabinet (British Empire Delegation).

When the subject was reopened at the meeting at 4 p.m. next day (January 13th), both Lloyd George and Wilson were in a more conciliatory mood. Lloyd George began by describing his talk with the Dominions Prime Ministers the same morning:

The latter were disappointed at the smallness of the representation allotted to them. They had not even received the same representation that had been granted to Belgium and Serbia, though they had supplied a larger number of troops, and their losses had been greater. He had explained quite frankly to them the reasons which had guided President Wilson in his desire not to accord a larger representation, as it would have the appearance of an over-representation of England, regarding her as a unit. He had informed them that they would be treated like the smaller States, and that one representative would be present whenever any question which affected them came under consideration. He had also agreed to add from time to time one or two of the Dominions representatives to the British panel of five.

Lloyd George also expanded on the claims of India.

This concession immediately elicited a conciliatory reply from Wilson. He

wished to remove any impression that he personally had any objection to the British Dominions being separately represented. He fully admitted that their claims were great. He had merely been guided by the desire to remove any cause of jealousy on the part of the other smaller States.

A little later in the discussion, the President went a step further by asking if Lloyd George would feel satisfied to give Canada two representatives, Australia two, South Africa two, and New Zealand one.

[1] *The Foreign Relations of the United States: The Paris Peace Conference 1919*, vol. iii, p. 483 *sq.*

Lloyd George agreed that such an allotment would be fair. But he would not care himself to make that proposal to the Conference. President Wilson said he would submit the proposal, and inquired whether Lloyd George would be satisfied if one representative was allotted to British India, and one to the Native States of India?

After Lloyd George had accepted, the conclusion was recorded as follows:

It was agreed that the British Dominions and India should have the right to be represented by the following number of Delegates:

Canada	2
Australia	2
South Africa	2
New Zealand	1
India, including Native States of India	2
Total	9

For Newfoundland, it was decided that, though it would not be given separate representation, a representative from that country could be included in the British Delegation.

Thus, by conciliatory diplomacy on the part of both Lloyd George and Wilson, a major obstacle to the launching of the Conference had been removed. The decision gave satisfaction to all the Dominions except one—New Zealand.

Massey, the Prime Minister of New Zealand, had been put in a quandary because the delegation selected by his Government included, in addition to the Prime Minister himself, Sir Joseph Ward, who was not only Minister of Finance and an ex-Prime Minister, but also leader of the other party in a coalition government. As a general election was due immediately after the Peace Conference, there had been a gentleman's agreement that they should have equal status at the Conference. As we shall see later, this dilemma did cause difficulties, but they were eventually solved by Lloyd George's nomination of Ward to fill one of the five British seats at the later Plenary meetings. This was rendered possible, and the claims of Morris of Newfoundland were also met by the inclusion of a special clause in the rules of the Conference providing that:

The representatives of the Dominions (including Newfoundland), and of India, can, moreover, be included in the representation of the British Empire by means of the panel system.

After this friendly and satisfactory solution of the problem of the representation of the Dominions and India, the few outstanding issues in the representation of the smaller States were easily cleared up. President Wilson got his way about Brazil. Montenegro was excluded from the list, as was Costa Rica, as her Government was not recognized by the United States. Neither of these countries was a signatory of the Treaty of Versailles.

The list of countries and the number of delegates for each, to whom invitations to the first meeting were to be sent, was as follows:

PLENIPOTENTIARY DELEGATES

The United States	5	Guatemala	1
The British Empire	5	Haiti	1
Canada	2	Hedjaz	2
Australia	2	Honduras	1
South Africa	2	Liberia	1
New Zealand	1	Nicaragua	1
India	2	Panama	1
France	5	Peru	1
Italy	5	Poland	2
Japan	5	Portugal	2
Belgium	3	Roumania	2
Bolivia	1	Serbia	3
Brazil	3	Siam	2
China	2	Uruguay	1
Cuba	1		—
Czechoslovakia	2	Total delegates	70
Ecuador	1		—
Greece	2		

Apart from the inclusion of the British Dominions as a new factor in world politics, the most important feature of that list is the omission of Russia. Russia was in chaos. In the Ukraine and other parts of south Russia, in the region of Archangel, and far away in Siberia, remnants of the old régime were putting up a fight with some sporadic aid from the Allies. In the centre the Bolshevists were slowly consolidating their position. But there was nowhere to be found any organized Government that could properly represent Russia at the Peace Conference. The subject was therefore reserved for later consideration.

Elated by the progress made in the first two days Clemenceau, on January 13th, sprang a proposal that the Plenary Conference should be summoned for Thursday, January 16th, only three days later. This proved impossible, for Sonnino, the Foreign Minister of Italy, who was the sole representative of his country so far, reported that Orlando had not yet completed his delegation, and could only reach Paris at the end of the week. So the date was fixed for Saturday, January 18th at 3 p.m. The notices were sent at once to the countries mentioned above, so as to silence the usual rumours of disagreement and delay.

The Italian Delegation's excuse for the later date was fortunate because, as some of us realized, a great number of questions remained for decision if the Conference was to burst into full activity after the opening meeting. These occupied the Council of Ten for three long meetings a day on January 15th, 16th and 17th. Some questions were easily settled, such as the precedence in which the Great Powers would appear, namely in alphabetical order in French:

> America—United States of
> British Empire
> France
> Italy
> Japan

A question which took a little longer was a demand from Belgium and Serbia, who had originally been allotted two delegates, to be given three. Because they had been the first nations to be attacked, and remained as belligerents to the bitter end, the appeal was conceded, but, on Lloyd George's insistence, a decision was taken that no further applications for additional plenipotentiaries should be considered. Belgium had a good reason in the fact that the Government was composed of three parties, each of which had to be represented if the cabinet was to function properly.

The official language of the Conference continued to be an obstacle, and was eventually narrowed down to a decision that delegates should be at liberty to speak or issue memoranda in French, English or Italian, but that in case of dispute about the meaning, the French texts should be taken as authentic. This led to a prolonged dispute.

The question of publicity, the admission of press representatives to Plenary meetings, the drafting of press communiqués and the like were discussed at great length, as they had been already at the low level of the Secretariat-General, and rules drawn up. But, as usual, it proved impossible to enforce them successfully, and it was not until the establishment of the Big Five meeting in complete secrecy that the problem was solved.

From the first, the Council of Ten had recognized that the Conference would, even at the first meeting, expect a lead on the method of handling the major problems of peace-making, and the following order of priority was adopted provisionally:

1. The League of Nations
2. Reparation
3. New States
4. Frontiers and territorial changes
5. Colonies
6. The responsibility of the authors of the war.

In the event, however, the first item was postponed, at the express wish of President Wilson, until the second of the Plenary Conferences. Reparation was reserved for preliminary consideration by the Council of Ten prior to the appointment of a special commission. On numbers 3, 4 and 5, Balfour, whose opinion always carried great weight, commented as follows:

If these questions were to be put to the delegates sitting at the full Conference, they would also have to be debated in full Conference. He asked his colleagues to imagine what would be the state of the full Conference if all these explosive subjects, full of difficulties and likely to lead to violent disputes, came up for discussion in this manner.

This view was not contested and, after a somewhat desultory conversation, the conclusion was reached that Clemenceau, as provisional chairman of the Conference, should invite the Delegations present to forward to the Secretariat reports setting forth their views on any question in which they might be directly interested. Their reports were to be transmitted by the Secretariat to the five Great Powers for their consideration. The chairman was also to invite special attention to the following subjects as requiring special consideration by all Delegations—(a) responsibility of the authors of the war, and penalties for crimes committed during the war and (b) international legislation on labour. Delegations could also suggest additional subjects for consideration.

The preparatory stage of the Paris Preliminary Peace Conference was now over; all was ready for its opening on Saturday, January 18th, and it is interesting to consider whether the criticisms of undue delay after the Armistice are justified. The accompanying circumstance must be taken into account—the terrible outbreak of influenza in France and Britain, and all over the world; the general election in Britain which Lloyd George had considered indispensable; adjustment of the date to the overwhelming responsibilities of President Wilson; the chaos of government in Germany, Austria and Russia and the sudden termination of the war. In spite of these handicaps the victor Powers had held a useful preliminary conference in London in December 1918, and had assembled in Paris on the evening of January 11, 1919, exactly two months after Armistice Day. Within less than a week they had put the final touches on their preparations, and the Conference held its first meeting seventy-six days after the signature of the original Armistice which had already been renewed once on December 13, 1918 and was due for a second renewal on January 15, 1919.

Could the Allies, with greater prescience, have provided a more solid foundation for the Conference? They had accepted, subject to a very few reservations, Wilson's fourteen points. The Armistice Convention was in order. The British, American, French, Italian and Japanese Governments had all, according to their respective methods, prepared their dossiers, assembled their experts and knew where differences were likely to arise. In London, for example, there was hardly a question that had not been thrashed out in great detail at the War Cabinet and/or the Imperial War Cabinet. A series of valuable handbooks had been prepared under the aegis of the Foreign Office by distinguished historians and experts. The American State Department had done the same, and the French Foreign Office had made a notable contribution to the general procedure of the Conference.

The reader can judge from the account in these pages whether our own preparations for the needs of the Supreme Control were seriously at fault. If, as I claim, the arrangements made for inaugurating the Paris Conference were successful, it was mainly because three great men, who had led their respective countries through the final and decisive stages of the greatest war in their history, had thought it worthwhile to come to Paris and for a whole week to devote themselves collectively morning and afternoon, and individually evenings too, to supervision and stimulation of the work of preparation. If only three of the four Heads of Governments are mentioned, it is because Orlando did not arrive in time to attend a meeting until January 21st, well after the opening of the Conference. But Sonnino had proved himself a first-class understudy. Much more will be heard on this subject of the immense personal application of the Heads of Governments before we reach the final scene of the signature of the Peace Treaty, and it is brought in here to emphasize that it is the key refrain of my story.

CHAPTER V

THE FIRST PLENARY MEETINGS

'Fourthly, in deliberations that ought to be kept secret (whereof there are many occasions in Publique Businesses) the Councils of many, and especially in Assemblies, are dangerous: and therefore great Assemblies are necessitated to commit such affairs to lesser numbers, and to such persons as are most versed, and in whose fidelity they may have most confidence.' (HOBBES, *Leviathan*, c. 25.)

'WE are here to repair the evil that it (the war) has done, and to prevent a recurrence of it. You hold in your hands the future of the world.' These words are from the final passage of the speech with which the President of the French Republic opened the Paris Peace Conference on January 18th. Needless to say, M. Poincaré played his part in welcoming the guests of France with dignity and eloquence. After the interpreters had translated into English he shook hands with all the guests and withdrew. Clemenceau, as President of the French Council of Ministers, stepped into his place and invited proposals for the choice of a president.

Wilson then proposed and Lloyd George and Sonnino (in Orlando's absence) seconded his election as President of the Conference. These speeches were permeated by a spirit of old 'friendship'. Lloyd George, I noticed, spoke '*on behalf of the British Empire Delegation*'.

Clemenceau then got down first to the business appropriate to the occasion, i.e. nomination of four vice-presidents, the secretary-general—this was M. Dutasta—and a secretary for each Great Power, a drafting committee, etc. Only then did he respond to the friendly speeches of the guests in a speech from which I need only quote the following:

A few days ago I said in the Chamber of Deputies and wish to repeat here, 'Success is only possible if we all remain firmly and united until the end. We have come here as friends—we must leave this room as brothers'.... Everything must yield to the necessity of a closer and closer union among the peoples who have taken part in this great war. The League of Nations is here. It is in yourselves, it is for you to make it live; and for that it must be in our hearts. . . .

After that he passed back to business—'The Rules of the Conference' laid on the table for distribution to delegates; and an announcement contained in it, that the 'Order of the Session' would be as follows:

(1) The responsibility of the authors of the war.
(2) The penalty for crimes committed during the war.
(3) The international legislation for labour.

Then, after announcing that the next session would begin with the question of the League of Nations, and that 'each member of the Conference is invited to present such observations as he may think necessary' and that 'the Bureau will welcome the expression of any opinion which may be manifested and will reply to all questions asked of it', he suddenly announced 'As nobody wishes to speak the session is adjourned at 16.35 o'clock!' and he brought down the hammer with such a resounding crash that no one could possibly attempt to speak!

Although, as the meeting dispersed, there were whispers in the corridors about the authoritarian attitude of the Great Powers, no notice was taken of them, and the Council of Ten, after a rest on Sunday, started work again on Monday, January 20th, and continued to meet twice a day as before.

Japan had now joined the Council and was represented by Baron Makino and Matsui, the Ambassador of Japan in Paris, with Saburi as Secretary, and on the Tuesday (January 21st) Orlando joined the Council as head of the Italian Delegation. During the greater part of the week the Council devoted itself mainly to the difficult question of Russia, and some acute problems in Poland, but in addition a good deal of attention was given to preparations for the second Plenary Session fixed for the coming Saturday (January 25th), and for which the League of Nations had been announced as the principal item. But there was a general desire that, in order to get the Conference into its stride, resolutions should be passed establishing commissions of the Conference on the other matters mentioned at the first Plenary Meeting. Lloyd George and I prepared (in consultation with the officials and experts of our delegation when necessary) a series of draft resolutions for setting up commissions on the following subjects:

> The League of Nations, which was intended to be the *pièce de résistance* of the meeting.
> Responsibility of the authors of the war and enforcement of penalties.
> Reparation for damage.
> International legislation on labour.
> International control of waterways.

There was of course a certain amount of discussion on details, and especially on the number of representatives on the proposed commissions of the Great Powers and the smaller Powers respectively, but the production at each stage by Lloyd George, 'out of his hat' so to speak, of a draft resolution, with typewritten copies for all, greatly facilitated agreement. It was the application of an old technique developed during the war which, strange to say, no one else had pirated. Sometimes, of course, the original drafts might have to be touched up or even re-written during the meeting, and I had Sylvester, my invaluable private secretary with his typewriter in an ante-room, ready to function. There is no doubt that this simple device, and especially the production of plenty of copies, helped to speed up the work of the Council of Ten.

By now many of the absentees from the first Plenary Session had arrived. The United States Delegation was complete. Of the British Empire Delegation, Bonar Law had gone home, and a seat was found for C. J. Doherty, Canadian Minister of Justice, and for Joseph Ward of New Zealand, which enabled Massey to occupy his rightful seat with a clear conscience. Thus the Dominions were present in full force. Japan still lacked the leader of the delegation, the Marquis Saionji, who did not appear until the fourth Plenary Meeting on April 11th, but Makino was a most competent substitute. Paderewski was, perhaps, the most notable absentee, and Poland was represented again by Roman Dmowski. The popular Venizelos took his seat for the first time for Greece. Altogether it was a remarkable gathering.

At the outset some surprise was caused by the President's announcement that at the request of the United States Delegation the approval of the Protocol (official jargon for 'minutes') of the first session would be postponed until the next session, as that Delegation had not yet received the English text, which it reserved the right to present to the Conference. That of course was just an American tactical move in the battle of the language of the Conference which was going on behind the scenes, unknown to most of the delegates, and consequently attracted little attention. After that, all went according to plan for some time.

President Wilson introduced the resolution setting up the Commission for the League of Nations. This was seconded by Lloyd George, Sonnino and by Léon Bourgeois; the last named in an over-long speech, considering that he was not a delegate, but, with Robert Cecil, had been allowed the privilege of a seat as a 'Special Delegate for the League of Nations'. A few more followed, mostly in the same strain with tributes to the idea of the League, apart from 'Billy' Hughes of Australia, an undisguised sceptic, who merely obtained a promise from the President that he would be at liberty to discuss the scheme when the Conference was complete.

About half-way through the meeting, the spirit of somnolent complacency that had set in was interrupted, and the smouldering doubts about the leadership of the Great Powers that had been suspected, sprang into flames.

The trouble started from a moderate speech by Hymans, the Belgian Foreign Minister who, after accepting the terms of reference for the commissions, as set forth in the resolution, questioned the general proposal that the 'Powers with General Interests' (i.e. the five Great Powers) should have two representatives apiece, making ten in all on commissions, and the numerous 'Powers with Special Interests' only five to be chosen from among them. He roundly claimed the special right of Belgium to at least one and in some cases two representatives on the commissions. He was followed immediately by a Brazilian representative who took the same line, but also went almost so far as to question the right of the self-constituted Council of Ten to lay down these rules. 'It is with some surprise', he began, 'that I constantly hear it said, "This has been decided, and that has been decided". Who has taken a decision? We are a sovereign assembly, a sovereign unit. It seems to me that the proper body to take a decision is the Conference itself. . . .' Then Borden gave weighty support to that attitude. While appreciating that there must be some limitation to the size of the commissions, and that their reports would have to be considered by the whole Conference before they went into effect, he continued:

but I do feel that the matter has been placed before the Conference in perhaps not the most appropriate way. We are told that certain decisions have been reached. The result of that is that everyone of us asks: 'By whom have these decisions been reached, and by what authority?'

Then he turned to the rules which, strictly speaking, were not yet before the Conference for reasons already mentioned:

Certain regulations have been formulated and passed by which, as I understand, two Conferences were established—one a Conference of the five Great Powers in accordance with the regulations thus adopted. . . .

That added fuel to the smouldering flame, and the representatives of one nation after another supported the criticisms and demanded representation on most, if not all, of the proposed commissions.

All this time, Clemenceau was getting more and more restive. The 'Old Tiger's' claws were beginning to show, and when the last speaker had sat down he sprang to his feet. A fearless debater, he turned first on his most formidable critic:

Sir Robert Borden has reproached me, though in a very friendly way, for having come to a decision. Well, we have decided, as regards the commissions, in the same way as we decided to summon the present Conference. With your permission I will remind you that it was we who decided that there should be a Conference at Paris, and that the representatives of the countries interested should be summoned to attend it. I make no mystery of it—there is a conference of the Great Powers going on in the next room. Sir Robert Borden has the less reason to be unaware of it since he yesterday did us the signal honour of making a statement before us on questions concerning the British Colonies.

The last sentence was a particularly happy thrust, because only on the previous afternoon Sir Robert had taken part in a most important discussion at the Council of Ten about the disposal of the captured colonies; he had put forward no claims on behalf of Canada, but, after hearing the claims of other Dominions, had wound up the discussion with some weighty observations in their support.

Clemenceau then made some pungent remarks in reply to the representatives of the smaller Powers who had criticized the initiative of the Great Powers:

The five Great Powers whose action has to be justified before you today are in a position to justify it. The British Prime Minister just now reminded me that, on the day when the war ceased, the Allies had 12,000,000 men fighting on various fronts. This entitles them to consideration.

We have dead, we have wounded in millions, and if we had not kept before us the great question of the League of Nations, we might perhaps have been selfish enough to consult only each other. It was our right. We did not wish to do this, and we summoned all the nations interested. We summoned them, not to impose our will upon them, not to make them do what they do not wish, but to ask them for their help. That is why we invited them to come here. But we have still to see how this help can best be used.

Having brought home to his critics how relatively insignificant were their pretensions, he went on to wider considerations, putting first the need for expedition:

Now, gentlemen, let me tell you that behind us is something very great, very august, and at times very imperious, something which is called public opinion. It will not ask us whether such and such a State was represented on such and such a Commission. That interests nobody. It will ask for results. . . .

Coming down to detail, he prefaced his remarks on the exorbitant demands for representation on the commissions by recalling his great age—he had entered the French parliament in 1871—and he continued:

I have seen many committees and commissions and have attended many meetings, and I have noticed—as most of you perhaps have also noticed— that the larger the committees are, the less chance they have of doing any work.

Then he went on very skilfully to explain the many ways and means delegates would have of bringing their views to the notice of commissions, or of the Conference as a whole, and concluded by describing in conciliatory tones the spirit of give and take that was already animating the Council of Ten and by an appeal that all should 'be animated by the same spirit'.

That powerful extempore effort silenced the critics, and added to the already great prestige of the permanent President not only among his colleagues in the Council of Ten but throughout the Preliminary Peace Conference, with echoes throughout the world. In addition, the prompt decision and action of the Council of Ten was vindicated, and after that speech no one could dare to contest its authority, as, for the time being at any rate, the directing and organizing bureau, the 'steering committee' of the Conference.

Under the plans of the Council of Ten, the five members of each commission to represent the 'Powers with Special Interests' (i.e. the Minor Powers), were to be selected at a meeting of those Powers. They met on Monday (January 27th) following the Plenary Session, under the chairmanship of the wise old French diplomat, Jules Cambon (brother of Paul Cambon, the trusted French Ambassador in London for many years), who, by his tact and wisdom, secured a satisfactory agreement by vote, so that the list of members of the four main commissions was circulated where necessary with the permission of the Council of Ten, to get the commissions established, and the Conference into its stride over a wide field.

But much more remained to be done before even the outline of a draft Treaty of Peace could be envisaged. For example, boundaries had to be drawn, involving most complicated issues in many countries, e.g. Poland, Czechoslovakia, the Saar, and many others, not to mention the Italian claims, which, although not usually connected directly with the German Treaty, had, for reasons that will become clear later, to be tackled before a treaty with Germany could be signed. Those could not be dealt with until the countries concerned had sent in their respective claims, which were certain to include many contentious issues. It was unavoidable, therefore, to wait until the memoranda which Clemenceau had called for at the opening meeting had been received, printed, translated and circulated.

There were, however, certain questions which were even more urgent, namely, (1) the representation of Russia at the Conference; (2) the disposition of the German colonies, which President Wilson wanted settled early as a basis for an article on mandates in the Covenant of the League of Nations that he was soon to tackle at the commission over which he was about to preside; and (3) a question of the transport of General Haller's Polish Division from the Western front to Poland which had become urgent for reasons that will appear in due course. To these we will now turn.

CHAPTER VI

THE CONFERENCE AND RUSSIA

'The Bolshevik Revolution was a portent transcending
in magnitude any movement of the kind of which
Europe had experience. Its efficacy, its ruthlessness,
the wide span of its ambition gave it a strange fascina-
tion. Even in conservative England, the Labour leaders
talked of workers' councils, of the supersession of Par-
liamentary government by direct action, and of the
General Strike.' (H. A. L. FISHER, *A History of Europe*,
vol. iii, c. 36.)

ACTUALLY the question of Russia arose, as it was bound to do, on
the first day (January 12th) of the meetings of the Great Powers to
organize the Preliminary Peace Conference. This was inevitable
because the question of Russia's representation at the Conference had
to be considered before the opening meeting on January 18th.

Russia had been one of the signatories of the guarantee of September 5, 1914, not to conclude a separate peace. The Bolshevist Government had broken this treaty by signing unilaterally a peace treaty with
the Central Powers at Brest-Litovsk on March 3, 1918.

Forces existed in various parts of Russia which were fighting the
Bolshevists, were opposed to the separate peace with Germany, and for
this reason were receiving a certain amount of armed support from the
Allied and Associated Powers. In Siberia there was Admiral Kolchak,
who had proclaimed himself dictator of all Russia at Omsk on
November 18, 1918; he had the support of large Japanese forces with
smaller numbers of Americans, two battalions of British troops at
Omsk, and a Canadian brigade at Vladivostok. In southern Russia
General Denikin commanded 40,000 men in what Lloyd George called
'a little backyard of the Black Sea'. He was said to have recognized
Admiral Kolchak. Behind him, in Transcaucasia, there were two British
divisions in occupation of the Batoum-Baku railway; in the Ukraine
there was General Petlyura, who stood for a separate Ukraine, and
had revolted against the previous Government of the Ukraine (which
had made peace with the Central Powers as early as February 9, 1918);
he had taken Odessa on December 11, 1918, and Kiev on December 20th, but his attitude was not entirely clear. Behind him at Odessa,

D

in the French sphere, there was a French division with some Greek troops. In northern Russia there were Russian anti-Bolshevist forces co-operating at Archangel and Murmansk with British, American, French and Italian forces 29,000 strong under the command of General (afterwards Lord) Ironside.

Up to now none of the contending parties had been formally recognized by the Allies as a *de facto* or *de jure* Government, and there existed no representative Government to which an invitation could be sent. In these circumstances, it was agreed on January 12th that Russia could not be represented at the Conference,[1] and in fact she never was represented there. Nevertheless, it was realized that a Peace Conference assembled to settle the peace of the world could not leave matters where they were. During the early discussions, a proposal was made that the representatives in Paris of some of the anti-Bolshevist movements in Russia should be heard first. Lloyd George urged that the first need was for the Allied and Associated Powers to decide whether to withdraw or to reinforce their troops in Russia. Without reinforcements they were useless. The difficulty about hearing the Russians now in Paris was that they represented every opinion except the prevalent opinion in Russia—the Bolshevists, who were the *de facto* Government in the greater part of the country. Lloyd George continued:

We had formally recognized the Czar's Government, although at the time we knew it to be absolutely rotten. We recognized the Kolchak Government, the Archangel Government and the Omsk Government, although none of them were good, but we refused to recognize the Bolshevists. To say that we ourselves should pick the representatives of a great people was contrary to every principle for which we had fought. . . .[2]

He would not agree with Pichon's proposal that people like Prince Lvov or Savinkov should be heard, for what they had to say, and not as representatives of Russia. 'To do so would give the public the impression that we considered they represented Russia.'[3] He proposed that if it was desired to know their views they should be obtained from a memorandum or a private conversation. This was agreed to.

Four days later (January 16th), i.e. two days before the first Plenary meeting, Lloyd George opened up at the Council of Ten the whole question of the relations between the Allied and Associated Powers

[1] *The Foreign Relations of the United States: The Paris Peace Conference 1919*, vol. iii, p. 491.
[2] *Ibid.*, p. 491.   [3] *Ibid.*, p. 491.

and Russia. He had no desire to recognize the Bolshevist Government by offering them a seat at the Preliminary Peace Conference. The first step in his view was to obtain a truce between the warring factions. After that their representatives should be invited to Paris to explain their position and to receive from the Allies suggestions for the accommodation of their differences. At present the facts about Russia were unknown, and the reports of the Allied diplomats varied from day to day. Without the facts it was impossible to form a correct judgment. It was only certain that there was misgovernment, and widespread starvation outside the grain areas. Which side was getting the upper hand was still uncertain, but the hopes of a Bolshevist collapse had so far been disappointed. He quoted evidence from British military sources, which could not be suspected of Bolshevist leanings, that their position had improved. The peasants feared that all other parties would, if successful, restore the ancient régime and deprive them of the land which the Revolution had put into their hands.[1] The Ukraine, the British Prime Minister continued, had not proved the barrier against Bolshevism that had been hoped. The former government of big landlords, only maintained by the Germans, had been easily overthrown by a mere adventurer (Petlyura) when the Germans withdrew.

There were, he suggested, three policies from which to choose:

(1) We could say that Bolshevism was 'a movement as dangerous to civilization as German militarism had been, and that we must, therefore, destroy it'. The Germans, while engaged in a death struggle on the Western Front, had been forced to keep a million men in the occupied provinces, a mere fringe of Russia, at a time when Bolshevism was weak. Now Bolshevism was strong. Which of the Western Allies, he asked, was prepared to keep a million men in the country? The Allied troops in northern Russia and Siberia 'were most unwilling to continue the campaign, and determined to return to their homes'.

(2) The second policy was a policy of insulation, the policy known as *cordon sanitaire*. That policy would involve a blockade and lead to the killing 'not of the ruffians enlisted by the Bolshevists, but of the ordinary population with whom we wished to be friends'. He could not support such a policy.

(3) The only other way he could think of was the plan he had proposed—that of asking representatives of the various Russian Governments to meet in Paris after a truce among themselves. . . .[2]

[1] *The Foreign Relations of the United States: The Paris Peace Conference 1919*, vol. iii, p. 581.
[2] *Ibid.*, p. 582 sq.

President Wilson strongly supported Lloyd George's views to which, in his opinion, there was no possible answer. In response, however, to suggestions pressed by the French and Italian Ministers, before reaching a decision it was agreed to hear Noullens, the former French Ambassador in Russia, who had just returned to Paris from Archangel, and Scavenius, the Danish Minister at Petrograd, who was also in Paris.

After an interval of a few days devoted to organizing and holding the first meeting of the Plenary Conference on January 18th, and prolonged discussions on press leakages, these two witnesses were heard on Monday (January 20th) and Tuesday (January 21st) respectively. The evidence of both was strongly anti-Bolshevist, and both suggested that the military power of the Bolshevists was much less than Lloyd George had suggested. Scavenius, who held that Bolshevism was a world danger and was himself frankly interventionist, admitted under cross-examination by Lloyd George, that the Russian troops of the anti-Bolshevist elements could not be depended upon without the support of foreign armies. Without claiming military knowledge he said that he thought that a stiffening of 100,000 or at the utmost 150,000 volunteers from the Allied countries would be sufficient to reinforce the Russian armies he had already enumerated, and to ensure success.[1]

The greater part of the afternoon meeting of the Council of Ten on January 21st was devoted to an admirable discussion on the Russian problem in the light of the evidence given and this prepared the way for an agreement.[2] At the outset, Wilson proposed, as a modification of Lloyd George's plan, that the eventual meeting, after a truce had been arranged between the contending forces in Russia, should take place not at Paris but in the Near East, at Salonica for example, where the Russians would be met by representatives of the Allies. Lloyd George at once accepted the amendment, though he preferred Lemnos to Salonica as the *rendezvous*. He pointed out that this would have the advantage of bringing the Russian representatives by sea direct without having to pass through other countries. Balfour gave a further reason that it would meet Clemenceau's objection to having these people in Paris. Clemenceau, for once, was rather hesitant:

In principle, he did not favour conversations with the Bolshevists; not because they were criminals, but because we should be raising them to our

---

[1] *The Foreign Relations of the United States: The Paris Peace Conference 1919*, vol. iii, p. 638.
[2] *Ibid.*, pp. 647–54.

level by saying that they were worthy of entering into conversations with us. The Bolshevist danger was very great at the present moment. Bolshevism was spreading. It had invaded the Baltic Provinces and Poland, and that very morning they had received very bad news regarding its spread to Budapest and Vienna. Italy also was in danger. The danger was probably greater there than in France. . . . To sum up, had he been acting by himself, he would temporize and erect barriers to prevent Bolshevism from spreading. But he was not alone, and in the presence of his colleagues, he felt compelled to make some concessions, as it was essential that there should not be even the appearance of disagreement amongst them. The concession came easier after having heard President Wilson's suggestion. He thought that they should make a clear and convincing appeal to all reasonable peoples, emphatically stating that they did not wish to interfere in the internal affairs of Russia, and especially that they had no intention of restoring Czardom. The object of the Allies being to hasten the creation of a strong Government, they proposed to call together representatives of all parties to a conference. He would beg President Wilson to draft a paper, fully explaining the position of the Allies to the whole world, including the Russians and the Germans.[1]

At this point, when the Council appeared to be on the brink of agreement, Sonnino made a strong appeal in favour of the policy advocated by Scavenius. Sonnino's idea was to collect together all the anti-Bolshevist parties and help them to make a strong Government, provided they pledged themselves not to serve the forces of reaction, and especially not to touch the land question thereby depriving the Bolshevists of their strongest argument. Should they take these pledges he would be prepared to help them . . . with soldiers to a reasonable degree or by supplying arms, food and money. . . . He would also point out that for Italy, and probably for France also, as Clemenceau had stated, it was in reality a question of self-defence. He thought that even a partial recognition of the Bolshevists would strengthen their position, and, speaking for himself, he thought that Bolshevism was already a serious danger in his country.

Lloyd George met this spirited sally by two deadly questions. Scavenius had suggested that an army of 150,000 Allied volunteers would be a sufficient stiffening of the Russian anti-Bolshevist forces. He asked what contribution America, Italy and France would make towards raising this army? President Wilson and Clemenceau each said none. Orlando agreed that Italy could make no further contributions.[2] Lloyd George then asked who would feed and equip the

[1] *The Foreign Relations of the United States: The Paris Peace Conference 1919*, vol. iii, p. 649 *sq.*
[2] *Ibid.*, p. 651.

army of 400,000 anti-Bolshevist Russians required to defeat the Bolshevists? Would Italy, or America or France do so? No answer was
forthcoming. It was clear that they would not.

That decided the issue. Orlando, throwing over Sonnino, agreed
that Lloyd George's objections to the use of physical force were
unanswerable. There remained, he said, the use of moral force. He
agreed with Clemenceau that no country could continue in anarchy,
and that an end must eventually come; but they could not wait; they
could not proceed to make peace and ignore Russia. He, therefore,
accepted Lloyd George's proposal, with President Wilson's modification. Makino, the astute Japanese statesman, who had been watching
the proceedings intently without saying a word, also supported the
proposal.

President Wilson then accepted Clemenceau's invitation to draft
a manifesto, which was adopted, subject to some small modifications
on the following day (January 22nd), for public transmission to the
contending Russian parties. The main difference contained therein
from the proposal discussed at the Council of Ten was the substitution
of the Princes Islands in the Sea of Marmara for Salonica or Lemnos;
the watering place of Prinkipo was actually the spot selected.

It was unfortunate that neither the Bolshevist Government nor any
of the contending parties in Russia responded to this overture in the
spirit in which it had been made, as years and years of misunderstanding might have been avoided thereby. It was a decisive moment
in the history of the world, and the failure to take advantage of the
offer was destined to weigh heavily on the future. But from their own
point of view the Bolshevists were undoubtedly right. They were
justified in assuming that they had nothing to gain from an accommodation with their enemies, that the Western Powers were too exhausted
to enter on a fresh major war in support of their scattered and half-
hearted opponents, so that in the end they were bound to win through
and force all Russia to accept their nostrums. That also was undoubtedly more apparent to the anti-Bolshevist leaders than it was
in Paris to the Allied Heads of Government, who by their own
admission were ill-informed about Russia. The response to the
proclamation proved completely disappointing, as is frankly admitted
in Lloyd George's account.[1]

---

[1] For later developments and Winston Churchill's sudden and unexpected arrival in Paris,
vide infra, p. 67.

CHAPTER VII

GERMAN COLONIES AND DOMINIONS MANDATES

'These Dominions were autonomous nations within an Empire, which might properly call itself a League of Nations.' (SIR ROBERT BORDEN at the Paris Peace Conference, January 25, 1919.)

IN the story of the Paris Peace Conference few episodes are more important to the history of the British Empire than the series of meetings of the Council of Ten described in this chapter. As already mentioned, the subject of the disposal of the German colonies had early become urgent in connection with the work of Wilson's Commission on the Covenant of the League of Nations, in which he wished to include an article on mandates. The first[1] of these meetings took place at 3 p.m. on Friday (January 24th), the day before the second Plenary meeting when the League of Nations Commission was established. Borden, Hughes, Massey, Botha and Smuts were all present. At the outset Lloyd George secured the unanimous agreement of all present to the principle that the colonies should not be restored to Germany. After that he outlined the various methods by which the colonies could be dealt with, viz., firstly, internationalization or control by the League of Nations, but he thought it was generally agreed that these territories could not be dealt with internationally; secondly, trusteeship on behalf of the League as mandatory; thirdly, frank annexation. He wound up a brief but telling summary of the position of each of the territories by stating

that he would like the Conference to treat the territories enumerated as part of the Dominions which had captured them rather than as areas to be administered under the control of an organization established in Europe which might find it difficult to contribute even the smallest financial assistance to their administration.

After that, Lloyd George wisely left it to the representative of each Dominion to state his case for whichever method he deemed most appropriate to the territories they had captured.

[1] The quotations in this chapter are all from *The Foreign Relations of the United States: The Paris Peace Conference 1919*, vol. iii, pp. 720–800.

Hughes led off with a powerful plea for the annexation of German New Guinea by Australia. He marshalled the strategical arguments effectively:

Strategically the Pacific Islands encompassed Australia like fortresses. New Guinea was the biggest island in the world save Australia itself, and was only 82 miles from the mainland. South-east of it was a string of islands suitable for coaling and submarine bases, from which Australia could be attacked. . . . It was obvious that five million people could not hold, against powerful enemies, a country larger than the United States with a coast-line as long as the distance between Australia and England. If there were at the very door of Australia a potential or actual enemy, Australia could not feel safe. . . .[1]

Later on he added prophetically that countries' policies were liable to change, and that 'history showed that friends in one war were not friends in the next'. He wanted to annex German New Guinea, which lay adjacent to Australian New Guinea, so that the administration of the two territories could be combined in one. He was not content to become a mandatory of the League of Nations, which, he apprehended, would overshadow Australia.

Smuts followed with the case for the annexation by the Union of South Africa of German South West Africa. The two countries, he pointed out, were geographically one. The reason why South West Africa had not been annexed to the Union was 'the dilatoriness of the Imperial Government'. It was they who had allowed Bismarck to steal a march in 1884. The German administration had been a failure. They had not colonized, and had done little but exterminate the natives. They had to a great extent fomented the rebellion in the Union at the outset of the war, and had seduced officers of the defence forces. Forty thousand men had been needed to suppress the rebellion before General Botha could invade German South West Africa. A good case could be made for the adoption of the mandatory system in tropical parts of Africa, but in the case of German South West Africa, 'a desert country without any product of great value and only suitable for pastoralists', there was not a strong case. It was on this ground that South Africa claimed the country. He appealed also to General Botha's loyalty in lining up with the Empire when many Dutch inhabitants of the Union would have preferred to remain neutral. Their position, however, was such that they could not legally or constitutionally remain neutral. If the territory in question were not ceded to the

[1] *The Foreign Relations of the United States: The Paris Peace Conference 1919*, vol. iii, p. 720 sq.

Union, the result would be 'the overthrow of General Botha and all his policy', a point that he developed at some length.

Massey began his case for putting Samoa under New Zealand control by an interesting story of the machinations by which Germany had established herself there. At one time, he said, there seems to have been a kind of internationalization. What happened was this:

A sort of protectorate was established of the three nations—Germany, the United States and Great Britain. To say the least, the result was by no means satisfactory. Germany was given the larger and much more important of the islands; the United States of America were given a small portion with a very good harbour. He did not wish to find fault with that. Great Britain was given some rights in other islands. Germany then became established there. He was delighted to notice the decision practically arrived at by the Council against German occupation of these islands in the future.

At this point Massey, like Hughes, had his prophetic moment. He was inclined, he said, to believe that we had not reached the last war. History had a knack of repeating itself and nations, just as unscrupulous as Germany had proved herself to be during the last few years, might make war. He developed the anxieties of, and the menace to, New Zealand when Germany, after establishing a great commercial position in the Pacific, with a powerful naval squadron and a huge wireless station, had declared war. But under the protection of the Australian battle-cruiser *Australia*, and the French cruiser *Montcalm*, New Zealand forces had occupied Samoa. He hoped that the League of Nations would be established successfully, but joint international control had again and again proved a failure—in the New Hebrides, Egypt and Samoa. He was very sceptical about the success of any joint arrangement for the German Colonies. . . . On behalf of his fellow citizens, and on behalf of the people in the islands of the South Pacific, for the sake of the native races, and for the sake of humanity, he most strongly urged that the claim he was making in regard to Samoa should be granted . . . and that the island should be allowed to remain under British control.

At that point it was left to Borden, who had no territorial claims on behalf of Canada, to wind up the meeting with a brief but weighty 'thought', which he presented 'on behalf of the claims put forward by the other Dominions':

Those Dominions were autonomous nations within an Empire which might more properly call itself a League of Nations. He realized that the

British Empire occupied a large part of the world, but the prejudice raised by the word 'empire' might be dispelled by considering the matter from the angle he had just suggested. All the cases advanced rested upon the plea of security and he considered that the arguments put forward deserved the closest attention of the Council.

These words, so prophetic of the famous Balfour Declaration of 1926, brought down the curtain on the first appearance of the Prime Ministers of the Dominions on the international stage. But only one side of the case had yet been heard, and they had to take part in a great deal more discussion before the question was finally decided.

Three days later, on the afternoon of Monday (January 27th), the question was taken up again. After hearing a short statement of the Japanese claims to the German Pacific Islands north of the Equator, the Council listened to a statement by the American President on the principles of the mandatory system:

The basis of this idea was the feeling which had sprung up all over the world against further annexation. Yet, if the colonies were not to be returned to Germany (as all were agreed), some other basis must be found to develop them and to take care of the inhabitants of these backward territories. It was with this object that the idea of administration through mandatories acting on behalf of the League of Nations arose.

The President went on to illustrate the principle by applying it to South West Africa with its sparse inhabitants, who had been so maltreated and reduced in numbers by the Germans that future development of the territory could not yet be determined, so that it must either be attached to its nearest neighbour, South Africa—

or some institution must be found to carry out the ideas all had in mind, namely, the development of the country for the benefit of those already in it, and for the advantage of those who would live there later. This he assumed to be the principle: it was not intended to exercise arbitrary sovereignty over any people. The purpose was to serve the people in undeveloped parts, to safeguard them against abuses such as had occurred under German administration, and such as might be found under other administrations. Further, where people and territories were undeveloped, to assure their development so that, when the time came, their own interests, as they saw them, might qualify them to express a wish as to their ultimate relations—perhaps lead them to desire their union with the mandatory power.

The President then went on to explain the general features of the proposed mandate, e.g. administration for the betterment of the inhabitants; no discrimination in access to the district against members of the League of Nations; no preferential tariff such as the Union's three per cent preference to the United Kingdom. With this limitation, he said, the Union of South Africa would 'extend such of its laws as were applicable to South West Africa, and administer it as an annex to the Union so far as consistent with the interests of the inhabitants'. His proposals for financing the administration were rather sketchy. He thought that in so far as the administration by the mandatory power became a financial burden, it was 'clearly proper that the League of Nations should bear a proportion of the expense'—a point that made little appeal to the hard-headed realists to whom he was speaking. He went on:

The fundamental idea would be that the world was acting as trustee through a mandatory, and would be in charge of the whole administration until the day when the true wishes of the inhabitants could be ascertained. It was up to the Union of South Africa to make it so attractive that South West Africa would come into the Union of their own free will. Should that not be the case, the fault would lie with the mandatory.

Botha, intervening for the first time, and Hughes strongly opposed the application of the President's plan to the territories in which they were interested. In fact Hughes made a powerful onslaught on the whole conception, summing up that 'there was nothing to be gained by the mandatory system that could not be got by direct government, except that the world was said to dread annexation. But he was positive that no one dreaded the annexation of New Guinea by Australia'.

Next day (Tuesday, January 28th) the controversy continued, Massey's opposition to the application of the mandatory system—in his case, to Samoa—was as strong as that of the Prime Minister of Australia and General Smuts.

The difference between the mandatory principle and that instituted by New Zealand was that between leasehold and freehold tenure. No individual would put the same energy into a leasehold as into a freehold. It would be the same with governments.

Another matter which increased the growing exasperation of Great Britain and the Dominions, was Wilson's absolute refusal to proceed there and then to the assignment of the mandates, for which Lloyd George had been pressing. 'His difficulty', the President explained, 'was to prevent the assignment of mandatories, if they were to be the Great Powers, from appearing to the world as a mere distribution of the spoils.'

The temperature, which had risen appreciably, was then cooled a little when the Council turned its attention to a controversy between Japan and China over Kiauchau. On the following day (January 29th) they heard French and British statements on the application of the mandatory system to the ex-German Colonies in which they were interested. Simon, the French Colonial Minister, ranged himself alongside the British Dominions in opposition to the mandatory system, and made a powerful plea for annexation of the Cameroons, etc. Lloyd George, however, pointed out that the difficulties were more imaginary than real. M. Simon, he said, had in the beginning of his speech appeared to be bitterly opposed to the whole idea, but in the end he had detailed as acceptable to France the whole list of conditions proposed for a mandatory except the name.

Clemenceau, the strong man, the statesman of big views, gave some approval to Lloyd George's interpretation, and added that the French Colonial Office had expressed its views, but that did not mean that he was not ready to make concessions if reasonable proposals were put forward. All his sentiments, he declared, were in agreement with those of President Wilson.

And for the United Kingdom, Lloyd George, after consulting the representatives of the Colonial Office in Paris, announced that Great Britain saw no difficulty in applying the system to British Colonies. With Britain and France favourably disposed towards the mandatory system, and Japan presenting no active opposition, the Dominions were rather isolated. On January 29th I wrote home as follows:

We have been greatly agitated during this week by the difficult questions raised by the disposal of the conquered German Colonies. It has been extremely difficult to reconcile the views of President Wilson and some of the Dominions. It involved many meetings of the British Empire Delegation, and an infinity of delicate negotiation. I have had to have nearly all my meals with the Prime Minister, in order to help him in squaring this or that party. Hughes and Massey, who insist on annexation of the German Islands in the South Pacific, are our principal difficulty, but President Wilson, in his insistence on the affiliation of these colonies, in some form or another, to the League of Nations, is even more obstinate. The trouble is that both are very unyielding. However, I am hopeful that we are now on our way to an accommodation.

As a matter of fact, after several exhaustive discussions, agreement was reached at the British Empire Delegation on that very day, and Lloyd George circulated to the Council of Ten a series of draft resolutions. In introducing them on January 30th he also insisted on the need to recognize three classes of mandates for the cases of the former Turkish territories, the tropical colonies and 'countries which formed almost a part of the organization of an adjoining power', respectively.

For the moment this compromise seemed likely to settle the question. But Hughes withheld his opinion until he had consulted his colleagues, and Wilson, exasperated at a mischievous leakage that had appeared in the press that morning, while accepting Lloyd George's proposals 'as practically clearing away all prospects of serious differences', wanted to accept them only as 'a precursor of agreement'.

In the course of a long comment Lloyd George said that Wilson's statement 'filled him with despair'. If every question was to be set aside for final decision until every other question was settled, the result would be disastrous. He emphasized the difficulty which the Dominions had found in accepting the draft submitted even provisionally. Hughes took fire, and in effect demanded a decision there and then. Massey backed him up. All the morning and half the afternoon the debate dragged on. At times it became acrimonious. Lloyd George describes how at one point, after some remarks by Hughes, the President asked him slowly and solemnly: 'Mr Hughes, am I to understand that if the whole civilized world asks Australia to agree to a mandate in respect of these islands, Australia is prepared still to defy the appeal of the whole civilized world?' and Hughes answered: 'That's about the size of it, President Wilson.' Massey nodded his assent to this abrupt defiance.[1]

That quotation brings the whole scene back to my memory—the stately, overheated chamber, the exasperated delegates, the feeling that there was some misunderstanding at bottom. At this moment Botha had one of his great moments. Speaking with great deliberation, but obviously under great emotion, in rather broken English that, if anything, added force to his remarks, he made an appeal to both sides for reason and forbearance. Perhaps the high point of his appeal was the following extract, which reveals the tone of the whole:

[1] D. Lloyd George, *The Truth about the Peace Treaties*, vol. i, p. 542. For the official version of Botha's speech, *vide The Foreign Relations of the United States: The Paris Peace Conference 1919*, vol. iii, p. 800.

He was one of those who would give up everything to reach the highest ideal. Therefore, he supported Mr Lloyd George, but he sincerely trusted that President Wilson would also agree. Do not let them stop at small things. If they could gain that bigger and higher ideal, then smaller versions of it ought not to stand in the way. He remembered that after the war in his own country, which was on a smaller scale than the present, but which was just as bloody and miserable, they got self-government; but he saw at once that four different self-governing bodies in that country must lead to war. He was one of the original promoters of the Union of South Africa. He had his ideals and they were very high indeed. When he assembled all the leading statesmen he found that the other people held views from which it would be impossible to persuade them. He had then personally investigated these and had come to the conclusion that these were smaller things. On that occasion he asked his colleagues to stick to one thing, to aspire to the higher ideal, and that was the Union of South Africa. They must give way on the smaller things. He would say the same on this occasion. They must give way now and get their higher ideal, get a better understanding, and bring all people together, and through that they would get all the things that they wanted to get. It was a small thing on which he had given way after the war in his own country, but unless they had done so they would have been in a very miserable condition today.

That statement, the official summary of which quoted above does scant justice to the eloquence with which it was expressed, at once lowered the temperature. Discussions were resumed on the usual businesslike footing. A number of points of detail were cleared. Hughes's opposition ceased. Massey accepted the draft. The discussion turned to less controversial aspects. The Belgian claims were heard. The Portuguese desiderata were mentioned by Balfour. A reference to the grossly exaggerated and tendentious reports in a newspaper of the proceedings of the previous day helped further to unite the principal delegates in condemning it. That raised the issue of the communiqué. President Wilson suggested that they should say that they had arrived at a satisfactory provisional arrangement with regard to dealing with the German and Turkish territory outside Europe. Then they should say that they had heard the Belgians with regard to the Congo, and that the military advisers of the Supreme War Council should make a report to the Conference on the best and most advisable disposition of troops to take care of the Turkish territories that were now outside Europe, and were now being occupied. This was agreed to.

That was all that was recorded of this momentous discussion by way of a decision, but it was enough. The documents which had been provisionally approved at the Council of Ten provided the basis for discussion at the League of Nations Committee. On them the Committee founded Article 19 of the draft covenant, which was presented to the Conference at the third Plenary session on February 14th, and which, without more than minor drafting alterations, eventually became Article 22 of the Covenant as incorporated in the Peace Treaties.[1] That was the eventual result of the discussion and the subject was never again brought before the Council of Ten. As we all trooped away from this long meeting, President Wilson said in my hearing that he had rarely listened to a more moving speech than Botha's. The South African Prime Minister had been the hero of the day.

At the six meetings described above the representatives of the Dominions had made their first appearance to defend their rights at a great international conference. They did not get all that they asked at the outset, but they one and all made a deep impression. They gave the assembled statesmen of the five Great Powers a magnificent example of how the British Empire does its business, by holding to its ideals and subordinating to them the smaller things, as Botha had shown. That is a lesson for all nations to this very day. In no manner could the Dominions have demonstrated more strikingly that they had reached full nationhood, but they had also shown with equal conviction their intention to concert their respective policies with the United Kingdom and the other self-governing nations of the British Empire. The machinery by which agreement was reached was the British Empire Delegation, that is to say, the Imperial War Cabinet projected into the Preliminary Peace Conference, a Cabinet of Nations, a prototype that might well be adapted to any world organization. That machinery continued until the end of the Conference, and hardly any great question was brought before the Conference that was not discussed first at the British Empire Delegation.

The original intention of the Inviting Powers in regard to territorial claims was that the Powers having these or other 'special interests' in such matters should, in the first instance, forward a memorandum on the subject to the Secretariat-General. In practice this plan did not always work out that way. For example, on the day after the first Plenary meeting (January 19th) the Japanese Delegation opened up at the Council of Ten the subject of their claims against China, but it

---

[1] *Vide* Appendix to this chapter, p. 65.

did not get very far that day in China's absence. On January 22nd discussions were opened on the Allied policy in Poland where of course, owing to the chaos in Russia, the position was one of great difficulty. On the following day Lloyd George on receipt of messages from London announced that it was becoming impossible to maintain the size of the British Army in Germany, which led to discussions with Foch and the Allied military authorities on Germany's capacity to re-open hostilities.[1] On January 30th Roman Dmowski, President of the Polish National Committee, came to represent the situation in Poland and next day Roumania weighed in with Bratiano to state her claim. He was present again on February 3rd.

February began with trouble in Teschen and a small committee had to be sent there to handle the dispute between Poland and Czechoslovakia on the possession of this important coalfield. And so it continued day after day, often a dreary business involving listening hour after hour to long statements in some language (e.g. Polish or Roumanian) which had to be translated first into French and then into English and *vice versa*. On February 5th the situation was alleviated by a very clear statement of the Czechoslovak claims by Beneš, an attractive figure with good knowledge of the French language, whom I was destined to get to know well in later years.

On February 6th we had a more sprightly entertainment when we heard the claims of the Hedjaz, presented by the Emir Feisal and interpreted by the famous Colonel Lawrence, who looked extraordinarily young and gay in the Arab clothes which he wore like Feisal and the other members of the delegation. But for me there was a pathetic discovery. In an inconspicuous corner of the room I found an old war-time friend, Sir Mark Sykes, MP, who had been brought to the meeting as a British expert, looking desperately ill as he indeed actually was with the influenza from which he died shortly after. That takes us to the last day (February 7th) before the departure of Lloyd George for London to deal with a difficult political situation there before returning to the Conference. After Lloyd George's departure the Council of Ten (meeting when appropriate as the Supreme War Council) continued the process on precisely the same lines until February 14th, the day on which Churchill's sudden arrival interrupted the routine and faced the Council with a series of formidable problems and proposals relating to Russia and the chaos throughout the East.

---

[1] *Vide infra*, p. 158.

APPENDIX TO CHAPTER VII

ARTICLE 22 OF THE TREATY OF PEACE BETWEEN THE ALLIED AND ASSOCIATED POWERS AND GERMANY: To those colonies and territories which, as a consequence of the late war, have ceased to be under the sovereignty of the States which formerly governed them, and which are inhabited by peoples not yet able to stand by themselves under the strenuous conditions of the modern world, there should be applied the principle that the well-being and development of such peoples form a sacred trust of civilization, and that securities for the performance of this trust should be embodied in this Covenant.

The best method of giving practical effect to this principle is that the tutelage of such peoples should be entrusted to advanced nations, who, by reason of their resources, their experience, or their geographical position can best undertake this responsibility, and who are willing to accept it, and that this tutelage should be exercised by them as Mandatories on behalf of the League.

The character of the mandate must differ according to the stage of the development of the people, the geographical situation of the territory, its economic conditions, and other similar circumstances.

Certain communities formerly belonging to the Turkish Empire have reached a stage of development where their existence as independent nations can be provisionally recognized subject to the rendering of administrative advice and assistance by a Mandatory until such time as they are able to stand alone. The wishes of these communities must be a principal consideration in the selection of the Mandatory.

Other peoples, especially those of Central Africa, are at such a stage that the Mandatory must be responsible for the administration of the territory under conditions which will guarantee freedom of conscience and religion, subject only to the maintenance of public order and morals, the prohibition of abuses such as the slave trade, the arms traffic, and the liquor traffic, and the prevention of the establishment of fortifications or military and naval bases and of military training of the natives for other than police purposes and the defence of territory, and will also secure equal opportunities for the trade and commerce of other Members of the League.

These are territories, such as South West Africa and certain of the South Pacific Islands, which, owing to the sparseness of their population, or their small size, or their remoteness from the centres of civilization, or their geographical contiguity to the territory of the Mandatory, and other circumstances, can be best administered under the laws of the Mandatory as integral portions of its territory, subject to the safeguards above mentioned in the interests of the indigenous population.

E

In every case of mandate, the Mandatory shall render to the Council an annual report in reference to the territory committed to its charge.

The degree of authority, control, or administration to be exercised by the Mandatory shall, if not previously agreed upon by the Members of the League, be explicitly defined in each case by the Council.

A permanent Commission shall be constituted to receive and examine the annual reports of the Mandatories and to advise the Council on all matters relating to the observance of the mandates.

CHAPTER VIII

THE CHURCHILL INTERVENTION

'It were better that in causes of weight the matter were
propounded one day and not spoken to till the next
day; *in nocte consilium.*' (BACON, *Essays: Of Counsel.*)

BACON's advice is very relevant to the course of an eventful day
(February 14th) at the Paris Peace Conference during which the
American President was the principal figure, an exceptionally exhausting day for him, for from 3 p.m. to 6.30 p.m. almost without stop he
was reading, or expounding, or answering questions about the report
of his Committee on the League of Nations at the third Plenary Session.
Only after the meeting closed at 6.35 p.m. did he or anyone else hear
from Clemenceau that he had felt obliged to summon a meeting of
the Council of Ten at Balfour's request to deal with a matter of
urgency, to take place immediately after the third Plenary, and that
Winston Churchill, British Secretary of State for War had arrived in
Paris without prior notice and would be present. Wilson at once
decided to attend the meeting, but neither Lloyd George who had
left for London on March 8th, nor Orlando who had slipped off to
Italy after the third Plenary were present; in Balfour, who was accompanied by Milner, and in Sonnino they had good substitutes. On
arrival we found assembled Foch, Henry Wilson, Bliss, Cavallero
and some other generals.

Balfour at once shouldered responsibility for the meeting, on the
ground that he had two urgent matters to raise before Wilson's
departure. The first related to the passage of Allied troops and supplies
through Holland. After a short discussion from which it transpired
that action had already been begun on the lines proposed without any
signs of difficulty, the decision was taken, without opposition, to
proceed as before unless trouble should arise.

Balfour next announced that the second question he had to raise
was a proposal that had been mentioned for a meeting between the
Allies and the various Russian Governments at Prinkipo. He only
wished to introduce the subject and he asked Winston Churchill, who
had come to Paris for that purpose, to explain the present view of
the British Cabinet. Churchill opened the proceedings with great

moderation. He said that at a meeting of the British Cabinet on the previous day:

great anxiety had been manifested concerning the Russian situation, particularly in respect of the Prinkipo meeting. In view of the imminent departure of President Wilson, the Cabinet had asked him to go over and obtain some decision as to the policy on this matter. Mr Lloyd George, he said, had expressed a wish to know whether the Allied policy which had led to the suggestion was to be pursued or, if not, what policy was to be substituted for it. If it were possible to go on with the original policy, so much the better; but if only the Bolshevists were to attend the Conference, it was thought that little good would come of the meeting.[1]

Churchill then passed to the military aspects, in which as Secretary for War and Air he was especially concerned.

Great Britain had soldiers in Russia who were being killed in action. Their families wished to know what purpose these men were serving. . . . The Russian anti-Bolshevist elements in those forces were deteriorating rapidly because of the uncertainty of the support they might expect from the victorious Allies. The Allied troops were intermingled with these Russian troops which were weakening and quavering, and they were themselves becoming affected. If the Prinkipo meeting was not going to procure a cessation of arms, this unsatisfactory condition might last an indefinite time.

After Clemenceau had observed 'that a matter of such importance could not be settled at a short and unexpected meeting', Wilson, flushed but tired from his successful launch of the Covenant of the League of Nations at the Plenary Session earlier in the afternoon, then expressed his views. Taking up the military point first he gave a clear opinion 'that the troops of the Allied and Associated Powers were doing no sort of good in Russia. . . .' His conclusion was that they ought to be withdrawn from all parts of Russian territory. As regards the Prinkipo policy

he would be quite content that informal American representatives should meet representatives of the Bolshevists. . . . If the other Russian Governments could not come to Prinkipo to meet the Allies, why should the Allies not imitate Mahomet, and go to them? . . . Some light on the situation might be obtained by meeting the Russian representatives.

In reply to an observation by Churchill that the consequence of withdrawal would be 'the destruction of all non-Bolshevist armies in

[1] *Vide The Foreign Relations of the United States: The Paris Peace Conference 1919*, vol. iii, pp. 1041–2.

Russia' numbering about half a million men, 'and an interminable vista of violence and misery . . .', President Wilson pointed out that the existing forces of all the Allies could not stop the Bolshevists, and that not one of the Allies was prepared to reinforce its troops. This was always the clinching argument and the President stuck to it firmly. Conscripts could not be sent and volunteers probably could not be obtained. He himself felt guilty 'in that the United States had in Russia insufficient forces but it was not possible to increase them. It was certainly a cruel dilemma. . . .'

In reply to suggestions by Churchill and Sonnino that, if the Prinkipo Conference proved a failure, the anti-Bolshevist forces could be armed, the President hesitated to express an opinion. He had, he said, explained to the Council how he would act if alone. He would, however, cast in his lot with the rest. On that note the meeting adjourned until the following afternoon.

When the Council of Ten met at 3 p.m. on Saturday (February 15th) —the day originally fixed for the abortive Prinkipo Conference—the situation had changed. Clemenceau was the only Head of Delegation left. Balfour was alone, as Milner who had been present as second string the previous day, had gone home. Orlando had left for Italy and Sonnino whose views on the Russian question were less conciliatory than those of his chief, was in sole charge for Italy. But above all Wilson had left Paris for Washington and America was represented by Secretary of State Lansing and House. When the cat's away, the mice will play—and all but one of the cats had gone home.

The discussion on Russia[1] began with an elaborate appreciation of the military situation by the French General Albi, the gist of which was that the Red forces were at present advancing on all fronts with the exception of Esthonia. The Red armies possessed a superiority over their opponents who lacked cohesion, were badly equipped and of low morale and were subjected to 'systematic propaganda for which no expense is spared, and which everywhere precedes military action'. But regular Allied troops being better officered and equipped, even though numerically inferior, could easily defeat the Red armies.

In this atmosphere Churchill adopted a more militant attitude than on the previous day. He urged that 'it was essential either to carry Prinkipo through to a definite result or to get it out of the way'. To this end he tabled the draft of a wireless message to the Bolshevists

[1] *Ibid.*, vol. iv, p. 12; the text of the Churchill draft is on pp. 13–14.

which, after setting out that the sole object of the Prinkipo proposal was to restore peace in Russia with 'the establishment of a Government based upon the broad will of the Russian people', and after insisting that fighting must stop forthwith, offered ten days more for a cessation of the fighting, failing which the Prinkipo proposal would be deemed to have lapsed.

The despatch of this message was to be accompanied by 'the immediate setting up of an Allied Council for Russian Affairs with political, economic and military sections, with executive powers within limits to be laid down by the present Conference.' Churchill laid stress on the formation and getting to work of the military section at once 'to draw up a plan for concerted action against the Bolshevists.'

Then if the Prinkipo proposal gave no results, the Supreme War Council would be in possession of a definite war scheme, together with an appreciation of the situation and an estimate of the chances of being able to carry through to success the suggested plan. The Supreme War Council could then make their choice; either to act or to withdraw their troops and leave everyone in Russia to stew in their own juice.

Churchill's eloquence, enthusiasm and personality produced an electrical effect. At first it seemed as though he would carry his point there and then. Nearly everyone present took up an 'I told you so' attitude, as is clear from the published minutes. Clemenceau said that *he had been completely opposed to Lloyd George's proposal*,[1] but he had accepted it in order to avoid the introduction of elements of discord into that Conference. Balfour *had never been sanguine about the issue of the discussions at Prinkipo*. . . . In any case the Allies had embarked on the Prinkipo proposal and, if abandoned, as Clemenceau proposed, all the advantages gained by the original proposal would be thrown away. . . . House said *he had never been in favour of the Prinkipo proposal* but it had been embarked upon, and therefore they must go along with it and, if eventually the Allies were compelled to embark on military operations, they would do so in a stronger and better position. . . .

Sonnino agreed that the Allies would have to get out of the Prinkipo business. *He himself had been opposed to it from the commencement* and he had then expressed the opinion that the Bolshevists would be the only ones to accept the Allies' invitation. They were all very brave and downright in the absence of Lloyd George and President Wilson.

[1] All this from *ibid.*, pp. 16 *sq.*; the italics are the author's.

Clemenceau was not altogether opposed to Churchill's draft message, but what was said in two pages could be put in ten lines. Personally, he would prefer to say nothing but, if the Conference insisted upon sending a message, it should be as simple as possible. Sonnino's attitude was rather similar. Churchill insisted, however, that the British Cabinet would never agree, having gone so far, to break off the Prinkipo policy without making it quite clear to the world that that proposal had been sincerely put forward and sincerely pressed, as long as any chance of its succeeding existed.

A proposed 'Allied Council for Russian Affairs' aroused no enthusiasm, but a suggestion that the policy should be discussed at the Council of Ten itself met with more support. Eventually both aspects of the question, the draft message and the proposed council, were adjourned until after the week-end, which would give time for contact with the home Governments. And those contacts so far as London was concerned produced notable results.

When the Prime Minister left for London, Philip Kerr had remained in Paris as watch-dog, and although Lloyd George's account is sparing in details and especially in dates, it is quite clear from it that by this time he had become very anxious about the news that was reaching him. He states, for example, that Kerr had telegraphed to him 'some alarming news as to the progress made under Mr Churchill's powerful impulse towards organizing an armed anti-Bolshevist intervention in Russia'.[1] This prompted the Prime Minister to send a very hot telegram expressing his alarm, stating that the Cabinet had never authorized anything beyond supplying the anti-Bolshevist areas with sufficient equipment to enable their armed forces to hold their own, and then only in the event of every effort at a peaceable solution failing. He violently repudiated operations which would consolidate and strengthen Bolshevist opinion and commit the country to a mad enterprise out of hatred of Bolshevist principles. 'An expensive war of aggression against Russia is a way to strengthen Bolshevism in Russia and create it at home. We cannot afford the burden.' In his message Lloyd George also stressed the disastrous effect of anything of the kind on the nation at large and especially on organized labour.

That telegram, although undated, must have been sent off on Saturday (February 15th) or Sunday (February 16th) for Lloyd George reproduces in his book a memorandum in reply dated February 17th sent by Philip Kerr which begins as follows:

[1] D. Lloyd George, *The Truth about the Peace Treaties*, vol. 1, pp. 370–1.

Your various telegrams and messages about the importance of not drifting into war against the Bolshevists have been received and have, I think, had their effect. There was a meeting of the British Empire Delegation on the Russian situation this morning at which Balfour set forth very much your view. The discussion showed pretty clearly that everybody was agreed that effective war against the Bolshevists was probably impracticable because of public opinion at home. . . .

The British Empire Delegation at Paris did go so far as to authorize Balfour and Churchill to press on the Council of Ten that afternoon the establishment of Churchill's military commission. But Churchill was out of luck that day for he had to spend the whole afternoon listening to a discussion of a number of tiresome but urgent details raised by Foch as the result of talks with the Germans over the renewal of the Armistice, from which he had just returned, and the Russian question was postponed for several days. Next day the Secretary for War returned home, and two days later Clemenceau was wounded by a would-be assassin and Pichon acted as Chairman of the Council of Ten in his absence.

The postponement of the Russian question is explained to some extent by the following telegram sent by House to Wilson on February 23rd:

George will not arrive in Paris until Friday, February 28th. No action will be taken respecting Russia until after his arrival. I have ascertained his views respecting this question and they are substantially as follows: 'No foreign intervention in Soviet Russia and no foreign troops to be sent to aid of non-Bolshevist Russia unless volunteers choose to go of their own accord, but material assistance to be supplied to these Governments to enable them to hold their own in the territories which are not anxious to submit to Bolshevist rule. Russia must save herself. If she is saved by outside intervention, she is not really saved. We are bound to give moral, material, and if necessary military support to protect Poland, Finland and other such states against Bolshevist invasion. The military party in France and England both favour intervention but have absolutely declined to commit themselves about how the expense thereof should be met. France surely cannot pay and I am sure we cannot either. Will America bear the expense? I do not think we shall have any difficulty reaching an agreement respecting our Russian policy after George arrives, inasmuch as his views apparently coincide with ours.'[1]

[1] *The Intimate Papers of Colonel House*, vol. iv, pp. 358–9. According to a footnote on p. 359, Wilson had cabled to House on February 20th: 'I hope you will make plain that we are not at war with Russia and will, in no circumstances that we can now foresee, take part in military operations there against the Russians'.

The Russian question did, however, come up unexpectedly a week later on Tuesday (February 25th) before Lloyd George's return, but only incidentally to a statement by Foch on the question of the return of Haller's Polish Division from France to Poland which had been troubling the Council for some time. But the reference is interesting because Foch gave a sketch of his ideas on the proper way to deal with Russia in the following passage:

The difficulties which the Allies had to face in Russia were due not only to the enormous distances, to which he had already referred, but also to the nature of the enemy that had to be dealt with. The enemy might be badly organized but he was scattered over an enormous territory, acting like a violent virus. Now, to fight against such an enemy, troops of a particular composition were required; and in great numbers in order to cover the whole territory involved; but these troops need not be strongly organized or of superior quality. The necessary conditions would be fulfilled by the employment of such armies as might be raised locally in the countries of Eastern Europe. For instance, the Polish troops would be quite able to face the Russians, provided the former were strengthened by the supply of modern appliances and engines of war. But great numbers were required, which could be obtained by mobilizing the Finns, Poles, Czechs, Roumanians and Greeks, as well as the Russian pro-Ally elements still available.[1]

However, with Churchill out of the picture, this rather nebulous suggestion cut no ice, and was never seriously discussed as it was subsidiary to the main issue before the Council. The subject did not come up again until March 17th when Foch proposed that, in order to clear up the situation in Lemberg, 'which was invested by the Ukrainians, and whose fall would entail that of the Polish Government', Polish troops should be brought from Odessa for the purpose and should be strengthened by the Roumanian army. But Lloyd George saw the red light in this proposal, which he said 'at bottom merely meant the setting up of a great army for the eventual invasion of Russia'. He came down so heavily against it that the proposal was dropped.

[1] *The Foreign Relations of the United States: The Paris Peace Conference 1919*, vol. iv, p. 122.

CHAPTER IX

THE FOREIGN MINISTERS SPEED
UP THE CONFERENCE

' I have heard oft times that it is more safe to hear and to
take counsel than to give it.' (THOMAS À KEMPIS, *The
Imitation*, c. 9.)

THE departure of Wilson and Orlando on February 14th was important to me for more than one reason. First, of course, owing to the
changes in the Council of Ten to which we shall pass anon, and second,
to the personal factor that my wife arrived in Paris on the evening of
Sunday (February 16th), which brought me great happiness and encouragement in the difficult period that was to come. As no official
accommodation was available, I had taken a room in a small hotel
within a few minutes' walk of my office but managed to convert my
bedroom in the Villa Majestic, adjoining my office, into a sitting-room
which was entirely at her disposal during her stay. She arrived in poor
shape, still suffering from the after-effects of 'Spanish' influenza but
a few weeks in Paris did her a power of good, and the food at the Hotel
Majestic, where we had our meals, was a vast improvement on the war
rations from which England was only very slowly recovering.

Turning to the political aspects of the change: Clemenceau was for
the moment the only survivor of the 'Big Four' (as they came to be
called) who had dominated the meetings of the Council of Ten. I had
formed a great admiration for him during the war, which had been
enhanced by his leadership at the Preliminary Peace Conference, both
in Plenary Session and at the Council of Ten. He also had a liking for
me, as illustrated by the following extract from a letter I wrote to my
wife on February 7th, a week before her journey to Paris:

Yesterday Clemenceau came up to me and *à propos* of nothing said: '*Restez
jeune, mon colonel, si longtemps que vous pouvez*' (remain young, my colonel,
as long as you can). I replied in English: 'If I can remain young half as
long as you, I shall be more than content!'

Perhaps as an introduction to the political events recorded in this
chapter the following continuation of the same letter is permissible:

I shall need my youth! Balfour is not in good health, and my responsibilities, with desperately difficult questions coming to their most acute

stage at the Conference, are very heavy. Luckily a good sound horse, Milner to wit, is to work in harness with Balfour at the 'hush-hush' meetings, still even the mechanical work is heavy and I work every day from 9 a.m. to 8 p.m. almost without cease. . . .

I had, however, under-rated, not for the first or last time in my life, Balfour's extraordinary aptitude for rising to the occasion.

After the departure of Wilson and Orlando, Clemenceau was left in charge of the Council of Ten which, apart from himself, included no heads of Governments but consisted mainly of Foreign Ministers, namely Lansing and House for the United States, Balfour with Milner for the British Empire, Pichon with Tardieu for France, Sonnino with the Italian Ambassador for Italy, Makino and Matsui for Japan.

On Saturday (February 15th) in accordance with a pre-arranged programme, the new Council first heard a statement of the claims of a delegation from the Lebanon, which did not detain them long and need not detain us at all. They took advantage of Winston Churchill's presence in Paris to continue discussions on certain outstanding military and air questions, including the renewal of the armistice, the negotiations with the Dutch Government for the passage of Allied troops to the Rhineland, and the attempts to secure a Russian representation at the Peace Conference. In the afternoon they heard a long report from Foch on the results of his successful discussions on the renewal of the Armistice with the Germans, who had accepted the conditions laid down by the Supreme War Council.

On Tuesday (February 18th) a very long hearing was given to the Serbian claims at the Peace Conference, which were presented with marked ability by the Serbian ex-President of the Council Pachitch and his colleagues, and were referred, as usual, to the appropriate committee.

On this occasion, Borden, who after the departure of Churchill and in the absence of Milner was acting as Balfour's colleague at the Council of Ten, made a very sensible suggestion that 'possibly time might be saved if the Council made up its mind what questions could suitably be sent to committees in anticipation of hearing statements beforehand and thereby, in each instance, a meeting of the Council might be saved'. Later, he explained that his suggestion had only been made with a view to saving time. In the same order of ideas he suggested that statements reduced to writing should not be read before the Council. The question, however, had, as Lansing pointed out, been discussed before Wilson's departure and it had been thought that many delegations, anxious to make statements, would be dissatisfied if referred direct to committees. The Foreign Ministers could hardly reverse a practice that had been deliberately adopted and established as a precedent on many occasions by their chiefs.

Undoubtedly they were right. Of course it was infinitely tedious for them to have to listen to the reading in French and English of long, written statements of each nation's claims which could have been read beforehand by conscientious members who had had the time, and after that, to hear the commentaries of the ministers concerned. But it must be remembered that each Delegation was led by a President of the Council or a Foreign Minister, with support from other distinguished figures, and it would have been an affront to these national representatives at the Conference to refuse to allow them to present their country's case and to reinforce it with their own arguments. The prestige of the Conference would have suffered throughout the world if Borden's very practical suggestion had been adopted. Although a lot of time was wasted by these hearings, they paid in the long run.

At the end of that séance, Balfour read out a list of the territorial questions still awaiting consideration which, in spite of the considerable number already discussed in a preliminary way, included Schleswig-Holstein, the Baltic Provinces, Poland (delimitation), Luxemburg, Albania, Zionism, Armenia. That was a formidable, although incomplete, list—especially when it is remembered that no territorial boundaries could be settled until after a detailed examination of each case by the expert committees, which could hardly be expected to produce unanimous recommendations in such controversial matters as national boundaries. It was after that long meeting on the afternoon of Tuesday (February 18th) that the attempt was made to assassinate Clemenceau, who was shot in the shoulder as his car was leaving his home.

The Council of Ten did not meet again until Friday (February 21st) when Pichon was asked to take the chair during the temporary absence of Clemenceau and the composition of the Council of Ten was now reduced, temporarily, to Foreign Minister's status, with Balfour as the outstanding figure. He at once rose to the occasion. The short respite from meetings of the Council of Ten from February 18th to February 21st was very welcome, for it gave Balfour an opportunity to overhaul our own organization, and more important, to hatch out in consultation with other members of the British and British Empire

Delegations and myself new plans for speeding up the work of the Conference. At this stage, six weeks after the start of the Conference, no less than nineteen subordinate committees or commissions had been set up to study detailed questions, and in addition the committees themselves had set up twenty-seven sub-committees making forty-six in all. Of the nineteen parent committees or commissions due to report eventually either to the Plenary Conference or the Council of Ten, seven dealt with major questions concerning the whole conference, viz. the League of Nations, authors of the war and penalties, reparations, international labour, ports, waterways and railways, financial and economic questions and the new Supreme Economic Council. All these seven bodies were due to report to the Plenary Conference which had set them up. Wilson's League of Nations Committee had already produced a draft of the Covenant, which had been discussed and accepted in principle at the Third Plenary meeting. There was also a group of four naval and military committees working under the general supervision of Foch, with whom Henry Wilson and his 'opposite numbers' in foreign delegations were in close touch.

In addition to those eleven commissions and sub-commissions, seven 'territorial' committees had been set up since January 29th, all of which, except the Inter-Allied Commission in Teschen and a Polish Affairs Mission, were resident in Paris. They were all due to report to the Council of Ten. For all these, nineteen British or British Empire Secretaries or members of a joint Secretariat had already been found with whom I was able to keep in touch at my daily informal meetings now held at 8.15 a.m. As we have seen, the number of territorial committees was being added to almost daily as the result of the preliminary hearings by the Council of Ten. This was not altogether a disadvantage as it gave time both for the Secretariat-General and for individual delegations (including our own) to find persons with the right qualifications as members, secretaries and interpreters, as well as accommodation. These inquiries had to be scattered all over Paris in French Government departments and sometimes even hotels.

The maintenance of an efficient up-to-date directory became a work of art, but my head clerk Rawlins, owing to his experience at imperial and international conferences (including the Supreme War Council) during the war, managed to produce successive up-to-date editions (printed at the Foreign Office press in the Bois de Boulogne) which were distributed widely in the British and British Empire Delegations and beyond. In addition to this, my small office was

reproducing in English the whole of the minutes of the Council of
Ten as dictated by the joint secretaries of the Supreme War Council
immediately after the meetings and circulating them with the least
possible delay—often the same evening—to all the delegations concerned. The French versions were dealt with by the Secretariat-
General. Besides that, my office was reproducing the minutes of the
almost daily meetings of the British Empire Delegation, prepared
under the direction of Clement Jones and his group of distinguished
Empire secretaries, as well as the agenda papers and documents for
the meetings. How this huge work was accomplished with such
efficiency and rapidity in so small an office was at the time, and still
remains, a mystery to me.

At any rate, Balfour found that our own organization was working
well and that this was equally true of the large inter-departmental
organization in the Hotel Astoria under Hardinge's control, with
whom we worked in perfect harmony; and that I had no doubt that
it would be equal to any additional strain thrown upon it by speeding
up the work of the Conference as a whole.

Balfour now decided to take the next step, namely the extension of
speeding up to the whole Conference. He left it to me to deal with the
Secretariat-General while he tackled Pichon. Fortunately the latter
was able to secure a bedside interview with Clemenceau who, he
reported, was most anxious to go ahead with the plan. This accordingly was presented to the Council the same afternoon. The Balfour
plan involved an extension of the principle that had been adopted just
before the departure of Wilson and Orlando, and accepted thereafter
by the Allied German Armistice Commission at Spa, namely, that
instead of the monthly revisions of the Armistice, the military terms
to be imposed on Germany should be drawn up in the form of a final
scheme which would definitely regulate her future armament. In view,
however, of the 'general feeling of impatience in all countries on
account of the apparently slow progress the Conference was making
in the direction of final peace', Balfour's suggestion was that the
principle should be extended to cover the whole of the ground so
that, when peace terms came to be discussed with Germany, a complete
document should be presented—including everything and not merely
a few naval, military, air and a few related other conditions.

Naturally, even in such a friendly atmosphere as that in the Council
of Ten, so drastic a proposal raised doubts. Pichon of course, after
the talk with Clemenceau, strongly supported it and added that Foch

and his military advisers were of the same opinion. House and Lansing took the same line. The doubts came from Sonnino who had replaced Orlando. He did not deny the advantages of speeding up the settlement of the peace preliminaries, but pointed out that Germany was not the only enemy with whom a comprehensive treaty had to be drawn up and that, in their case also, many complicated questions presented themselves. For example, for Italy, the Austrian question was more complicated in that the Austrian Empire was now divided into various states, some of which were friendly, others semi-friendly and others hostile. . . . 'Should the military, economic and financial conditions to be imposed on Germany first be settled, what,' he asked, 'would happen to the other questions requiring settlement?. . . .'

That led to a prolonged discussion during which many amendments were suggested to Balfour's original draft and eventually the final decision was adjourned until the next meeting. On Monday (February 24th) at 3 p.m., however, the plan was adopted with small amendments, and extended so as to apply in identical terms to each of the ex-enemies by means of separate drafts for Germany, Austria, Hungary, Bulgaria and Turkey respectively. Thus the resolution relating to Germany was as follows:

RESOLUTION NO. 1[1]

1. The Conference agree that it is desirable to proceed without delay to the consideration of preliminary peace terms with Germany and press on the necessary investigations with all possible speed.

2. The preliminary peace terms, other than the naval, military, and air conditions, should cover *inter alia* the following points:

   (a) the approximate future frontiers of Germany and the renunciation of colonies and territorial rights outside Europe;

   (b) the financial conditions to be imposed on Germany;

   (c) the economic conditions to be accorded to Germany; and

   (d) responsibility for breaches of the laws of war.

3. In order that the Conference may have at its disposal, with the least possible delay, the results of the labours of the various Commissions which have been investigating these subjects, it is requested that the various commissions will send in their reports to the Secretary-General, not later than March 6th. This will not apply to commissions set up after February 15th which would be unable to render their final reports at so early a date, but it is requested that in these cases, interim reports may be presented dealing with all matters affecting the preliminaries of peace with Germany.

[1] *The Foreign Relations of the United States: The Paris Peace Conference 1919*, vol. iv, pp. 104–111.

As Germany was the only ex-enemy country that had possessed colonies, the resolutions were re-worded (para 2(*a*)) to meet the conditions of Austria-Hungary, Bulgaria and Turkey.

No well-informed person, of course, was under any illusion that there was the slightest hope of making serious progress with the treaties with Austria, Bulgaria or Turkey for some time to come, but Sonnino's apprehension that concentration on the German Treaty might leave Italy in the lurch over the Austro-Hungarian settlement was understandable. Still, the reduction of the German army to limits where it was no longer a danger to peace was obviously the first objective, and the Council of Ten showed foresight in realizing that the completion of the rest of the Treaty at the same time would render it easier for Germany to swallow.

Swift action was taken by the Secretariat-General to translate this important decision into action. Committees that were hanging fire were stirred up and emphasis on the need to push ahead, hitherto confined to the more important commissions, spread a better tone to all parts of the Conference. In the last three days of February, the Foreign Ministers followed up this valuable initiative by tackling and deciding, with the aid of Foch and Weygand, the difficult problem of the despatch of Haller's Polish Army from France and other Polish troops from Italy, by sea to Danzig, and *via* Danzig to Warsaw, moves involving concerted arrangements with the Allied Maritime Council in London and the Allied Commission in Poland. In addition, the question of the boundaries of the Polish State was discussed and referred for examination and report to the Committee on Polish Affairs (February 26th). The discussion of this question, however, brought into sharp relief the difficulties arising from the fact that, both in Poland and other countries in Eastern Europe, the question of the boundaries with Russia was undetermined, and indeed indeterminable, owing to the failure of the Conference to secure the presence of any representative from Russia, in view of the chaotic state of that country.

After considerable discussion it was decided on February 27th, in order to expedite the work on defining future frontiers of enemy countries, to set up yet another small and rather high-level committee of one representative from each of the principal Powers with the following terms of reference:

(*a*) to draw up for the consideration of the Preliminary Peace Conference the frontiers based on the recommendations of the territorial commissions which have been, or may be, appointed.

(*b*) to make recommendations as to any part of the frontiers of enemy states which are not included in the scope of any commission, excepting such frontier questions as any of the powers concerned may reserve for discussion in the first instance at the Quai d'Orsay Council (i.e. the Council of Ten).

The committee appears in the Directory of the Conference under the title of 'The Geographical Frontiers of Germany Committee', and consisted of Dr S. E. Mezes (United States), Sir Eyre Crowe (British Empire), André Tardieu (France), Count Vannutelli (Italy) and Mr H. Ijuin (Japan), but was sometimes spoken of as the 'Boundaries Co-ordinating Committee'.

Besides those very useful accomplishments, the Foreign Ministers did some good spade work in clearing up an awkward question of an Austrian debt payment of coupons, due March 1st; in ventilating some French difficulties over Moroccan affairs; by giving a hearing to M. Tardieu, Chairman of the Belgian Commission on 'certain hesitations, and doubts' that had already arisen; in approving—with slight modifications—a report from the military representatives of the Supreme War Council on the creation of a neutral zone in Transylvania; and by listening to very long statements by an American delegation (February 26th), and by a Zionist deputation which included M. Sokolow, Dr Weizmann and several others (February 27th). On most of these it was not found possible to make much progress at the moment.

Altogether, when February closed, the Foreign Ministers of the five principal Powers who had been left by their respective chiefs in charge of the Preliminary Peace Conference and the Council of Ten had done a fine job in speeding up the work; for this they did not receive the credit they deserved.

F

CHAPTER X

ACCUMULATING DIFFICULTIES

'And coming events cast their shadows before.' (THOMAS CAMPBELL, *Lochiel's Warning*.)

IN March the Heads of Delegations returned one by one—Clemenceau on March 1st, Lloyd George on the 6th, Orlando on the 11th and Wilson on the 17th. All that time the Council of Ten's plans for speeding-up were coming into effect, but a good deal of time had to be devoted to a settlement of questions of principle such as the distribution of functions between the different commissions so as to avoid duplication or a hiatus between them. Such problems arose at once between the Economic, Financial and Reparations Commissions and the sub-committees they were setting up, and sometimes decisions had to be given on important questions of principle. For example, the Commission on Reparations by Germany was instructed to prepare its report on alternative hypotheses that war costs were or were not included. Questions had to be cleared up between the Transport Commission and other bodies, such as those concerned with supplies for the starving people of Germany, Austria and Central Europe. These, in turn, involved expenditure which reacted on the Economic and Financial Commissions. Of course, the Commissions and the Secretariat-General did their utmost to adjust such problems but the hard cases had to come to the Council of Ten as the supreme authority of the Conference.

In the wide field of territorial committees where, at the beginning of March, the preliminary hearings by the Council of Ten itself had not been completed, many problems of adjustment between the different committees arose—particularly in the case of existing or prospective countries with many frontiers, like Greece, Poland, Czechoslovakia and Jugoslavia. Even the decision of the Council of Ten on February 27th[1] to set up a Central Territorial Committee to co-ordinate the work of the other territorial committees, and to draw the frontiers resulting from their recommendations, though it proved a useful piece of machinery, did not relieve the Supreme Council from having to decide hard cases.

[1] *Vide supra* pp. 80–1.

Even more hampering, however, in the day-to-day work of the Council of Ten on the Peace Treaty was the stream of problems that arose owing to the unsettled state of Central and Eastern Europe. Thus, in Russia, although the Communists were slowly getting the upper hand, there was still civil war in several centres. This reacted severely on all the border-countries. In Poland for example, Paderewski, the patriotic pianist who had formed a struggling government, was threatened by the Germans on the west, the Lithuanians on the north-east, the Ukrainians in Galicia, where the key town of Lemberg—described as 'a Polish island in a sea of Ukrainians'—was cut off from Przemysl, its main source of supplies, and where the important Galician oil-fields were in Ukrainian occupation. There were also troubles over Teschen, and elsewhere in the south. In these circumstances, much time had to be devoted by the Supreme War Council of Ten to such measures as the transport through Danzig of Haller's army and other Polish troops, to which the Germans were putting up every possible obstruction at the Armistice centre at Spa. This was only overcome by very drastic insistence, and by the expedient of describing Haller's troops as 'part of an Allied force to help restore and maintain order'.

There were other difficult problems of the same sort in the Banat, in Croatia and elsewhere in connexion with the transport and distribution of food to the starving populations of Central Europe. Awkward problems of payment were also constantly arising, and were dealt with as a rule by the appropriate financial, economic and transport organizations of the Conference though, now and then, they would have to be decided by the Council of Ten as the Supreme War Council. These aspects cannot be discussed in detail here but must be mentioned owing to their collective importance as a factor overlooked by critics who have charged the Supreme Council of the Peace Conference with sloth. In very many cases, the sole object of the trouble-makers, in the various countries, was to jump their claim to territories in dispute in the hope that the Conference would be influenced by the proposition that 'possession is nine-tenths of the law'.

The result of these and other factors was that the optimistic hopes of the Foreign Ministers proved too sanguine and on March 6th, the date fixed by the Council for the completion of reports by committees and commissions appointed before February 15th, the Secretary-General had not received a single report from any of the territorial groups, except one of relatively minor importance on the Belgian

Treaties of 1839, nor from any of the large groups dealing with reparations, economic and financial subjects, transport and the like.

Rather unexpectedly, Foch threatened to upset the programme of the Council of Ten with his report on the all-important naval, military and air terms of peace to be imposed on Germany, which the military members of the Supreme War Council and the corresponding naval and air groups had, for some time, been hammering out in secrecy under the marshal's direction. This very long and important report had only been submitted to the President (Clemenceau) and distributed to the representatives of the five Great Powers on Friday (February 28th); yet on Saturday (March 1st), at his first return to the Council of Ten (still lacking the presence of any other heads of Government), Clemenceau opened the meeting by asking the Council to consider it there and then and even to take a decision without delay.

There had, of course, been no time to study this long and weighty report in detail or for the Foreign Ministers to discuss it with their respective naval, military and air advisers, none of whom were present with the exception of Foch and his chief of staff, Weygand. Balfour, therefore, expressed the general view of the meeting in demurring to this proposal tactfully and adroitly, without any hint that it was suspect of being a 'try-on' to rush through the French view before the return of the other Heads of Delegations. The subject was, therefore, postponed until the next meeting on Monday (March 3rd) and, for the moment, the Council of Ten passed to a complicated report by a Financial Drafting Committee on the group of financial, economic and reparations questions, in which my old friend Edwin Montagu was playing a prominent part.

On Monday (March 3rd), after disposing of an aftermath of the financial questions, the Council of Ten automatically resolved itself into a meeting of the Supreme War Council for consideration of the report on naval, military and air terms of peace, with the result that the numbers present in Pichon's moderately-sized room at the Quai d'Orsay rose from its normal average of 20 to 25 to over 50, including a great array of admirals and generals in uniform. This time Clemenceau supplemented the report by a paper, sent by Foch, purporting to summarize the full report. Once more, Balfour had to ask for further time to examine in detail the report, as well as Foch's summary, with his advisers, particularly as there were points (Clemenceau only admitted *one* point) on which the military authorities were not agreed. Balfour also remarked that 'it is not unlikely that Lloyd George would like to examine the report'. A few days' delay would, he thought, be enough. His real object of course was to gain time for Lloyd George's return. Foch, who probably knew that his report was not likely to be acceptable to Lloyd George, protested against the delay on the grounds that the present rate of demobilization in the Allied armies required that the discussion with the Germans should not be delayed after April 1st. The Allies could impose their will on Germany until that date; if they were not to be in a position to do so, the whole plan of demobilization would have to be altered. He, therefore, begged the council to agree upon the terms early enough to allow a meeting with the Germans by March 20th.

That argument did not cut much ice because everyone present at this meeting on March 3rd knew that the Treaty, which was now to be presented to the Germans as a whole, could not possibly be ready by March 20th or even April 1st. Clemenceau decided that he could not refuse Balfour's request for a short delay and, after a lengthy and not very fruitful discussion, the subject was postponed until Thursday (March 6th) when Lloyd George was expected back. In the meanwhile, Foch was to assemble the Military, Naval and Air Commissions to co-ordinate their reports.

The Council of Ten, in adjourning the all-important question of military, naval and air terms until March 6th, had left quite enough material for digestion by members to occupy them for the whole of the two days' interval in discussions with their respective delegations, to say nothing of the heavy jobs referred back to Foch and his Committee. But such was the pressure of other urgent questions that yet another meeting of the Council had to be held on Wednesday (March 5th). In order not to interrupt the story of the military, naval and air terms, it will suffice to mention that that meeting resulted in decisions: (*a*) to refuse a Belgian claim to be represented at all meetings of the Council of Ten; (*b*) to refuse a demand for a hearing for a Danish Commission on Schleswig and to delegate it to the Belgian Commission; (*c*) to defer a Luxemburg claim to be heard for the present; (*d*) to relegate for later consideration a paper by Foch on the cost of the Allied Army of Occupation in Germany. In addition, an excellent proposal from the American Delegation that commissions and committees should attach to their reports a special drafting of articles to find a place in the preliminary draft of the Peace Treaty was reserved for discussion on March 8th together with the naval, military and air terms, when it was at once approved. Further demands for certain South American representation on the Economic and Financial Commission were rejected; useful decisions were taken on the financing of supplies for Austria, some aspects being reserved until Friday (March 7th), and a hearing was given to a statement by the King of Montenegro.

Those comparatively uninteresting and unimpressive details are mentioned to illustrate the pressure under which the Council were working at the time when their minds were occupied with one of the most thorny and difficult questions of the Peace Treaty, namely the military, naval and air conditions, to which we must now return.

CHAPTER XI

MILITARY TERMS OF PEACE

'These are the three great chords of might,
And he whose ears are tuned aright
Will see no discord in the three
But the most perfect harmony.'

(LONGFELLOW, *The Singers.*)

As neither President Wilson nor Signor Orlando had yet returned, the Council of Ten met on March 6th as the Supreme War Council, a procedure which was followed for four consecutive meetings. Once more the room was overfull with naval, military and air uniforms for discussion of the military and air terms. Henry Wilson, who had not been present at the previous meeting on this subject, headed the British contingent, with Admiral Wemyss. On the return of Lloyd George the atmosphere was charged with a note of expectancy.

However, Lloyd George opened the proceedings quietly by announcing that he had just received a message telephoned from Spa to the effect that negotiations relating to the supply of food and stores to Germany as well as the surrender of merchant ships by Germany had been broken off, and that the Allied delegates were returning to Paris to report. As Foch had received no information as yet, this subject was adjourned until the morrow.

On passing to the military, naval and air terms the Council was informed that agreement had now been reached by Foch's groups on the outstanding issues, but that this had only involved slight alterations in certain sentences. General Degoutte, Foch's spokesman, claimed that 'the military advisers had from the beginning been in complete agreement as regards the principles advocated'. The changes in the texts, indeed, were so trifling that Clemenceau suggested that they might be discussed at once, one by one.

At that point Lloyd George weighed in and soon showed how right Balfour had been in suggesting at the previous meeting on the subject that he 'thought it not unlikely that Mr Lloyd George would like to examine the report'. The atmosphere now became electric. Having extracted from Foch the admission that the maximum German army proposed would be 200,000 men and that they would be raised by annual recruitment and serve only for one year, our Prime Minister pointed out that under this system in ten years 2,000,000 men would have been raised, in fifteen years 3,000,000 and in twenty years 4,000,000. Foch's reply was that the personnel for these large armies would have only short training and that the number of officers, and especially staff officers—the really important factor—would be small. Lloyd George's rejoinder was that trained officers were already plentiful in Germany and that would be the case for the next twenty-five years. They 'would be ready to come forward, thirsting for revenge, at the first opportunity'—and much more in the same vein. 'Surely that ought not to be called disarmament', he said. 'He himself would be very sorry to leave France after the signing of peace with that threat facing her across the Rhine. . . . He would inquire, therefore, why a present of this great force should be made to Germany. He thought history would be repeating itself, and the Allies would be doing exactly the same thing as Napoleon had done after the battle of Jena. . . .' Lloyd George then explained that what he had in his mind was that 'Germany should not be permitted to maintain a larger army than Britain possessed', and he ended by asking for a postponement until the next morning in order to give him time to submit an alternative proposal to the Council. In spite of Foch's objections this was agreed to.

The Council then turned to the draft of the naval conditions to be imposed on Germany, to which Lloyd George raised the same doubts as in the case of the military terms and stated that 'he was not prepared to agree to 15,000 men being trained every year'. Apart from that, however, he had not very much to say on the proposed naval terms and left the British case to Balfour as an ex-First Lord of the Admiralty. The main criticism came from Leygues, the French Minister of Marine, who was very concerned at a provision that German warships surrendered to the Allies should be broken up, instead of being divided among them.

The result of this discussion, however, was much more satisfactory than in the case of the military terms for 'the Naval Clauses for the Conditions of Peace with Germany', were approved subject to a number of reservations, including Leygues' point mentioned above and three points which were referred to special committees, namely: the Kiel Canal to the International Ports, Waterways and Railways Commission; the German submarine cables to a special judicial committee to be created; and reparation for Allied shipping losses to the Inter-Allied Commission on Reparations. Altogether Lloyd

George had celebrated his return to the Conference by a real 'day out', and his advisers, including Henry Wilson and myself, had a 'night out' to help him prepare a practical plan for the resumed discussion on the morrow. We all agreed, however, that he was absolutely right.

At the outset of next day's meeting (March 7th) there were, as usual, a certain number of difficult matters affecting the condition of Europe to be disposed of. First, there was a piece of good news, namely that the report of the Belgian Commission had been received. Next, however, the interrupted discussion on the Spa negotiations had to be taken up, for which Robert Cecil and Admiral Hope, both old friends of mine, had come from Spa to present the case, but the subject had to be postponed until next day. Then the terms of reference to the new Legal Committee, as well as its composition, had to be settled.

After that the American delegation paraded the famous Mr Hoover to ventilate a serious problem affecting the blockade in the Adriatic which was hampering the transport of urgently needed relief for the starving Jugoslav population. This subject did not admit of postponement, but was complicated and controversial and took some time to settle by concerted instructions to a commission of four generals and other relief organizations concerned with transport and so forth.

So much time had been lost in settling these emergency questions that on Lloyd George's suggestion, to their great disappointment, the audience of technical naval and military advisers was asked to withdraw, except Foch and one general, one admiral and one air officer for each nation. Lloyd George then propounded the following draft resolution:

The military, naval and aerial terms of peace shall be based on the following principles:

1. The German naval, military and air forces shall be raised by voluntary service.
2. The minimum period of service for all ranks shall be twelve years with the colours.
3. The strength of the German army and air force shall not exceed 200,000 men of all ranks, organized in not more than fifteen infantry divisions and three cavalry divisions.
4. The strength of the German navy shall not exceed 10,000 men of all ranks and ratings.

Thus Germany would not have an annual contingent of troops. With the substitution of long service for short service 'she would not be able to play the same trick on Europe as she had after Jena'. A voluntary army would cost much more than a conscript army. That, in addition to paying compensation to the Allies, would leave her no money for adventures. That, much condensed, was the pith of Lloyd George's statement. His audience was dumbfounded. As the now published official minutes reveal: 'There being no dissentient, the resolution was adopted.'

There was a moment of tension after Clemenceau had announced that, as there was no objection, the resolution would be sent to the Military, Naval and Air Committees for adaptation to the body of their recommendations. Then Foch pointed out that there were no advocates of Lloyd George's principles. He would, therefore, press that the British Delegation should be asked to report on the matter. He had received Lloyd George's proposals at mid-day and found that they dealt with other than military proposals. 'Was his Commission', he asked, 'to report on these also?' Degoutte then spoke up and said that 'he personally would never agree with the views expressed by the British Delegation in favour of a voluntary army in Germany. He thought this would make Germany stronger than a short-term conscript service'. But no one else supported him—neither Henry Wilson, nor the experienced Bliss nor Cavallero, nor any of the admirals. So the subject was referred back to the military advisers 'to draft a scheme on the basis of the resolution'. The redraft, it was specified, was to include the naval and air aspects, but the French General Duval remarked that the Air Committee had proposed to suppress the whole of the German air force. Was he to understand that a different report was now required? Lloyd George said that he had no objection to the entire suppression of the German air force and there the subject was left for the time being, but subsequently the Air Committee's recommendation was adopted.

Before adjourning, however, Wemyss, chairman of the Naval Commission, secured approval to a number of revised naval clauses, including such important provisions as the limitation of German replacement vessels to 10,000 tons for armoured ships, 6,000 tons for light cruisers, 800 tons for destroyers, 200 tons for torpedo boats and 'no submarines for any purpose whatever, commercial or otherwise . . .'. Important limitations on German coast fortifications were also approved. Altogether, in spite of the interruption of the early part of the meeting by extraneous matters, a great advance had been made and Lloyd George had had a big triumph and decisively strengthened his position in the Conference. In effect the ruling of March 7th proved decisive on the military, naval and air terms.

The committees under Foch got to work with their usual energy on the preparation of a re-draft of their original effort based on Lloyd George's principles which was circulated in time for discussion at a meeting of the Supreme War Council (Council of Ten) on Monday (March 10th). In an introductory declaration, actually read by Clemenceau, the French Marshal still maintained that his original draft, based on the principle of short service, was preferable to the new plan. He urged, however, that if the Governments insisted on adherence to the principle of short service the strength of the German army should be reduced from 140,000 in the new draft to 100,000.

This point was immediately taken up and led to considerable discussion. Bliss supported the reduction and Clemenceau made a strong appeal for its adoption. Lloyd George, who had at first felt no objection to 140,000, then stated that, in view of the burden of defence which must fall in later years on France, he could not refuse the appeals of Foch and Clemenceau. Lansing took the same view and the reduction to 100,000 was accepted. Balfour, while not contesting the decision, pointed out that this would reduce the German army to a police force basis, and a small one at that. If Germany were to be left powerless for defence, while France, Poland or Czechoslovakia could have as many troops as they wished, would she not be entitled to demand some guarantee from the Allied Powers against her being left at the mercy of her small neighbours? Clemenceau agreed that this was an important question but its solution ought to be left to the League of Nations, one of whose functions was to prevent sudden aggression by any of its members. Balfour said 'that if this was the solution it should be communicated to Germany'.

After discussions and amendments to the earlier articles, and acceptance without discussion of the air terms, the whole convention—military, naval and air—as amended was referred to the Drafting Committee of the Conference, assisted by Generals Weygand, Henry Wilson, Bliss and Cavallero. At the fag end of the meeting protests were made against the redraft by the French Generals Degoutte and Weygand and the Italian Cavallero. As they received no support from any delegate Clemenceau refused to discuss them, but allowed them to be recorded in the Minutes.

The military, naval and air terms of peace did not come back to the Supreme War Council (Council of Ten) from the Drafting Committee until Wilson's return on March 17th, when they appeared first on the agenda paper. Orlando who had just missed the previous discussion on the 10th by returning on March 11th also had his first opportunity to discuss it with his colleagues. Clemenceau therefore decided that the interpreter (M. Mantoux) should read it article by article, which he did admirably, pausing at the end of each article for discussion. Nothing could have been more thorough.

At the outset President Wilson asked for assurances that the number of 100,000 would be sufficient to cope with 'exterior dangers from the Bolshevists' and was assured by Foch that it was sufficient with the gendarmerie for 'the maintenance of order within the territory of Germany and the defence of her frontiers'. No one of course was thinking of what kind of a Russia might develop out of the chaos prevailing at the time. The President also objected to the use of the word 'never' when laying down the limitations of armament, and the word 'not' was substituted. This affected several articles of the Treaty.

The President also, with strong support from Lloyd George, secured the removal from Article 10 (manufacture of arms, munitions and war material) of the following sentence: 'All orders shall be notified to the Allied and Associated Governments and may not be carried out until after such notification'. This was considered as too humiliating and unworkable. A slight clash occurred between the President and Lloyd George whether Article 12 forbidding importation of war material to Germany was not already provided for in the Covenant of the League of Nations, the British Prime Minister claiming that it was and the President that it was not. The difficulty was resolved by the following re-draft:

Importation into Germany of arms, munitions and war material of every kind shall be strictly prohibited. The same applies to the manufacture for export of arms, munitions and war material.

Other articles were discussed and many were amended to meet Wilson's comments; he had obviously studied the draft with the utmost care. I should like to add the words 'and had obviously been well briefed' if I had not learned by later experience that he relied very largely on himself for briefing.

The net result of that long and very thorough re-examination was that the military, naval and air clauses were approved, subject to the reservation of five subjects for further consideration, namely:

Art. 25   The disposal of the German warships to be surrendered.
Art. 35   Heligoland (the destruction of the harbour).

Art. 38 On enemy cables, under consideration by a legal committee which was meeting with difficulties.

Art. 47 Providing for the modification by Germany within three months of the signature of the stipulation of German laws and administrative or other measures required to give effect to the stipulation.

Art. 48 Providing for the Armistice of November 11, 1918, and conventions subsequent thereto being kept in force so far as they are not inconsistent with the Treaty.

That list was not perhaps as formidable as it appears at first sight, as several of the reserved points were liable to be dealt with in sections of the Treaty other than the military, naval and air clauses.

In telling the story of the naval, military and air conditions of peace up to March 17th when, at the first meeting after President Wilson's return, they had been brought to a sufficiently advanced stage to justify their remission to the Drafting Committee of the Conference, it has been found necessary to pass over some other important achievements of the Council of Ten. These need not be described in the same detail as the military terms but cannot be ignored, for they occupied much of the time of the Conference on the few days on which the military terms were not the main subject of discussion and obtruded themselves only too often at meetings allotted to the military terms.

For example, the group of questions arising out of German obstructiveness at the Armistice Enforcement Commission at Spa, which resulted in peremptory demands on the Germans to fulfil their obligations, continued, as they developed, to necessitate further instructions from Paris on matters of vital importance, sometimes bearing on the possibility of getting a Treaty at all. Among other such subsidiary, but important, matters were questions of supplies to the starving population of Germany and Austria, the use of German merchant ships as well as the use of German, and in Central Europe other, railways for their transport and distribution, the incidental payments, the conveyance of Haller's army and other troops to Danzig and beyond that port into Poland, and the negotiation of an armistice with the Ukrainians at Lemberg. These questions, which have already been mentioned, were all passing through various stages of solution and at times giving rise to situations so critical that, in spite of the invaluable efforts of such bodies as the Armistice Commission at Spa, the Commission on Ports, Railways and Waterways, the Supreme

Economic and Financial Commission, the Polish Commission, and so forth, many difficult problems had to be referred for decision to the Council of Ten. As some of them were liable to involve the use of force, or conceivably a recrudescence of war, they were usually discussed and recorded by the Council of Ten under the title of the Supreme War Council with Foch and generals and admirals in attendance.

Among questions affecting the Treaty which found a place on the agenda of the Council of Ten on March 12th was the position of the Austrian Emperor which arose out of information received by Balfour from the British representative at Vienna to the effect that the Austrian Government was about to introduce a bill providing for 'the abdication and banishment of the Emperor Charles'. This subject brought the Council to the verge of the contentious question of responsibilities for the war, but no one showed the smallest desire to try the Emperor Charles, and Lansing, the president of the Committee on Breaches of the Laws of War, reported that his Committee

had not attempted to draw up a list of war criminals because the sub-committee dealing with the responsibility for the war had decided that no one could be tried under that head. That is to say, the sub-committee had come to the conclusion that the accused could not be brought before any legal tribunal, since they were only guilty of moral responsibility.

This gives the impression that the sub-committee were wiser than their successors after World War II.

The result of the discussion was that Balfour was asked, on behalf of the five Great Powers,

(1) To telegraph to the British Mission in Vienna to grant facilities for the Austrian Imperial family's journey to Switzerland, and

(2) To ask the Swiss Government to give hospitality to the Imperial family, a guarantee being given, if so required by the Swiss Government, that no difficulties would be raised.

On the same day (March 12th) important progress was made in the settlement of the conditions to be imposed on the German Government in regard to military and maritime aviation—including civilian aviators.

After the provisional settlement of the naval, military and air terms several efforts were made by Foch and friends of his way of thinking to clear up the situation in eastern Poland, which was becoming more and more dangerous. At one time he suggested the despatch of Allied troops through Danzig to co-operate with and stiffen Haller's Polish troops. He attached especial importance to restoration of the much discussed and dangerous situation in Lemberg, actually proposing (March 17th) the transport thither of part of the Polish troops at Odessa, and the support of the Roumanian Army, 'for which purpose a force of ten to twelve divisions at least could be obtained of good physique and good morale'. The Roumanian Government, the marshal reported, was agreeable provided clothing, equipment and food were supplied. Lloyd George's comments were scorching:

The proposal at bottom merely meant the setting up of a great army for the eventual invasion of Russia. It would be agreed that Roumania had nothing to do with Lemberg, but it was hoped that, once the Roumanian troops had been brought to that place, they would be available for operations against Russia. He was entirely opposed to any such operations which could only be carried on at the expense of the Allies. Even supposing the policy was correct, who was going to pay? Roumania could not finance even their own justifiable operations. The Poles were starving and unable to defend Lemberg against an untrained mob of Ukrainian rebels, unless they were organized, furnished with supplies, and paid by the Allies. He, therefore, personally would have nothing to do with the proposal, which merely, being interpreted, meant that in the first place the Roumanians and the Poles would be assembled in Galicia and, under the guise of relieving Lemberg, Russia would be invaded. . . .

His constructive policy was that the Committee on the Frontier of Poland should report whether Lemberg ought to belong to Poland, and he was entirely in favour of using all sources of persuasion to bring about the temporary settlement of the dispute between the Poles and Ukrainians in the same way as had been done in the case of Teschen.

The latter proposal was supported by Pichon and Jules Cambon, the president of the Committee for Polish Affairs which, after hearing General Bartholomy and the British General Carton de Wiart, had decided to support Pichon's plea. The result was the adoption by the Council of Ten of a resolution by the Polish Commission for implementing the policy favoured by Lloyd George of an attempt to obtain an armistice. A proposal by Foch that with the consent of the Conference he should study the possible utilization of Roumanian troops in Poland was rejected, though his other proposal regarding transport of Polish troops from France and Odessa to Poland was approved.

Among other important decisions taken about this time (March 11th to 24th) after discussion were the postponement until later of the boundaries and constitution of a Turkish State; the reservation from the reference to the Territorial Committee on Greece of the frontiers of Albania and Jugoslavia; the remission to the League of Nations Commission and the Committee on International Labour Organization of a demand from a group of ladies representing the Suffrage Association of the Allied countries to take part in the work of the Conference. They had already been received by President Wilson.

The last meeting of the Council of Ten in this series for current day-by-day business relating to the details of the Peace Treaty took place on March 24th when there was a well attended meeting at which, characteristically, was discussed the report of the committee on the controversial but rather secondary subject of enemy-owned submarines, which was referred to the Drafting Committee to put up for early submission a draft clause for inclusion in the Treaty of Peace. The meeting closed with an instruction, after considerable discussion, to the Inter-Allied Teschen Commission on the next step in its efforts to mediate between the claims of the Czechoslovak and Polish Governments. The text of communications to be made to the two Governments was included in the instruction—a useful piece of work.

Before that meeting, however, developments were taking place which brought to an end the position of the Council of Ten as the Supreme Council of the Paris Peace Conference and led to its replacement by the Council of Four, a self-constituted group unknown to the constitution of the Conference which started informally, but, after a preliminary period of 'growing pains', took control and completed the Treaty which, after approval in the Plenary Session of the Preliminary Treaty of Peace, was presented to the Germans and, after some haggling, became the Treaty of Versailles on June 28th. The story of how this came about will now be told.

CHAPTER XII

ORIGIN OF THE COUNCIL OF FOUR

'A new chapter in an old story.'

THE Supreme Control at the Preliminary Paris Peace Conference had been handled from January 12th to March 24th, that is to say for twelve weeks, by the Council of Ten with competence and with a considerable degree of success. It had held long meetings every week-day, morning and afternoon, as well as three Plenary Sessions of the whole Conference. Even in the absence of the Big Four, or some of them, from February 8th to March 16th the work had not been inter-rupted, and, during the short period when the Council consisted mainly or exclusively of the Foreign Ministers, important measures had been inaugurated for speeding up the work and the Council had got the whole Conference working with great activity.

Still the fact remains that, whether due to ignorance of the difficul-ties, or to faulty publicity or other causes, there was widespread discontent in France, Great Britain, America and other countries, as well as within the Conference itself. There was also a good deal of leakage and rumour about what was happening which did not help. No one was more acutely conscious of this situation than Lloyd George and his closest advisers, who at that moment were Philip Kerr, Henry Wilson and myself, and it is not surprising that we came together to try and help our chief. Henry Wilson[1] took the initiative by inviting Kerr and myself to listen as the only audience to a lecture on Tuesday (March 18th), which was followed by a long exchange of views. Next day (March 19th), I sent Lloyd George a memorandum covering most of the ground, the object of which was thus described in the first paragraph:

For some time I have felt a vague but indefinite uneasiness whether the Peace Treaty was developing on sound lines of policy. Philip Kerr has several times pointed out to you and to me that, while every exaction on Germany was justified on its merits, the accumulation of these will put Germany in an utterly impossible position. Last night I had a long talk with the Chief of the Imperial General Staff on the subject, and I found that he holds this view very strongly. I do not agree with all his views, but I was enormously impressed by his presentation of the case, and I

G

should like you to hear it at first hand. The views I give here are not his but mine.

My views are perhaps worthy of a brief mention because they formed the basis of my remarks at the subsequent Fontainebleau Conference. My general thesis was that in the coming years Bolshevism was the greatest danger to Europe. Already it had gripped most of Russia and was spreading to neighbouring countries from the Baltic to the Black Sea and Mediterranean. These countries were too weak to resist and too divided to combine. Germany and Austria were the only countries capable of providing a line of resistance unless the Peace Treaties were so drastic as to deprive them of the power to do so. After describing the situation in detail I urged the adoption of the following principles as a basis of the German Treaty:

First: The enormity of their crimes must be brought home to the German people.

Second: Means ought to be found for providing them with the physical force for resisting Bolshevism.

Third: We ought to try and build up the self-respect of the German people so that they may resist the approach of Bolshevism and believe in their own civilization rather than in that which comes from Russia.

Those principles were followed by many detailed suggestions, including an assurance that the disarmament of Germany was part of the disarmament of the world; that Germany should in due course be permitted to become a probationary member of the League of Nations; and that vindictiveness should have no place in the Peace Treaty. How much effect the joint efforts of his advisers had on Lloyd George I do not know, but there is no doubt that two days after receipt of my minute he embarked on a programme of drastic reforms to improve the prospects of the Conference.

The Prime Minister opened his campaign after a long and rather irritating meeting of the Council of Ten on Friday (March 21st) at 3 p.m., which was mainly devoted to the transport of troops to Poland and at which fifty-three people were present. After Clemenceau had adjourned that meeting, the word was passed that a second meeting would be held, which would be attended only by the members, the secretaries and a minimum of personal advisers to ministers. By these means the numbers were halved.

This meeting began at 6 p.m. and Lloyd George at once explained that it had been summoned at his request to enable him to raise the following question, though with considerable disinclination. He recalled that, at the meeting on Poland on March 18th, it had been necessary for members to express themselves freely and clearly. He was, therefore, surprised next morning to find in three important French newspapers, one of them supposed to be in close touch with the French Government, not only a full report of the Committee's finding, illustrated by secret maps, but, in addition, a garbled account of his own remarks, including some passages in quotation marks, giving a very wrong impression of what he said, as well as an opportunity for violent attacks against him. He recalled an earlier case complained of at the time by President Wilson, where a leakage had been traced to a British source and appropriate action had been taken, and he asked that, this time, the French should take action, which of course Clemenceau and Pichon agreed to do.

This let loose a flood of evidence of other leakages. From a good American source it was learned that the daily disclosures in the press were driving the Germans to desperation, and even putting acceptance of the peace terms in jeopardy. It was stated that leakage was occurring in the commissions and committees throughout the Conference. Balfour gave an example where, at a meeting of the Council of Ten, he had mentioned that the port of Danzig presented a difficult problem, and in consequence Dmowski had called on him and talked of his 'supposed anti-Polish feelings', though as a matter of fact he was a great supporter of the Poles. Wilson then chimed in and said he had often learned of the decision about to be taken by commissions 'first from outside parties'.

It transpired that the French still had a press censorship in force and that a great number of articles and paragraphs were being suppressed by the censor, but Clemenceau and Pichon agreed to institute a strict and severe inquiry into the leakage mentioned by Lloyd George about Poland. In addition, the Secretary-General was instructed to send a circular to the whole Conference impressing on everyone the need for reticence.

That bid for less leakage was the first step in Lloyd George's plan. The second step was to obtain an official list of all questions ready for immediate discussion, which the Secretary-General was instructed to prepare for consideration at a morning meeting next day, Saturday (March 22nd). The third step, decided on by Lloyd George only the day before (March 21st), was a visit to Fontainebleau, for which we managed to arrange that Saturday's business should be limited to a short meeting at 11 a.m., instead of 3 p.m. as usual, and that Monday's business should begin at 4 p.m. instead of 3 p.m.

The main reason assigned by Lloyd George for the Fontainebleau visit was a hitch in very secret discussions he had been holding *in camera* with Clemenceau and Wilson about his own proposal for a joint military guarantee by the United States and Britain to France, owing to the opposition of Tardieu and Foch, backed by the President, to some of his conditions. As he himself states:

> I, therefore, decided that it was desirable that the British delegation should make quite clear in writing the limits to which they were prepared to go. I retired with some of my advisers—General Smuts, Sir Henry Wilson, Sir Maurice Hankey and Philip Kerr—to the seclusion of the Forest of Fontainebleau, to work out definite proposals for the kind of Treaty of Peace to which alone we were prepared to append our signature.[1]

Such were the background and origin of the famous Fontainebleau visit, which exercised considerable influence on the eventual Treaty of Peace with Germany. It was only after we reached Fontainebleau on the Saturday afternoon that my colleagues and I realized what a tremendous task we were to undertake—namely, nothing less than a complete synopsis of the future Treaty.

After our arrival, in order to establish the camouflage of a pleasure trip, we paid a brief visit to the Palace and the sights. Then Lloyd George summoned us to a private sitting-room in the hotel to give us his instructions. After telling us that we had been brought there to discuss the subject of peace with Germany, he proposed to begin with a rather general inquiry on a plan in vogue at that time, and sometimes resorted to by Henry Wilson at Staff conferences, namely, to assign a particular rôle, e.g. ally, enemy or neutral, to selected individuals present who would be invited in turn to address the meeting from the point of view allotted to them. On this occasion Henry Wilson was to give both the German and the French points of view; I was to speak for the average Englishman; and Philip Kerr was to act as secretary and editor of the results, which of course Lloyd George would sum up. We were given about half an hour to prepare our thoughts and to meet again for a cup of tea and discussion. So each went his way, I for some fast walking and rapid thinking round the Palace grounds.

[1] *The Truth about the Peace Treaties*, vol. 1, p. 403.

I am unable to describe the speeches in detail as I have little to guide me except my own memory and a few smatterings from Henry Wilson's diary, where he recalls that on the Saturday evening he spoke as a German. I remember well that he wore his military cap back to front (i.e. with the eye-shade at the back of his head), which gave him the appearance of a German officer! In that part of his statement he would have developed among other aspects the threat of Bolshevism from the German point of view. At a subsequent meeting he spoke as a French *woman*, for, as he insisted, the unenfranchised French women were the real source of French public opinion. The losses of so many of their husbands, sons and men folk, the unbearable anxiety and long separations, the financial losses, and the desperate struggle and over-work to keep their homes going, the wanton destruction, and frequent prolonged occupation by German, British or French troops were his themes. These all contributed to an overwhelming insistence on restitution and full reparation by the enemy above everything else, the punishment of the guilty and absolute guarantees that Germany should pay the bill and make up all losses, and that the terms of peace should ensure the complete disarmament of Germany and that a war of the kind should never happen again. In his delivery pathos and humour were skilfully blended.

To the best of my recollection my own contribution began with insistence on the average Englishman's belief that our sea-power had once more proved itself a decisive factor in victory, that he had an instinctive dislike of compulsory military service, that the years in the trenches had been a long agony to the whole nation. We must in our terms of peace concede nothing to the doctrine of freedom of the seas and we should avoid any return to Germany of her colonies, or any permanent military commitments on the continent of Europe. I was at the time unaware of the Anglo-American offer to France. The rest of my remarks were based on my memorandum of March 19th.[1]

After a general discussion Lloyd George summed up his own con-clusions, and Philip Kerr got down to his heavy task as draftsman which, with typing, took most of the Sunday. The morning of Monday (March 24th) gave us a few more hours to discuss and touch up Kerr's memorandum, which is dated March 25th and was sent at once to Clemenceau and President Wilson. The completed document was in two parts: (1) some considerations for the Peace Conference before

---

[1] Summarized *supra*, p. 98.

they finally draft their terms, and (2) an outline of peace terms. It is reproduced in full in Lloyd George's book[1] and only the briefest indication of the contents of Part 2 need be given here:

The League of Nations: All parties to the Peace Treaties to become parties also to the Covenant, subject to an agreement by the principal members of the League to end competition in armaments.
Political:
  Eastern Boundary of Germany: Poland to be given a corridor to Danzig so as to embrace the smallest possible number of Germans. Rectification of the Bohemian frontier;
  Western Boundary of Germany: Rhenish provinces to remain part of Germany but to be demilitarized;
  France: To be compensated for this by the guarantee of the British Empire and the United States, lasting until the League of Nations provided adequate security, and by the cession to her by Germany of Alsace-Lorraine, as well as the 1814 frontier, or, in the alternative, compensation for the destruction of her coalfields, etc.
  Germany: To cede certain portions of Schleswig to Denmark as recommended by the Danish Commission of the Conference.
  Germany: To cede all rights in the ex-German colonies as well as in Kiauchau.
Disarmament of Germany, and the naval, military and air terms as already approved by the Council of Ten.
Restoration of prisoners of war and interned persons, and waiving by Germany of claims on their behalf.
Germany to undertake to pay full reparations—with a tentative scheme for the settlement of the amount and the methods of payment.

The Fontainebleau proposals, of course, gave rise at once to a tremendous controversy, which began by an exchange of letters between Lloyd George and Clemenceau (who was less extreme than his advisers, especially Tardieu and Foch). President Wilson, according to Lloyd George, in the main favoured the proposals though considerable pressure was put on him by the French, through House, to modify his attitude.

We are concerned here, however, with the machinery of the Supreme Control rather than with the merits of Lloyd George's plan. Once the plan had been launched it was bound to be discussed at the highest level of the Supreme Control of the Conference. At the moment that was still vested in the Council of Ten, which Lloyd George, partly owing to the large numbers of officials it attracted, did not consider

[1] *The Truth about the Peace Treaties*, vol. 1, p. 404.

to be a suitable body to discuss such an important and highly secret subject. I do not doubt that that was the reason for his savage attack on the leakage of its secrets. However that may be, the Council of Ten did not meet after March 24th until April 16th (when Lloyd George was not present) and thereafter only on four occasions, though some important and essential work was continued by a Council of Five composed of Foreign Ministers.

What, then, took its place? The answer is that from March 24th onwards the Supreme Control passed, *de facto*, gradually and for some time unnoticed by the press or the general public, and without any formal instrument of approval by the Conference, to the Council of Four.

For his speech to the House of Commons Lloyd George was so well informed that he rarely required help from Philip Kerr and myself, and our duties were almost confined to listening to the debate from the Official gallery. So I was able to devote some time to thinking over whether it would be advisable for me to apply for the post of Secretary-General of the League of Nations, a subject which I had been considering for some time. The matter is more germane to this book than appears at first sight for, after discussions with highly placed friends in London and in Paris, I discovered that, if I was accepted as prospective Secretary-General, I should have to relinquish my work with the Council of Four, which was very promising, and join House and Robert Cecil in working out the details of the organization of the League. I came to the conclusion that I could make a greater contribution to peace and security by continuing my services to the Supreme Control in Paris than in the superficially attractive post at Geneva. So, in spite of the attractions of a salary of £10,000 a year, a beautiful house near the lake and an enticing bathing place, a congenial work that offered great prospects for the promotion of world peace, I decided to drop the idea.

It is perhaps worth mentioning that before reaching this decision I had consulted a great many friends in Paris, including Lloyd George and Balfour who promised support but did not want to lose me, President Wilson who was favourable, and some of my colleagues in the Secretariat-General, who agreed to serve with me if I accepted the post. But when I discussed it with Cecil Hurst, he advised strongly against it on the ground that his American colleague on the Drafting Committee was certain that, in spite of Wilson's confidence, the United

States would never be allowed by the Senate to become a member. That decided me against acceptance.

April 18th, Good Friday. Returned to Paris yesterday with P.M. after a busy three days in England for his speech. The principal development from a personal point of view is that I have definitely chucked the League of Nations. My visit to London has convinced me that the British Empire is worth a thousand Leagues of Nations. They are a sound nation over there —the sheet anchor of the world. I can do more for the peace of the world there than in Geneva. . . .

On the same day (April 18th) I wrote to my wife in England and, after describing my journey back to Paris with Lloyd George on the 17th, added—'I had a long talk with the Prime Minister about the League of Nations and he agrees in my chucking it'. The text of my letter to Lord Robert Cecil which I marked 'Private and Confidential' and dated April 18th was as follows:

Dear Lord Robert,—It is only this afternoon that I have had the full talk with the Prime Minister on the Secretary-Generalship of the League of Nations, which I always insisted was an indispensable condition to a decision whether I would formally offer myself as a candidate for the post. The result of the conversation, following on a most earnest and anxious consideration of the question in all its bearings (including, as you know, the elaboration of a partial scheme of organization of the Secretariat), has brought me to the decision that my duty is to remain in the post I now occupy. In these circumstances I must ask that my name will not be put forward officially as a candidate.

I very much regret this decision because I realize the delay in reaching it may cause great inconvenience. Yet, on so important a subject I could not give an affirmative decision until I had all the necessary data before me. Those included, on the one hand, a closer perception of the duties and responsibilities which would fall to the Secretary-General of the League of Nations, and of the conditions under which he would work. These latter could not be ascertained until the Covenant had been revised, until the seat of the League was fixed and until the Treaties of Peace had reached an advanced stage of development. Most of these factors were indeterminate until within the last few days, while some are still unsettled, including perhaps what, rightly or wrongly, I always regarded as an essential condition, namely, the certainty of the acceptance of the Covenant by the United States of America. The development of all these questions has, on the whole, been steadily in a direction contrary to my conception.

I wish to thank you personally for considering me as a possible candidate and for your forbearance in the uncertainty in which I have kept you.

I need hardly say, in conclusion, that, if I can render any assistance to you in finding a British candidate, I will do my utmost, and that, if he should be selected, he will have not only my interest and sympathy, but all the practical assistance that I can give him. Yours very sincerely,

M. P. A. HANKEY.

On my return I had the impression that my status had in some way altered. I fancy that during the period April 3rd to 10th my efforts to speed up the work and give greater precision to the decisions of the Council of Four, and to translate them into effective instructions, had not remained unobserved. Moreover, the lapse to the former lack of system during our absence in London did no harm, so far as I was concerned, and the threat of an immediate crisis over the Italian claims, concurrently with the urgency to complete the Treaty before the arrival of the Germans, must have helped Lloyd George and Balfour to get me installed.

In addition, my experience during these days had resembled a rehearsal enabling me and my staff at the Villa Majestic to try out and tune up to concert pitch the whole organization, and to do so without umbrage to the Secretariat-General, the Drafting Committee, the numerous commissions and the foreign delegations, so that we took over our new responsibilities without anxiety or misgiving. In my diary for April 18th, I wrote:

I was called into the Council of Four to advise as to procedure and told them some plain truths. They still sit without secretaries and cause an infinity of chaos and confusion in consequence. We have to get the peace treaty ready for the Germans in a week and yet we cannot ascertain the decisions.

And on April 19th

I functioned as secretary of the Council of Four. I gather that Aldrovandi and I are to officiate in future, which will ease matters.

The latter statement is confirmed by a footnote to Professor Mantoux's version: 'It was from this *séance* that Sir Maurice Hankey functioned regularly as Secretary of the Council of Four and that Count Aldrovandi accompanied the representation of Italy'. Count Aldrovandi preludes a very full account of the meeting in the Italian language by mentioning my presence and accounting for his own by stating that 'Wilson personally invited me to take part (*intervenire*) given the gravity of the discussion'. Aldrovandi's primary function at this stage was to interpret for Orlando, whose knowledge of French was not great and of English even less. But he combined this with taking notes and prompting his Prime Minister when required. His duties were essentially with the Italian delegation, and he never interfered with my own self-constituted function as international Secretary to the Council, but he gave me all the help he could as the good comrade he was. Neither Clemenceau nor Wilson introduced a permanent secretary at this stage.

CHAPTER XIII

SUMMIT REORGANIZATION

'Then was called a Council straight,
Brief and bitter the debate.'
(BROWNING, *Hervé Riel*, written in March 1871.)

THE inauguration of the Council of Four, which was about to become
the Supreme Council of the Preliminary Peace Conference, could
hardly have taken place in circumstances of greater obscurity, and that,
as will be shown, was even more true of the Council of Five, which
was an afterthought, though a valuable one. As we have seen, Lloyd
George, who was the prime mover in this development, had prepared
the way by his protest a day or two before on leakage and by obtaining
the adoption of measures to bring it to an end, as well as by the
preparation in great secrecy of the famous 'Fontainebleau Memorandum' as a guide to his own policy and to give the new Council
pabulum for its discussions on the shape of the Treaty as a whole.
But he had done more than that in a series of personal unrecorded
talks with Clemenceau, Wilson and Orlando, either individually or
in small groups, some of which are mentioned, without much detail,
in Lord Riddell's diary of the Conference.

On his return from Fontainebleau on Monday (March 24th) the
decisive step was taken. It will be recalled that the time of the usual
Monday meeting of the Council of Ten had been postponed from
3 p.m. to 4 p.m. ostensibly to give Lloyd George time to get back
from Fontainebleau and prepare for the meeting. What actually
happened was that the Big Four, Clemenceau, Lloyd George, Wilson
and Orlando, met together at 3 p.m. secretly for an hour and took
the decision to start up the new Council of Four to supersede the
Council of Ten. We owe our knowledge of what occurred entirely
to the fact that, with his usual prescience, Clemenceau had brought
with him the indispensable chief interpreter of the Peace Conference,
Professor Paul Mantoux, who, fortunately, kept a record. This was
printed and published some years later. The keynote was struck in
the first sentence by President Wilson in the following words (translated from the French):

There is at the moment a veritable race between peace and anarchy, and the public begins to manifest its impatience. Yesterday in the ruins of Soissons, a woman addressed herself to me and said, 'When will you give us peace?' My opinion is that we should take in hand the most difficult and most urgent questions, such as the question of reparations, the protection of France against aggression, the Italian frontier on the Adriatic side, and discuss them among us four. Once the more important and difficult subjects are settled the road will be opened and the rest will go quick.

After Clemenceau had added 'German Austria' to President Wilson's list of urgent questions, Lloyd George, the real originator of the plan, accepted the proposal and expanded a little on 'reparations' which was the most difficult question, the only one he thought (prophetically) that was likely to embarrass the Council, and one on which the experts were never likely to reach agreement. He concluded by proposing that the meetings between heads of Governments should take place twice a day, if that was necessary to speed up the Conference, and should begin next day. This was accepted by his colleagues.

Before leaving that historic day (Monday, March 24th) it should be mentioned that at 4 p.m. they, all four of them, appeared at the Council of Ten and with the exception of Lloyd George, who left the presentation of British interests to Balfour, took some part in the proceedings. But not a hint was dropped about the all-important decision they had just taken, or that the Council of Ten was to be superseded by a Council of Four in the Supreme Control of the Peace Conference. Presumably that information was left to the Heads of Delegations to pass on direct to their deputies, as Lloyd George did in the case of Balfour. But when the meeting ended nothing was said about the date, time, place or agenda of the next meeting of the Council of Ten. Such was the modest and almost furtive inauguration of the famous Council of Four.

At this point, however, it is necessary to mention that three days later the Big Four changed their minds, while assembling for their sixth meeting, and in a short exchange of views decided to set up in addition a Committee of Foreign Ministers of the five Inviting Powers; this came to be known as the Council of Five. Mantoux, in his usually reliable and full notes of this meeting of the Council of Four, does not mention this episode, which probably took place before his arrival. The only official record of it is in the following note, drafted by myself, at the head of the printed minutes of the first meeting of the new Committee of Five on March 27th, after the list of those present and in brackets:

(*Note.*—This meeting was arranged at short notice at the beginning of a meeting between President Wilson, Mr Lloyd George, Clemenceau and M. Orlando held at 11 a.m. at President Wilson's house at the Place des États-Unis.)

That procedure was as furtive as the inauguration of the Council of Four.

The moment I learned from Lloyd George at President Wilson's house that the Big Four were to meet at once and that I should not be required, I dashed off to the Quai d'Orsay, whither Balfour had proceeded at very short notice on the request of Pichon. This was very fortunate, for this proved, as I had guessed, to be the first meeting of the new Council of Foreign Ministers. For the next meeting on the following day (March 28th) I arranged with the Secretary-General that the now famous international secretariat from the Supreme War Council should keep the minutes exactly as they had done in the case of the Council of Ten, and thereafter I handed over the secretarial duties I used to render to that Council to my Foreign Office colleagues, Messrs Norman, Phipps and Spring-Rice, according to the subjects of discussion.

It will be convenient to describe the development and procedure of the Council of Five at this stage and to proceed thereafter to the Council of Four. The new Council of Five held twenty-eight meetings between March 27th and June 25th and virtually became the successor of the Council of Ten. In fact, on rare occasions, the Council of Four and Council of Five met together to co-ordinate their activities, in which case their proceedings were included in the records of all three—the otherwise defunct Council of Ten, the Council of Four and the Council of Five. That was occasional only.

Broadly speaking, however, they relieved the Council of Four of many essential subjects that had to be decided, notably acting as the Summit authority on most of the territorial boundary issues, for which they were better qualified than the Big Four, as well as a long list of other subjects including Heligoland, the Kiel Canal, the Suez Canal, etc. Without this relief the Council of Four could never have got the Treaty ready for the Germans in time. In all three cases, the Council of Four, and the Council of Five and the Council of Ten, the whole of the mechanical work, reproduction and distribution of agenda papers, minutes, etc., was undertaken in the Villa Majestic under my supervision.

To sum up, from now to the end of the Preliminary Peace Conference the Summit organization consisted of the Council of Four and the Council of Five, with occasional joint meetings for purposes of co-ordination. Between them they correlated the work of the numerous commissions and committees and decided the general policy and procedure, and succeeded within six weeks in presenting to the Germans a draft Treaty of Peace which, with modifications, was signed at Versailles on June 28th. No more need be said about the organization and procedure of the Council of Five, which was identical with that of the Council of Ten, and we can pass straight to that of the Council of Four.

The Council of Four, as the new Supreme Council of the Paris Preliminary Peace Conference, had at its disposal, of course, the huge, if somewhat cumbrous, machine already brought into existence by the Council of Ten. So far as treaty-making was concerned, there were few subjects that came before the Big Four that had not been under consideration at some stage by an appropriate commission of international experts of high competence, mostly operating in Paris, but some 'in the field', so to speak, in Spa, Danzig, Warsaw or Teschen, each with an able chairman and competent secretariat, the whole of them in close touch with the Conference Secretariat-General. Perhaps it was the most powerful international organization that had ever existed, and, judged by results at any rate, superior to most of its successors. At this stage it had gained sufficient momentum to carry on for a time without much guidance. Yet the four new usurpers of power set out on their tremendous task without establishing any link with the machine they were to control, except that of the sturdy, competent, seventy-five-year-old Chairman of the Conference, Clemenceau. The subjects of organization, procedure and secretariat were not mentioned, either at the first meeting or thereafter, until the Big Four got into difficulties,[1] as described later, and called on my services.

To add to the aloofness of their meetings they met as a rule in President Wilson's study in the Place des États-Unis, or occasionally in Lloyd George's flat on the opposite side of the Rue Nitot, or in Clemenceau's bureau in the Ministry of War, but hardly ever at the Quai d'Orsay, the *siège* of the Conference. The President's study was a small room on the ground floor, facing north and rather gloomy. The Four sat at ease in comfortable chairs. There was no large table,

[1] *Vide infra*, p. 115.

only a small one for the interpreter, and when later I joined them as Secretary, I wrote my notes on a pad on my knees. Large maps were usually spread on the floor and had to be explained with a pointer or by lying on all fours. The procedure was delightfully informal. Clemenceau, as President of the Paris Peace Conference, took the chair.

The point that made me anxious was that they began their meetings without a secretary of any kind. Some others were of the same way of thinking. On March 24th, the day of our return from Fontainebleau, Riddell made a long entry in his diary which includes the following:

L. G. back from Fontainebleau. I met Henry Wilson, who painted a gloomy picture of the position in the East. He said 'We are drifting to disaster. I have told the P.M. that, if the Conference don't take charge of affairs, affairs will take charge of them. . . . They are going to suspend the Council of Ten, and L. G., Clemenceau, Wilson and Orlando are going to meet every day and try and settle the terms. *But* (continued Sir Henry) *I told the P.M. that*[1] he ought to have Hanky Panky (Sir Maurice Hankey) with him. The trouble is that the four meet together and think they have decided things, but there is no one to record what they have done. The consequence is that misunderstandings often arise and there is no definite account of their proceedings and nothing happens.

That is exactly what I was fearing and I frequently warned Lloyd George who shared my views, for like Henry Wilson and myself he had not forgotten the shortcomings of British Cabinets before his own establishment of the War Cabinet Secretariat in December 1916. But he was in a quandary because, if he asked his colleagues to allow him to bring a secretary (even myself, so familiar to them all) they would have been forced by pressure from their own delegations to follow suit, and the whole object of small numbers, intimacy and secrecy would have been frustrated at the outset. What he decided, therefore, was that I should accompany him to the meetings, morning and afternoon, with my famous black box packed with all the documents and papers which might possibly be required, in accordance with my invariable practice, and remain in an ante-room until for some reason my presence was required. Neither he nor I had much doubt that sooner or later I should get my opportunity, though it was rather long in coming.

As Lloyd George never knew of the existence of Mantoux's notes, which were published after his death and I was equally ignorant of

[1] Author's italics.

their existence, I have preferred to use only the information we had at the time and to refer to Mantoux's book only for occasional confirmation and in cases where there is no other information to explain what happened. This applies also to Aldrovandi's excellent diary.[1]

From March 25th onwards the new Council of Four started regular meetings, twice a day, beginning at 11 a.m., lasting for about two hours, and in the afternoon at 3.30 p.m., often sitting late. My own dreary vigil in an ante-room began at the same time. Every morning and afternoon I called at Lloyd George's apartment in the Rue Nitot half an hour or so before walking across the road to the meeting, to discuss the subjects and to give him the latest information. After the meetings I walked back in order to ascertain what decisions, if any, had been taken. Often I extracted but little, because a Prime Minister has little leisure. I then returned to my office in the Villa Majestic and dictated an official minute recording who had been present, what subjects had been discussed, what documents had been used and what (if anything) had been decided. If any action was required, I checked up with the Secretary-General or the Drafting Committee of the Conference whether they had received any instructions from the Council. It did not provide a satisfactory substitute for minutes. Soon, however, it appeared that Henry Wilson's forecast was proving correct, as shown by the following jotting in my diary:

March 26th. Paris (Villa Majestic). Since I came to Paris, this is my first entry in the diary. The fact is I have generally been too busy as British Secretary of the Preliminary Peace Conference to keep a diary. I only attempt it now because of the method, or rather lack of method into which the Conference has drifted. Discontented with the slow progress of the Council of Ten, and disgusted with the leakages to the Press, Lloyd George, Wilson, Clemenceau and Orlando are now sitting *in camera*, with no secretary at all. It is frightfully inconvenient from a secretarial point of view. They reach decisions and fail to communicate them, so that the required action is not taken.

The second entry in my diary, was a continuation of the first:

March 30th. (My début at the Council of Four.) I was interrupted in writing the above. The 'conversations' have been continued but have been entirely without result. I try to keep touch with what is going on, and keep

[1] L. Aldrovandi-Marescotti, *Guerra diplomatica: ricordi e frammenti di diario 1914–1919* (1936).

a sort of record of such progress as is made from the scrappy accounts I get from the P.M. I also append all documents. Yesterday I was called in to draft some instructions to Marshal Foch on his attitude towards the German plenipotentiary who has been asked to meet him on the subject of the transport of the Poles through Danzig. It was very difficult as I had not heard the previous discussion, but I acquitted myself sufficiently well, and my draft was accepted. I remained in the room afterwards for a discussion about reparations and was able to help. It is rather pathetic to me to see them groping about. A good secretary would help them prodigiously. . . .

As in the case of the Council of Ten a large proportion of the discussions of the Council of Four had to be devoted to urgent current issues, many of them brought up by Foch in connexion with his responsibility for the fulfilment of the terms of the armistice. For the first three or four weeks these accounted for about one-third of their time, leaving only two-thirds for the Treaty, in spite of the fact that some of the less important current affairs were diverted to the Council of Five.

Coming to the Treaty, reparations by Germany, which as we have seen had been given first priority, took up nearly as much time as the current questions for these early weeks. The subject had, of course, been divided into its component parts by the appropriate commission, with sub-heads such as evaluation of damage, the financial capacity of enemy states, measures of control and guarantees, etc., each of which tended to throw up a host of subsidiary questions. Over the whole field, as Lloyd George had foreseen, there were wide differences of opinion, and the Council of Four found themselves baffled on every phase by this fact. For example, how much could Germany pay, over how many years could the payments be spread, how much were the different countries entitled to demand, and how much of that was it wise, economically and politically, to include, how did the demands of France with the destruction of towns, villages, house property, agricultural lands and so forth compare with the British claim for the huge destruction of ships, where did Belgium, Italy, Serbia and other countries come in, and so forth?

Day after day the unfortunate Council of Four had to grapple their way through this tangle of conflicting claims, on which their technical advisers were so divided as to afford them singularly little help. In fact, the differences within the commissions and sub-commissions concerned were transferred very largely to the Big Four themselves, until eventually it was found that the material did not exist, and would

H

take months or years to collect, for a just appraisement of the various factors. And ultimately much had to be delegated to a long-range body, namely the ill-fated Reparations Commission, which ended a stormy and somewhat inglorious career at the Lausanne Conference of 1932. But we are going too fast.

In the intervals between the opening of that baffling question in the early days, the Council of Four managed to open up a certain number of other questions. 'Responsibilities', the title for 'war crimes trials', and particularly the subject of the trial of the Kaiser, had produced a divided report by the commission on the subject, where Lansing and the American legal authorities were critical of trials by the victor of the vanquished, as Balfour and Sonnino and some others had been at the pre-Conference discussions in London. I was myself so strongly moved by this subject that I was positively glad that most of the discussions at the Council of Four took place before I became *de facto* Secretary of the Council. But, a week before that development, in a letter home dated April 11, 1919, I find the following highly indiscreet passage:

The Big Four have reached some more conclusions, but I horrified them rather yesterday by pointing out that their conclusion on breaches of the laws of war would involve rather difficult legislation in our country and America at any rate. It rather amused me to pose as a lawyer, but as it was a question of military law and naval law, I was all right.

Still, after two meetings of obstinate resistance, President Wilson, who had originally shared Lansing's objections to the majority report, agreed to waive them. My instinct was right, however, and in the end very little came of it all.

Other matters which occupied much time at these early 'Summit Talks' were the very difficult subject of the Saar and the Belgian claims both on reparations and other questions on which the King of the Belgians volunteered to appear before the Big Four and, *inter alia*, made a powerful plea for uniting Luxemburg to his kingdom, to which no support could be given until the opinion of Luxemburg was ascertained. Eventually it proved unfavourable. An important decision on April 3rd was to hold a special plenary meeting on April 11th to secure approval to the report of the Commission on International Labour Organization which was completing its admirable work under the chairmanship of George Barnes, the Labour member of the British War Cabinet, who put his heart and soul into the task. He had taken the place, as chairman, of Mr Gompers, an American Labour man, who had had to return to his own country.

On Saturday (April 5th, 11 a.m.) I had my first opportunity to follow up my original début at the Council of Four on March 30th. The meeting was held for the first time in the large over-decorated salon on the first floor of President Wilson's house, and among a team of nine international authorities were Sumner, Baruch, Norman Davis, Klotz and Loucheur. Three secretaries slipped in with the crowd, namely my good friend Auchincloss of the American State Department, Aldrovandi and myself. The other two confined their services to their respective delegations, but I sought to render services to the meeting as a whole and, as a result, my first long *procès-verbal* occupies ten pages of the American published version of the proceedings. The meeting was continued that afternoon and occupies another eight pages.

Perhaps this lapse from the usual exclusiveness of the Council of Four was due to the fact that President Wilson was absent, suffering from indisposition, and House who took his place may well have needed a reliable man like Auchincloss to take a note to keep the President abreast of what was being settled. But President Wilson's indisposition continued and on Monday (April 7th), the place of the meeting was changed to Lloyd George's apartment in the Rue Nitot. This time there was no team of experts and the subject was not German reparations but current affairs, and Foch and Weygand were there to receive the plaudits of the Council on their success at Spa in settling the plaguey question of the transport of Haller's army to Poland. In addition a message was sent to Smuts in Budapest, requesting him to visit French and Roumanian Headquarters before returning to Paris.

That afternoon the business was continued in Lloyd George's apartment, into which the whole of the reparations group was crowded, and my *procès-verbal* records a large number of conclusions and articles for inclusion in the Treaty. They constitute, I think, the longest step forward that had yet been made at any single meeting of the Big Four on reparations.

Next day (April 8th) President Wilson being still on the sick list, the Council of Four met again in Lloyd George's flat and, as part of his campaign for speeding up the Conference, he produced a list of the subjects remaining for consideration by the Council of Four which I had prepared for him and which, as intended, precipitated a discussion on the future of the Conference. There were no less than thirty-one questions that had to be decided by the Council before they could be dealt with by the Drafting Committee and included as draft articles in the various Treaties. My list had the effect of sobering for the moment Lloyd George's insistence that the Germans should be invited within a matter of a few days to Paris to receive a Treaty which was so incomplete, and House went so far as to suggest that it should be 'some weeks hence'.

That afternoon (April 8th) my temporary assumption of the post of secretary came to an end, for President Wilson returned to the Council of Four and the meeting was held again in his study. Neither I nor any other secretary was present, and I was back in my vigil in the ante-room. They returned to the subject of war crimes but the President stuck to his guns and, after a meeting described by Orlando as 'serious and even stormy', refused to accept the majority report of the Commission until he had discussed it with Lansing, who had dissented from his colleagues. At the morning meeting on the 9th, however, Wilson put up a compromise proposal which provided for a demand that Holland should hand over the Kaiser for trial by the Allied and Associated Powers.

That same afternoon at 4 p.m. I was back at the Council of Four, without my American and Italian colleagues, and officiating as the sole secretary at a meeting on German reparations. Klotz and a large team of experts of the four nations were present. The subject was now narrowing down and the nature of the provisional settlement —for it never reached a *final* settlement at Paris—was coming into sight. That was the last occasion on which I functioned as *temporary* secretary until April 19th when I was tacitly accepted as permanent secretary and attended all meetings of the Council of Four.

Between April 10th and April 19th, however, I paid my first visit to England in the following circumstances.

Ever since his return from his long visit to London in March, Lloyd George had been anxious about the unrest in Great Britain, which he attributed largely to the apparent lack of progress at the Paris Conference. His anxieties were increased at the beginning of April by a debate in Parliament, in which the public complaints sedulously fostered by the Northcliffe press were presented in a vigorous form and were by no means allayed by Bonar Law's reply. Soon after the debate the Prime Minister received a telegram signed by no less than 233 supporters of his own coalition, which, though moderate in tone, left no doubt of the seriousness of the situation. This brought Bonar Law to Paris for consultation, in pessimistic mood,[1] and Lloyd George decided to return to London before Easter to confront his critics as soon as possible. As Good Friday that year fell on April 18th, he decided to speak on Wednesday the 16th. There was no time to lose, for much remained to be done. First he wanted to persuade the Council of Four to agree to make an announcement of the date when the Treaty would be presented to the Germans *before* his speech, to which he attached the utmost importance, in order to improve the atmosphere, and he realized that this would create difficulties for the Council of Four. He, therefore, had to act with the utmost promptitude and, on the morrow of his talk with Bonar Law, i.e. on Friday (April 11th) at 11 a.m., at the outset of the meeting he announced his intention of leaving Paris on the following Monday (April 14th), and gave his reasons. At first no objections were raised even by Orlando, who intimated that it would give him a good opportunity for a preliminary talk with President Wilson on the Italian Treaty claims. But he begged Lloyd George to return as soon as possible, as he himself had to meet the Italian Chamber on April 23rd.

Next day (April 12th) Lloyd George reopened the subject, which gave rise first to a discussion whether the Treaty should be published as soon as it could be ready. This course was unanimously rejected and that view was accepted by the Foreign Ministers who were invited to join the meeting shortly after. On the question of summoning the Germans, Orlando made a strong point that, before that was announced, he must be in a position to reassure the Italian Chamber that the broad lines of the Italian settlement had been agreed. The question of Danzig was also raised as one which ought to be settled before any announcement was made. But no decision was taken about summoning the Germans either at that meeting, or at a short meeting on a detail of reparations that afternoon.

Lloyd George had told me that nothing would stop him from leaving Paris on the 14th, even if he had to compel the Council of Four to work all day Sunday, which was contrary to their habits. In the event he did not go as far as that, but he did induce them to meet at President Wilson's house at 6 p.m. on Sunday (April 13th), and to hold a very long session.

The question of the invitation to the Germans was raised at the outset by President Wilson who stated that Orlando had been to see

[1] Lord Riddell, *Intimate Diary of the Peace Conference*, p. 41.

him and had asked that no announcement should be made until the Council had decided on the principles of the Italian settlement. Orlando then said bluntly that, if he had to announce that five months after the Armistice the Germans had been invited to receive their treaty and that the treaties in which Italy was interested had not been touched, the effect on Italian public opinion would be disastrous. He had been very patient; he did not demand a complete treaty with Austria before the Germans were summoned, but he must insist on agreement on the principles of the ultimate settlement of the Italian claims. Clemenceau pointed out, also, that it would not be safe to announce the date before they were certain to be ready. Lloyd George agreed that all these questions must be examined—but the date of the convocation of the Germans must be announced before his departure on the morrow.

After Wilson had suggested that Orlando should agree to an invitation to the Germans on condition of an undertaking by his colleagues to settle the principles of the Italian Treaty before their arrival, the Italian Prime Minister suggested a delay of forty-eight hours, in which he thought a settlement on principles might be reached. Lloyd George would not look at that. The Germans, he recalled, had been the first to conclude an Armistice, and the drafting of their Treaty had taken weeks and months, and it was only reasonable that the Austrians and the other former belligerents should bide their time. In any event the date of the meeting with the Germans must be announced before he reached London. Were his colleagues so sure, he asked, that they could reach agreement on the principles of the Austrian Treaty so rapidly? Clemenceau replied, 'Non', and added that they would need all their time to complete the German Treaty in ten days, but between the moment of the arrival of the German Plenipotentiaries and the beginning of negotiations with them, he was ready to examine the Italian question. That proposal, said Orlando, was even less favourable to him than the other.

Eventually, an offer by President Wilson to suspend the usual meeting on Monday (April 14th), during which he would spend the whole day in examining the Italian claims alone with Orlando, was adopted and Orlando undertook to notify his position to Lloyd George before his departure for London.[1] So the meeting closed at a late hour in some uncertainty.

[1] We arrived in London on the evening of Monday the 14th after a rough passage in a destroyer, and on Tuesday (the 15th) the press stated that President Wilson had announced that it had been decided to summon the German Plenipotentiaries to Versailles on April 25th.

At the time I never heard what had happened at the projected whole-day interview between President Wilson and Orlando on Monday, April 14th, but found later that Aldrovandi's diary for that date contains the following passage (translated from the Italian):

On the 14th there took place a private and very tempestuous (*molto tempestuoso*) conversation between Orlando and Wilson. Wilson that day handed Orlando a memorandum of his own conclusions on the Italian question, a question to which more than any other he had given his most attentive and serious thought, and had included a suggestion, or request, that it should be presented to the Italian Parliament. After examining the document (Aldrovandi continues), Orlando declared that the proposal therein, in the judgment of his Italian colleagues, to whom he had communicated it, and himself, was not and could not provide a basis for discussion and the situation on these terms was hopeless.

CHAPTER XIV

ITALY'S CLAIMS: ORLANDO'S DILEMMA

'Deo et Patriae omnia debeo.' (Inscription on an old and
dilapidated palazzo in Venice behind the Abbezzice.)

WHETHER by chance or design the beginning of my continuous
association with the Council of Four at the Paris Peace Conference
coincided in date with the most acute, distressing and prolonged
crisis of the story, namely, the disagreement on the Italian claims on
Saturday and Sunday, April 19th and 20th, just after our return from
London.

On the Saturday (April 19th) Orlando, who was about to return to
Italy to confront his Parliament, began quietly with a sober review
of the Italian claims in the light of the resolutions taken by the
Supreme Council on other questions, in the past history of which the
United States had taken no part.

His first claim was that Italy should be allotted her natural boundaries, namely the watershed of the mountains which encircled her
northern limits, notwithstanding that the present population included
a certain number (which was not excessive) of people of non-Italian
races. His second claim—unexpected to me at that stage—related to
Fiume, and was defended on the principle of self-determination,
though he admitted the population was small, and compared it to
that of the State of San Marino. On the economic aspect he compared
Fiume to Danzig and emphasized its importance as a port. He claimed
that only 7 per cent of the port was devoted to the commerce of
Jugoslavia, compared with the 50 per cent previously stated by
Trumbitch. His third claim—to Dalmatia and the islands off the
coast—was based on strategic considerations, founded on the experience of the World War in which the Allies, in spite of their numerical
superiority at sea, had been unable to protect the coast of Italy from
sporadic raids or to navigate the Adriatic freely owing to the raids
of Austrian warships issuing from the shelter of the islands. To this
he added historical claims. In Dalmatia, however, he insisted that
Italy's demands were modest, including only a small port, and leaving
to Jugoslavia the ports of Spalato, Ragusa and Cattaro. He only asked
that in Dalmatia 'the existing agreement' (i.e. of April 1915) should

be adhered to and that was his only hint of the secret Anglo-French-Italian agreement of April 26, 1915 which had brought Italy into the war.

President Wilson, who spoke next, recalled that 'it had been his privilege as the spokesman of the Associated Powers to initiate the negotiations for peace. The basis of the peace with Germany had been clearly laid down. It was not reasonable—and he thought his Italian friends would admit this—to have one basis of peace with Germany and another set of principles for the treaties of peace with Austria-Hungary, Bulgaria and Turkey.' He insisted that they were trying to make peace on an entirely new basis and to establish a new order of international relations—something that no other body of statesmen had ever tried before. He brushed aside all economic arguments, but admitted that 'natural boundaries, such as those included in Signor Orlando's first point, deserved consideration. Nature had swung a great boundary round the north of Italy. It included Trieste and most of the Istrian Peninsula on which Trieste lies. Here he had no great difficulty in meeting the Italian views.' South of this, however, all the arguments led the other way, especially in the case of Fiume, a point he developed at great length. The claim to Dalmatia, and particularly the strategic argument, came in for heavy criticism by the President. For security Italy must rely on the new order, one of the essentials of which was that the control of the Great Powers must be withdrawn from the Balkans, another point that he developed in considerable detail.

Sonnino then countered the President's stragetic arguments with ability and some asperity. Without the islands 'the east coast of Italy was helpless. The League of Nations could not intervene in time'. He recognized the importance of the League of Nations and the general sentiment in favour of a better state of things but 'the League was a new institution and had many difficulties to face'—Russia, for example. 'How could it be relied on until it was fully established?' Its guarantees were not sufficient and it had no force under its control. Altogether his comment was a courageous reversion to common sense. Like Orlando and the President he avoided any reference to the Treaty of London of April 26, 1915.

Clemenceau spoke next. He, too, had his doubts, and in listening to President Wilson 'felt we were embarking on a most hazardous enterprise, but with a very noble purpose. . . . It was not possible to change the whole policy of the world at one stroke. This applied to France just as much as to Italy. He was ready to make concessions to his Allies, but he reminded his hearers that Great Britain and France were bound in advance. The 1915 treaty with Italy had not been signed by him but it bore the signature of France. In that treaty Dalmatia had been given to Italy, and that was a fact he could not forget. In the same treaty, however, Fiume was allotted to Croatia. Italy had at that time no pretentions to Fiume. She had allotted it as a gift to Croatia. . . .'

Lloyd George, speaking, like Clemenceau, not as a signatory of the Treaty of London but as representative of a country that had signed it, left no doubt of his intention to honour his country's signature. 'He realized the strength of President Wilson's arguments, but he thought he was entitled to say that if we felt scruples about the Italian claims they should have been expressed before Italy had lost half a million gallant lives. He did not think we were entitled to express these doubts after Italy had taken part in the war. He wished to say that Great Britain stood by the treaty, but she stood by the whole of the treaty.' Those words were followed by confirmation of the allocation in it of Fiume to Croatia, which he elaborated by producing a map which had been attached to the treaty and which showed Fiume in Croatia. He also took up another point already touched on by Clemenceau that Italy could hardly hope to justify her threat to leave the Conference on the grounds of the refusal of her Allies to hand over to her possession of a town with a population of only 25,000, in which the Italians predominated, especially as the majority were doubtful if the suburbs were taken into consideration, and where, if the surrounding country was included, the population was overwhelmingly against Italy. After elaborating this point with a wealth of detail and reminding Italy of the heavy sacrifices which other Allied countries were being asked to make, for example, France in conceding her ambition for a frontier on the Rhine, he made a strong appeal to Italy not to leave the Conference on such a doubtful issue as her claim for Fiume. Shortly after, however, he mentioned 'that some time ago he had told Orlando that the British Cabinet had decided that they would stand by the Pact'.

At that point, Orlando speaking in conciliatory terms observed that 'if what Lloyd George said meant that the Conference would take its decision on the basis of the Treaty of London, leaving Fiume to be settled as the Conference might think fit, then a new situation would be created, and he would be prepared to discuss it with his colleagues on the Italian Delegation and return to give a reply'.

That roused President Wilson to make a statement of such importance that it must be quoted in full:

The President said that the solution would place a burden on him that was quite unfair. He did not know and he did not feel at liberty to ask whether France and Great Britain considered the Treaty as consistent with the principles on which the Peace Treaty was being based. He was at liberty to say, however, that he himself did not. To discuss the matter on the basis of the Pact of London would be to adopt as a basis a secret treaty. Yet he would be bound to say that they were establishing a new order in which secret treaties were precluded. He could not see his way to make peace with Germany on one principle and with Austria-Hungary on another. The Pact of London was inconsistent with the general principles of the settlement. He knew perfectly well that the Pact of London had been entered into in quite different circumstances and he did not want to criticize what had been done. But to suggest that the decision should be taken on the basis of the Treaty of London would draw the United States of America into an impossible situation . . . he was willing to state, and might have to state to the world the grounds of his objections. He could not draw the United States into principles contrary to those which now animated them and which had brought them into the war.[1]

At last all the cards were on the table. The secret Treaty of London, which for so long had escaped mention, had at last been brought into the open, and the effect obviously needed time for consideration. After a final appeal by President Wilson to Italy to take time to consider the matter, the meeting adjourned until the next morning, Sunday (April 20th), at 10 a.m.

When the discussion was resumed Orlando opened the proceedings by reading a statement, intended to be conciliatory, to the effect that the withholding of Fiume would create among the Italian people 'a reaction of protest and of hatred so violent that it will give rise to the explosion of violent contrasts within a period that is more or less close'. Nevertheless, to save the Alliance he would declare formally that 'in the event of the Peace Conference guaranteeing to Italy all the rights that the Treaty of London has assured to her, I shall not be obliged to break the Alliance, and I would abstain from every act or deed which would have this signification'. All three accounts (French, Italian and my own in English) agree that this was followed by a long silence.

This was broken by a very long and eloquent and well-balanced

[1] All the quotations, except where otherwise specified, in this chapter are from the account of the discussions in *The Foreign Relations of the United States: The Paris Peace Conference 1919.*

protest by Wilson, starting from the fact that France, Great Britain and Italy, which had undoubtedly borne the brunt of the war, had found the co-operation of the United States essential to victory. This was followed by the story of the principles on which the United States had joined in, which he had written to express the point of view of the people of the United States and were found to be identical with those of all the Allied and Associated Powers. The Peace Treaty must reflect the views of the whole world, not of a very few nations. All this he said in order to pile up the case against Orlando's demand for the Treaty of London conditions and particularly for Dalmatia, which was inconsistent with paragraphs ix and x of his fourteen points, which he read.

Lloyd George then intervened. This, he said, was the most difficult question that had yet confronted the Conference, and it was hard to see a way out. On the one hand was the possibility that Italy was feeling that she could not continue her association with her Allies in making peace owing to the Austrian question, and on the other the United States would not assent to a Peace Treaty based on principles inconsistent with those for which they had entered the war. He himself could not discuss the question on merits, because he was bound by his bond, which 'had been honoured by Italy, in blood, treasure and sacrifice'. Putting Italy's case to Wilson, he said that he had been profoundly moved by Orlando's reasoning and by what Sonnino had said. The latter had been in the war from the outset, when he had taken a heavy responsibility in rejecting Austria's offers. What could he say to the Italian people? If he returned without fulfilment he would almost have to leave the country. After incurring heavy losses and large debts he only got little more than he could have had without risking a single life. He concluded that the representatives of the Powers signatory to the Treaty of London should meet separately to consider Wilson's grave decision. The President accepted this proposal—and that is what was done.

It was during this discussion that Orlando's feelings got the better of him and that, to quote Mantoux's very restrained account '*M. Orlando donne des signes de la plus grande émotion*' (M. Orlando showed signs of the greatest emotion) or according to Aldrovandi's version '*Orlando è talmente angosciato che singhiozza lungamente*' (Orlando was so afflicted that he sobbed for a long time), which is more accurate. Personally I decided not to refer to this breakdown in my official account. I regarded myself as the official secretary of the Council of

Four and knew that my notes (which were being circulated to the principals) were being treated very seriously, and might be passed round by any of them within a narrow circle. It is not unlikely that I acted after consulting Lloyd George, for in his version of the meeting Orlando's breakdown is not mentioned.

There is, however, a slight difference between the French and the Italian accounts on the timing of the episode, which is of some importance. Mantoux places it midway in Lloyd George's speech, after the words 'Personally I am not free, since I am bound by the engagement of my country', while Aldrovandi times it at the end of Orlando's short reply to President Wilson's long speech. I think it practically certain that the French version is correct on this point, and there is a good deal of evidence to support this view, for, although the episode is not mentioned in my official printed version published by the American State Department, it is referred to in several contemporary accounts, including Riddell's diary and in my own diary. Under date April 20th Riddell writes:

Telephone message asking me to go with L. G. and party to Noyon, starting at 11 o'clock. We waited until after 12, L. G. being kept at a meeting at President Wilson's. As I looked over the road, I saw Orlando standing at one of the windows, apparently weeping. When L. G. returned I said, 'Evidently you people have been putting it over poor Orlando. Have you decided against the Italian claims (the subject of the discussion)? Orlando looked as if he were weeping.'

L. G.: 'He was. He was overcome by a speech I made. It was a touching scene. He began to gulp and then got up and walked to the window and regularly broke down. Wilson was very touched. He went and shook him by the hand.'

R.: 'What did you say'?

L. G.: 'Well, as you know, Wilson is strongly opposed to the Italian claims, not only to Fiume, but also to the territories comprised in the Treaty of London. I said "We stand by that treaty. I must uphold the honour of my country. I think the Italians are making a mistake in taking over territories comprising so many Germans, and particularly the Tyrol. But, at the same time, what we have signed we stand by".'[1]

The reason why I have described the incident is that it was a notable illustration of the part that the human factor can play in public affairs, even on the highest level. Orlando, by his engaging personality, had won the liking and confidence of his three great colleagues. He had

[1] Lord Riddell, *Intimate Diary of the Peace Conference*, c. 7, p. 53.

co-operated helpfully and wholeheartedly in the German Treaty, which to Italy was of secondary importance, leaving until dangerously late his main concern, the Austrian Treaty. Now he suddenly realized that, after all their sacrifices and sufferings, the hopes of his people, which he had espoused, were to be dashed to the ground by Wilson's vague internationalism. It was the loyalty of Clemenceau and especially Lloyd George to their plighted word that touched his heart and precipitated this outburst.

The stormy atmosphere at the Council of Four on that Sabbath morning was relieved by the arrival, at the fag-end of the meeting, of news that brought all four back into complete harmony. That was a reply from the German Government to the invitation to send envoys to Paris on April 25th. In form it purported to be an acceptance of the date, but they only proposed to send an unknown minister and two officials with power to receive the text of the proposed Preliminaries of Peace and to take them back to the German Government. This aroused general indignation and there and then President Wilson, at Clemenceau's request, drafted the following reply on his private typewriter:

The Allied and Associated Powers cannot receive envoys merely authorized to receive the terms of peace. They must require that the German Government shall send plenipotentiaries fully authorized to deal with the whole question of peace as are the plenipotentiaries of the Allied and Associated Powers.

Thus it was on a more cheerful note that soon after noon on that Sabbath day we adjourned and went our several ways—Lloyd George to Noyon to visit a battlefield of the late war with Pétain, I to my office for a hard day's work, and the others I know not where.

On the next day (Monday, April 21st), in accordance with Lloyd George's suggestion, we met in groups, as described in the following contemporary diary note:

April 21st. Two meetings. One (informally) at Lloyd George's flat at 23 Rue Nitot (at 10 a.m.); the other at President Wilson's house, Place des États-Unis (4 p.m.) with the Americans and French, both on the Italian claims. We have now reached an impasse. The Italians say they won't sign the German Treaty unless they are promised Fiume and the whole Treaty of London. No one will give them Fiume, and President Wilson won't give them Dalmatia, which, he says, would contravene the ethnical principle. During the afternoon meeting I was sent to see Orlando and Sonnino at the Édouard VII Hotel, where they lodge, to ask if they thought it worth while to come and discuss their claims again on the basis of retention of the islands off the Dalmatian coast, in order to provide the security they demand as the object of their claim (i.e. Lloyd George's proposal).

My verbal report of my visit is summarized in the published proceedings of the meeting as follows:

Sir Maurice Hankey reported that he had seen M. Orlando, Baron Sonnino and Count Aldrovandi. He had delivered his message in the very words that President Wilson had used. After recalling Mr Lloyd George's proposal made at the morning meeting, which they had had some time to consider, he had asked whether they would think it worth while to discuss the Italian claims on the basis of the cession of a series of strategic islands off the coast. M. Orlando had asked him if he could give the proposal in writing, but he had replied that he only had authority to deliver a verbal message. The proposal had not commended itself to M. Orlando and Baron Sonnino, who had absolutely rejected it as a basis for discussion. They had said, of course, they were always prepared to discuss anything with their colleagues if asked to do so, but they would be in the wrong if they encouraged any hopes that this could be a basis for a solution. M. Orlando had elaborated his objections to the proposal a little. He had explained that, even from the point of view of defence in its narrower strategic aspects, the proposal did not commend itself. He had, however, always regarded defence in the wider aspects of the defence of the Italian towns on the west coast of the Adriatic. He mentioned in this connexion especially Fiume, but also referred to Zara and Sebenico. Questioned about the precise terms of Mr Lloyd George's suggestion, Sir Maurice Hankey said he had been given to understand that it did not include islands such as Pago, which were almost part of the mainland, but would doubtless include the other islands allotted to Italy in the Treaty of London. Sir Maurice mentioned that M. Orlando had said the question had rather retrograded within the last two days, owing to the proposal for the establishment of a free port and city at Fiume similar to that at Danzig having been dropped.

Count Aldrovandi, who was taking notes during my talk with the two Italian statesmen, includes a long account in his *Guerra Diplomatica*, which adds nothing of material importance, unless the following passage (translated from the Italian) bearing on his own personal relations with myself is considered as such:

Hankey, with whom I have always maintained, during years of common labours, the most cordial confidential relations, when leaving Orlando's room was clearly disturbed. He grasped me firmly by the hand and began to say; '*A rivederci*. . . . .' I have a notion he wanted to add something more; then he concluded by saying simply. . . 'Aldrovandi'. . . But the naked word, by the tone in which it was spoken and the look that accompanied it, reflected emotion, sympathy.

What I actually had in my mind to say was—'I wonder if you and I could not find a way out'—but I had to hurry back to the statesmen awaiting me.

After hearing my report some discussion took place on a proposal by Wilson to publish a statement on the Italian claims that he had drafted and which had been discussed during my absence. Clemenceau and Lloyd George thought it premature, and the President, in deference to his colleagues, agreed not to publish immediately. A short preliminary discussion followed on the Japanese claims.

In spite of the failure of all attempts to find a solution Lloyd George continued his efforts, keeping his colleagues continuously informed, and on Tuesday (April 22nd) at an afternoon meeting of the Council of Three (the number to which it was now reduced) he was authorized to see Orlando at once and to ascertain from him whether Italy would discuss the following conditions:

(1) Fiume, together with the surrounding territory, to be a free city;
(2) The islands of strategical importance to Italy, excluding such islands as Pago, which are almost an extension of the mainland, to go to Italy; and
(3) Zara and Sebenico to be free cities without any definite provision for a plebiscite, but with the power all countries have under the League of Nations to appeal to the League for an alteration of their boundaries.

Orlando replied at once with a counter-proposal, which Lloyd George read to the President and Clemenceau at 11 a.m. next morning (April 23rd). It was as follows:

(1) The line of the Alps (Brenner) to the sea, east of Volosca (which is close to Fiume).
(2) Fiume under the sovereignty of Italy. Italy will establish in the port of Fiume free zones in accordance with the terms of Articles 8, 9 and 10 of the Peace clauses drawn up by the Commission of Ports, Waterways and Railways, and will extend to Fiume those facilities which may be arranged for later on in a general convention with reference to free ports.

(3) Italy will have all the islands mentioned in the Treaty of London except Pago.

(4) Zara and Sebenico will be placed under the League of Nations with Italy as the Mandatory Power.

The new Italian plan was, of course, totally unacceptable and had the effect of deciding Wilson to publish that same evening the memorandum on the Italian questions that he had held back for a few days at the request of his colleagues, and in consequence Lloyd George and Clemenceau decided to send the Italian representatives a joint memorandum prepared by Balfour, subject to certain amendments. No date was decided for forwarding it to the Italian delegates. There was a further exchange of views on the grave problems that would arise for all concerned, including Italy (e.g. on her reparations claims against Germany), if the Italian delegates were not present when the German delegates appeared to receive the Treaty.

On the same evening (Wednesday, April 23rd) I dropped in at Lloyd George's flat in the Rue Nitot to introduce Captain Gibson, an emissary from Germany with news that Lloyd George ought to hear. There I found quite a musical party—Riddell, Auckland Geddes, young Spring-Rice of the Foreign Office, Miss Stevenson and J. T. Davies. On my arrival Geddes's Scottish songs and other music came to an abrupt stop and I felt a terrible spoil-sport. Lloyd George and I retired to the study, where the Prime Minister dictated and signed a letter to Orlando asking him urgently to come to breakfast next morning bringing with him Sonnino and Aldrovandi. Davies, who acted as messenger according to Lord Riddell, who took him in his car, 'found Orlando surrounded by his compatriots all in a state of great excitement'.[1] The breakfast invitation was declined. But Lloyd George himself visited Orlando early next morning at the Hotel Édouard VII (April 24th). At 11 a.m. he reported to the Big Three that Wilson's manifesto had reached Orlando, but that publication had been held up until Orlando's reply could be published with it. Orlando had yielded to Lloyd George's insistence that his reply should be couched in moderate language and should not commit the Italians to Fiume. Orlando was willing to leave Sonnino in Paris but had intimated that it would help him to stay if a communiqué could be issued to the press to the effect that, at the request of Clemenceau and Lloyd George, as representing two countries signatory of the Treaty of London, he had agreed to defer his departure. This was

[1] Riddell, op. cit., p. 59.

I

agreed to and the text of the communiqué was accordingly drafted and sent, there and then, by the hand of Philip Kerr to obtain Orlando's agreement to its publication forthwith. But Orlando 'ratted' on it. Then, just as the meeting of the Big Three had concluded, and while they were dispersing, Aldrovandi arrived with a message from Orlando that he and his colleagues had come to the conclusion that the best plan would be for them to meet the Supreme Council that afternoon at President Wilson's house.

So all other business was cancelled and at 4 p.m. the Big Four met again, this time with three secretaries, Aldrovandi and myself, as usual, and, for the first (and last) time a Mr Close for the United States. The meeting began with expressions of mutual goodwill and personal liking between Orlando and Wilson and gradually ranged over the whole area, tending more and more to accentuate the difficulties in spite of Lloyd George's and Clemenceau's efforts to find a solution and, more especially, to bring home to the Italian Ministers the dangers of putting the Germans, before or on their arrival in Paris, in a position to exploit these grave differences among the Allies. But Orlando stuck to his point that, before he could meet the Germans or sign a Treaty with them (which did not greatly concern Italy, except their relatively small claim for reparations) he must confront his own Parliament and ascertain how far he could go in the matter of the Austrian Treaty. There was much discussion about how he was to present the situation.

Naturally no clearcut binding decision was or could be taken, but the following passage from my published Minutes shows the trend:

President Wilson said that the Italian representatives could go to the Italian Parliament and tell them that neither the Allies nor the Associated Powers could consent to give them Fiume. The British and French felt bound to stand by their agreement as allies. In regard to the agreement they could state that he, himself, understood the difficulty of his colleagues and was ready to agree with anything consistent with his principles, although he had no proposal to make. Signor Orlando re-stated what President Wilson had said in almost the same words.

Further Orlando added that he had received a copy of the President's memorandum and had announced his intention to read it to the Italian Chamber. Then Orlando announced that he must leave to catch his train; and before he left I handed him a copy of the letter signed by Clemenceau and Lloyd George. A press communiqué was also agreed to.

Orlando and most of the Italian Delegation left Paris that evening (April 24th). According to Aldrovandi Orlando called out from the window as the train left '*À bientôt*'. And on Saturday (April 26th) Sonnino, after refusing to see anyone in Paris, left at 2 p.m., taking Aldrovandi with him. Sonnino was received with great demonstrations at Chiavari, Pisa and Grosseto and on arrival at Rome from the station to the Consulta (the Italian Foreign Office).

The spinning out of the Italian claims had been very embarrassing to the Council of Four and to the Secretariat-General and myself, as many other questions were arising in connexion with the German Treaty. The Japanese Delegation, however, also had claims against Germany, which were known to be disputed by China, and as early as April 20th, that is to say, five days before Orlando's departure, Wilson was informed by them that they must insist on a settlement of their dispute with China before the completion of the German Treaty. The Drafting Committee also reported that the section of the Treaty dealing with Germany's overseas possessions was held up until the matter was settled.

The Council of Four at once realized that the subject could not be postponed. It would be bad enough before handing over the German Treaty to lose the Italian Delegation, but if the fifth of the Inviting Powers (Japan) had also withdrawn its representatives, the three remaining Powers responsible for the Treaty would be in a very awkward fix. In the circumstances they had no alternative but to open up the Japanese question while the Italian claims were still at a pressing stage especially as the arrival of the German Delegation to receive the completed Treaty was approaching. It was not a pleasant outlook for the Council of Four—nor for their secretary! However, postponement was impossible, and, as early as April 21st, the day following the Japanese approach to Wilson, the subject came before the Council of Three just after my little report had been made about my visit to the Italian delegation.[1]

Baron Makino and Viscount Chinda described their claims as lucidly as they had done before the Council of Ten on January 10th, namely (*a*) to the leased Territory of Kiauchau together with possession of the railways and other rights possessed by Germany in respect to Shantung Province, and (*b*) to the former German islands, with the rights and properties connected therewith.

[1] *Vide supra*, p. 127.

At the discussion on April 21st Wilson was confronted with much the same opposition as before. Japan, he claimed, should have the same treatment at Kiauchau as the other Powers had received in the case of German colonies, to which indeed they had pledged themselves. As France had given Japan a corresponding pledge, *mutatis mutandis*, Wilson was again left in a minority of one. But on this occasion he was more cautious than in the case of Italy and had better luck for, at this point it was remembered that China was also represented at the Peace Conference and had a right to be heard. Makino agreed, but asked to be excused from attending as he did not wish to bandy words with the Chinese delegate. As at that moment the Italian claims were still at a critical point the Council of Three could not possibly find time for another meeting on the same morning; they instructed me to try and arrange the meeting for that same day and it took place at 4.30 p.m.

That meeting was notable for the appearance of Wellington Koo, a most remarkable man. Skilfully interrogated by Wilson, Koo replied with a complete mastery of the English language and an admirable delivery which made a deep impression on his hearers of the strength of China's case. After this Japan's claims for Shantung looked rather different. Especially effective was Koo's description of the so-called 'twenty-one points', which had been formulated by Japan as recently as 1918, when the Western Powers had been too busy with the final stages of war with Germany to pay much attention to the Far East. The argument was long and complicated. At last a question was put to Koo whether China would be better off under the maintenance of the Treaty forced on her by Japan (the twenty-one points) than under Japan's present claims, which were supported by France and Great Britain.

After a short adjournment Koo replied that both alternatives were unacceptable, but that perhaps the German rights were more limited than the rights claimed by Japan in the Treaty and the exchange of notes between the two countries. After that the argument lasted so long that, without any sign of an agreement, all accepted Lloyd George's suggestion for an adjournment.

The Chinese Delegation did not appear again before the Council of Four but both sides were clamouring for a decision, not to mention the Drafting Committee, and something had to be done.

To Balfour and Wilson belongs the credit for achieving a settlement by informal good offices, which included the establishment of a committee of three knowledgeable officials, Jean Gout for France, B. T. Williams for the United States and Ronald Maclean for Great Britain. With astonishing celerity they made a report (undated) which was considered by the Council of Three on April 24th, advising that it would be advantageous for China to agree to accept Japan's succession to the rights and position which Germany had possessed at Kiauchau and Shantung in 1914 on the outbreak of war, provided that Japan's rights, both in the leased territory and in the province, were confined strictly to those accorded to Germany by the Treaty of March 6, 1898, and by subsequent Sino-German agreements on mines and the railways.

The report was the starting point of fresh discussions, some of them 'behind the scenes' and others at the Council of Three, but it was not until Wednesday (April 30th), after a final discussion by the Council of Four, that I had the pleasure of forwarding agreed articles to the Drafting Committee.

This addition to the work of the Council of Three had been an almost intolerable strain to all concerned coming on top of the Italian claims and a spate of urgent questions pouring in about the compilation of the German Treaty, to which we must now turn. Before leaving the subject, however, I must pay a tribute of admiration to all concerned in this business, to my chiefs in the Council of Three and to Balfour, to the Japanese delegates and especially their secretary Saburi, with whom I was laying the foundations of an intimate and precious friendship, and to the members of the expert committee that rendered such good service.

CHAPTER XV

COMPLETION OF THE DRAFT
TREATY WITH GERMANY

'More haste, less speed.'

THE final stages of the draft Treaty raised a number of delicate questions in relation, first, to the members of the Preliminary Peace Conference and, second, to the reception of the Germans.

On the first point it must be borne in mind that the final stages for completing the Treaty had been so rushed that, apart from the members of the Drafting Committee, no one in the Conference, not even the Council of Three nor their secretary, myself, had the slightest idea of its size, shape or total contents up to the eve of its presentation to the Germans. Moreover, the members of the Council of Four were unanimous that on no account must its contents be published before its communication. All were agreed that advance communication to the members of the Plenary Conference would be tantamount to publication and, in some shape or form, would reach the Germans prematurely.

It was decided therefore, in principle, that a Plenary meeting of the Preliminary Peace Conference should be summoned only just before the handing over of the Treaty to the Germans, and that Tardieu, who had been working in collaboration with the Drafting Committee, should prepare a summary covering all points in the Treaty to read to the Plenary meeting.

Turning to the second point—the arrangements for the reception of the Germans—the initiative had been taken beforehand by the Secretary-General, and the group of representatives from the five Inviting Powers, on which I was represented by H. Norman, my deputy from the Foreign Office.

It will be remembered that, after rejection of Lloyd George's proposal of April 8th as the date for the arrival of the Germans in Paris to receive the Peace Treaty, Clemenceau had invited them for April 25th through Foch and the Armistice Commission, which was the only official channel of communication at that time when, technically, we were still at war. The German reply, received late on April 21st, offering to send certain officials to receive the Treaty was rejected because the Council of Four insisted on Germany being represented by responsible authorities, and, the date was postponed until April 28th, as the German representatives could not leave before April 27th.

That was very fortunate for the Conference, since we were hard put to it to stage the opening meeting even on the new date. Ever since Lloyd George's return from London, in spite of my heavy preoccupations with the Italian and Japanese claims, I had been watching for opportunities to squeeze a place on the agenda for arrangements for the reception of the Germans. On April 22nd, on consideration of the German acceptance which was conditional on 'liberty of movement and free use of telegraphs and telephones for communication with the German Government', it was decided to grant to the German delegates full freedom of movement for the execution of their mission and unrestricted telegraphic communication with their Government (Wilson's draft). Clemenceau entered a *caveat*, however, that he would have to take precautions that they should *not* have free movement *at Versailles* as there would be a grave danger of their being mobbed.

On April 26th Clemenceau informed his colleagues that the Germans were due to arrive on April 30th, and that the first meeting would be on May 1st at Versailles. That nearly gave me a fit, for there was still much to be done, but, owing to the arrival in the Council Chamber of a huge group of reparations experts, I should not get in a word of warning. Every subsequent day, after that and until the eventual meeting on May 7th, was to confirm how right I was. Thus on the next day (Monday, April 28th) numerous changes in the Treaty mostly raised by Hurst on behalf of the Drafting Committee, were approved. One came from Borden in the articles relating to the Labour Commission's report and others on the suggestion of the Drafting Committee. Then a number of outstanding objections were raised relating to China, which were referred to the three official experts on China.[1] Next the need for the preparation of draft articles on Luxemburg was brought to light, for which a special *ad hoc* sub-committee had to be set up. I myself raised a new question relating to prisoners of war, which had to be postponed until next day. I also called attention to a suggestion from the Council of Five (Foreign Ministers) for a modification in the naval, military and air terms to safeguard the recruitment by France of Germans for the Foreign Legion. Then Lloyd George proposed an additional article designed

[1] *Vide supra*, p. 133.

to compel the German Government to disclose the means employed for manufacture of poison gases.

All that arose out of a discussion on my list of subjects still out-standing. The Council now began to realize that there was much more to be done before completion of the Treaty than they had thought. That was confirmed when they turned to a memorandum by the Secretary-General on the revised arrangements prepared by the Credentials Committee for the communication of the peace terms to the Germans. The list of nations to be invited to the ceremony pre-sented a number of problems and eventually the following were included—Belgium, Brazil, Czechoslavakia, Greece, Poland, Portugal, Roumania, Serbia—to sit with the five Inviting Powers (including the Dominions and India).

The question of Jugoslavia, whose delegation had not yet arrived and which presented peculiar difficulties, was referred to the Council of Five for advice. As we shall see the list had eventually to be extended.

It was arranged that on arrival the Germans should proceed to Versailles where they were to stay, and that the first task to be under-taken by the Credentials Committee under Jules Cambon should be an exchange and examination of the credentials of all the states to be represented at the actual handing over of the terms of peace.

Tuesday (April 29th) was more or less a repetition of Monday. The morning already had been devoted to Japan's claims, after which I brought up an important point raised in a telegram from the British Admiralty, insisting that the Treaty should provide for the surrender of the surface ships '*at such Allied ports as the Allied and Associated Governments may direct*', as, otherwise, the Allies would have to fetch them from German ports themselves. This important change was approved.

An important alteration recommended by Headlam-Morley and Haskin (the British and American experts) in the articles relating to the Saar settlement was also approved almost without discussion. In the afternoon changes were approved in the articles on prisoners of war. In addition a difficulty about recognition of the Jugoslavs was cleared up, as it had been ascertained that the mere acknowledgment of their credentials would be equivalent to recognition, and would give no occasion for a special declaration by the Allied and Associated Governments. This seemed to me an odd and rather furtive way of recognizing the birth of a new nation, but the jurists insisted, and it sufficed. Articles on Luxemburg were also approved.

Just before the dispersal from this meeting I had to raise the question of Heligoland, which had been decided on April 15th during the absence of Lloyd George and myself in London, and no secretary had been present. No one was quite certain what the decision had been, but Wilson eventually supported a recollection given me by Balfour who had deputized at that meeting for Lloyd George, that the naval harbour as well as the fortifications were to be destroyed, and that the island was not to be re-fortified; this I undertook to pass on to the Drafting Committee. On looking into it today, in the light of the French interpreter's notes, which were only published in 1955, I feel less sure. These notes record no decision, but confirm that Balfour strongly pressed for a decision as recorded above, and Clemenceau supported him, but mention is also made that Wilson was not on that occasion convinced that the destruction was absolutely necessary, though he added that, if it was absolutely necessary, he would not refuse. There is no doubt, however, that on April 29th, he did confirm Balfour's recollection. This is a good example of the danger of holding meetings to take decisions without the presence of a secretary.

At 4 p.m. on Wednesday, April 30th, Lloyd George, apparently oblivious of the fact that we were already five days past the original date contemplated for the arrival of the Germans (April 25th), and that the German Treaty was still far from complete, sprang a proposal that the delegates of Austria and Hungary should be invited to Paris for the following week, and Wilson and Clemenceau approved without discussion. This so alarmed me that I broke from my usual secretarial taciturnity so far as to enter a protest, which is recorded in the published Minutes as follows:

Sir Maurice Hankey said that, as he was the only official present he thought he ought to put the point of view of the officials. The Drafting Committee was so overworked in bringing out the German Treaty that he felt confident they could not possibly prepare the Austrian Treaty in so short a time.

That made some impression and we gained a few days, namely, until May 12th, which sufficed. The Austrians would be invited to come to Chantilly, a rendezvous which was changed later to St Germain.

Afterwards I obtained approval to a scheme I had prepared in consultation with Dutasta for dealing with the many points that were certain to be raised by the Germans on reading the Treaty. Under my plan each of the thirteen principal commissions of the Preliminary

Peace Conference was to nominate a committee composed of four persons (one each for the United States, British Empire, France and Italy) to whom the Secretary-General would send copies of the German observations on points of detail in their respective sections of the Treaty. Questions of policy would be dealt with by the Council of Four, who could of course refer these, if they thought right, to the committee or committees concerned.

In addition, more last-moment amendments were made to the naval, military and air clauses, and memoranda were called for on the possibility of reopening communications with Russia, through M. Tchaikowski, the head of the Archangel Government, who was in Paris. The afternoon meeting had to be devoted to the clauses on Alsace-Lorraine, and some Belgian claims. And so it went on throughout Thursday (May 1st) when loopholes were plugged in the clauses on 'Responsibilities' (war crimes) and outstanding points were settled on Belgium and reparations.

As the Germans had been due to arrive on the previous day, the difficult question was raised on May 1st what attitude the Credentials Committee should adopt if the Germans asked for the Italian credentials. For the moment no decision was taken, as a considerable number of outstanding questions had to be dealt with, including such important matters as submarine cables (which was referred to the Council of Five); a protest by Pichon against the decision to invite the Hungarians as well as the Austrians for May 12th (which was left for Clemenceau to decide); the addition in some of the treaties of clauses for the protection of religious minorities, and arrangements for the relation between the Anglo-French armies and the civil populations during their occupation of certain areas in Germany as provided in the Treaty.

I had just time to set in motion the action required on each of these points and to dictate the minutes, before the Big Four met again at 5.45 p.m. to hear a report from Jules Cambon, accompanied by White (United States), Hardinge (Great Britain) and Kimura (Japan), of first contact with the German delegates, all of whom had arrived as arranged on the previous day (April 30th). Before the meeting he had received a message that the head of the German Commission would be represented at the exchange of credentials by the German Minister of Justice and two high officials, who would be at the Palais Trianon to hand over German credentials and would ask to receive the credentials of the Allied and Associated Powers in return. But Jules Cambon had replied by suggesting that Brockdorff-Rantzau should come himself—which he did. The credentials had then been handed over reciprocally, and it was arranged that, if the Germans had any remarks to make on the credentials of the Allies, they should meet again. After that they had separated. Cambon had received the impression that Brockdorff-Rantzau and his colleagues were profoundly moved and that their attitude towards the Allied and Associated Powers was what it should be. Brockdorff-Rantzau, who knew and spoke French fluently, as well as his officials, had spoken in German, and had brought an interpreter. That immediately provoked the question whether, when the Treaty was handed over to the Germans, he should be permitted to speak in German or should have to speak in French or English.

Clemenceau ruled that they could not be forbidden to use their own language and recalled that in the negotiations of 1871 Bismarck had spoken French when he was pleased and German when he was not. Cambon had not fixed a date for another meeting but, from his knowledge of the Germans, he felt sure that it would take them some time to examine all the credentials of the Allied and Associated Powers. That applied also to his own commission, which was to meet the following afternoon. He asked for forty-eight hours for examination of the German credentials, and said he would not be prepared to make any report on them before Saturday (May 3rd).

At that moment Wilson received a message that the Drafting Committee would probably require to ask for Tuesday (May 6th) to be the date for handing over the Treaty. He suggested, therefore, that Cambon's committee should make a careful scrutiny of the German credentials—which Cambon undertook to do. After the withdrawal of Cambon and his group, the position of the Italian Delegation was discussed and it was decided that Pichon should inform the Italian Ambassador in Paris that the Drafting Committee did not expect to have the Treaty ready for the Germans until Tuesday (May 6th) and that the Treaty would probably be handed over on that date. This was to be merely a message from the French Minister of Foreign Affairs to the Italian Ambassador and not a formal message from the Conference to the Italian Government.

The question of the date for the arrival of the Austrian and Hungarian delegates[1] was then cleared up, namely, May 12th for the

[1] In the event, owing to the disturbed state of Hungary and the fall of the Bela Kun Government, the Hungarian Treaty was not presented until long after the period covered by this commentary.

Austrians and May 15th for the Hungarians, as the two countries were
not friendly at the moment. I was instructed to speed up the various
commissions dealing with subjects affecting peace with Austria.

That brings us to Friday (May 2nd) when I reported the difficulties
that the Drafting Committee were meeting in cutting out all mention
either of Italy or of 'the *five* Allied and Associated Powers' (of whom
Italy was one) throughout all sections of this vast Treaty. I had myself
asked Hurst to look into it, but as yet nothing had been done. Now
they asked for instructions. I also mentioned that one of the commissions dealing with economic questions had sent a telegram to Rome
warning the Italian representatives that Austrian questions were about
to be discussed; this was deemed irregular. There was also an awkward
question about the status of Crespi, the Italian economic delegate, who
had stayed in Paris when the other delegates had levanted to Rome.
Nothing was known yet about the intentions of the Italians, and
eventually it was decided that a firm but tactful letter should be sent
by Klotz, as chairman of the Reparations Committee, to Crespi asking
him to define his position. Philip Kerr, who had now replaced me
'outside the door', was called in and instructed to draft the letter. This
he did very rapidly and adroitly and the letter was approved and
passed by Clemenceau to Klotz for signature and despatch.

Meanwhile the Italian situation was discussed in some detail and it
transpired that they had sent a battleship, two cruisers and a destroyer
to Smyrna and were making suspicious troop movements, both in
Turkey and in the direction of Fiume. At the end of the afternoon
meeting the Council was informed that American, British and French
warships had been ordered to Smyrna, and that Venizelos wanted to
send Greek ships too, but had been advised to wait. That was the
beginning of a disastrous chapter in the history of Greece.[1]

At the last moment of the morning meeting also an emergency
recommendation from the Drafting Committee was approved adding
Bolivia, Ecuador, Peru and Uruguay to the list of nations to be
represented when the Treaty was handed to the Germans and directing
that their credentials should be handed over to the Germans.

In the afternoon meeting at 4 p.m.—not in Wilson's house but at
the Quai d'Orsay—a further series of alterations and additions to
the Treaty were made on such varied subjects as the naval, military
and air terms, Belgian reparations, the ports of Kehl and Strasburg
in the Alsace-Lorraine articles, and instructions were approved to

[1] *Vide infra*, p. 162.

help the Drafting Committee in last-moment alterations which would be made in the Treaty with the Covenant of the League of Nations, in writing if necessary, according as the Italians were present or not at its handing over to the Germans. The Drafting Committee was also instructed to aim at handing over the whole Treaty to the printer by the evening of Sunday (May 4th). Important new articles were approved also to safeguard the eventual position in Russia, including cancellation of the Treaty of Brest-Litovsk, as well as providing for German respect for the independence of Austria within the frontiers covered by the Treaty, except by consent of the Council of the League of Nations.

The meeting on Saturday (May 3rd) began at 10 a.m. with a talk in Wilson's study on the Italian situation. A request by him for the publication now of the letter by Clemenceau and Lloyd George to the Italian delegation before their departure in order to let the world know that there was no rift between the Anglo-French position and that of the United States led to discussion so frank and so outspoken that it might have made a rift between them, had they not been so fundamentally united in their desire for peace. But it led nowhere, and I was relieved when at 11.30 a.m. they had to adjourn to the big drawing room upstairs to approve a belated article on the renunciation by Germany of her submarine cables, a report covering new articles on the position of new States submitted by Philippe Berthelot, Millar and Headlam-Morley, and a claim by Belgium for an indemnity to be paid to her by Germany and by Poland for reparations.

These questions, tiresome in themselves, were a useful antidote to the acrimonious earlier discussions on Italy. Even more useful was a long discussion the same afternoon (4 p.m.) at Wilson's house when the first direct, but extremely tentative, move by the Italian delegates to return to the Conference was disclosed. It had taken the form, that very day, of an informal approach by the likeable Marquis Imperiali[1] to Lloyd George and a more formal one by the Italian Ambassador to Clemenceau, as President of the Peace Conference. Both of them had adopted an attitude of straight speaking and complete refusal of these overtures. Lloyd George, in particular, had insisted that, with or without Italy, the Allied and Associated Powers had every intention of making peace with Germany and Austria. The only hint of a conceivable concession was when Imperiali had reminded Clemenceau of the question of giving a mandate to Italy for certain

[1] The Italian Ambassador in London, who was on a visit to Paris.

towns on the Dalmatian coast. At the Council of Four a very long discussion followed, much of it being devoted to the question whether Clemenceau should send a formal letter to Orlando, but the decision was first passed for the preparation of drafts, and for reasons that will soon appear it was never sent.

Other important questions then came up, e.g. the assignment of the mandates for ex-enemy colonies, etc., to the different nations, on which the Dominions were anxious for a settlement; a troublesome issue whether I was to send the Chinese Delegation a copy of the clauses in the Treaty of Peace about Shantung and Kiauchau; a Chinese proposal about payments by countries with a silver currency in the financial clauses, and matters relating to the dispersal of German ships captured in American ports. The only point in all these worth mentioning is my report that Edwin Montagu had resigned his position as chairman of the Financial Commission. Having thus landed the Drafting Committee with the well-nigh impossible job of sending the complete Treaty to the printer on Sunday evening, the Council of Four took a Sabbath rest and Lloyd George wisely went off to Fontainebleau with a picnic party.

The Council of Four met again on Monday (May 5th) at 11 a.m. After disposing of two last-moment changes in the Treaty, Clemenceau introduced a Colonel Henri, officer in charge of the arrangements for the security of and communications with the Germans at Versailles. He reported that on the previous evening the Germans had sent him a message to the effect that they had been kept waiting so long that they proposed to return to Berlin. That morning he had been informed that fourteen people would be leaving the same evening.

The Secretary-General of the Conference, who was also present, then stated that the Drafting Committee considered that Wednesday (May 7th) was the earliest safe date for handing over the Treaty. At that very moment Clemenceau reported that he had just received news that Orlando had announced that he was coming back, which would involve altering the first two pages of the Treaty. After a short palaver the decision was taken that the Germans should be informed that the Treaty would be handed over on Wednesday afternoon (May 7th) and Colonel Henri was authorized to inform them of this decision, also that the delay in printing was due to the time taken in examining the full powers, and that the Treaty was being printed. It was also decided that no alteration should be made in the first two pages of the Treaty owing to the fact that the Italians had announced their intention of returning. I asked for confirmation of that decision, which was given; any alteration would be made in manuscript at the last moment. Then Imperiali arrived to give Lloyd George the same message from Orlando. It was at this point that the decision was taken that the Plenary meeting to communicate the gist of this Treaty to the members of the Preliminary Paris Peace Conference would be held the next day, Tuesday (May 6th).

Another decision taken at short notice late in the morning (May 5th) was that the Council of Four should spend the same afternoon on a visit to the Trianon Palace, Versailles, where the ceremony of handing over the Treaty was to take place, to discuss the final arrangements with the Secretary-General on the spot—a good example of the care devoted by the Council to details. The most important result of this visit was a decision to admit to the ceremony a limited number of journalists. A strong resolution to this effect had been passed at a meeting of British correspondents at the Maison Dufayel on May 2nd, and next day Riddell, who had been in the chair, handed it to Lloyd George who took it up informally with Clemenceau and Wilson. In the result forty-five international journalists, including five Germans and ten for Great Britain and the Dominions, were admitted.

After leaving Versailles Lloyd George decided instead of returning straight to Paris to drive to St Germain to investigate in a general way its possibilities as a substitute for Versailles in connexion with the Austrian Treaty, which he was anxious to press on with. The following, quite irrelevant note, is perhaps of less interest to my readers than to myself:

May 5th. 11.45 p.m. I only make this entry in order to record that this day in a motor between Versailles and St Germain the Prime Minister (Lloyd George) said: 'I suppose you would not have cared for a peerage.' I at once said: 'No!' because I had not the means to carry it on. I said I would gladly have accepted a life peerage, if such a thing had existed. He replied that we ought to have them.

In a postscript to a letter to my wife I added: 'The P.M. says that he and I are an indispensable combination.'

The excitements of that particular day (May 5th), however, were by no means ended with our return to Paris. At about 11 p.m. that evening, just after I had dined at the Hotel Majestic, after some hours of intensive work in the office, a distinguished French Minister descended on me with another alteration in the Treaty, which he himself deemed urgently necessary, and to which, he said, Clemenceau had assented on condition that his colleagues in the Council of Three agreed. After a brief word with Hurst of the Drafting Committee I suspected a 'try-on' but I felt I had no alternative but to try and see Lloyd George and Wilson, late as it was. The result was recorded that night before I went to bed as follows:

Tonight between 11 p.m. and 11.30 p.m. I saw, first Lloyd George, who was half undressed, and then Wilson, who was in bed, about some alterations at the eleventh hour and fifty-ninth minute in the Treaty of Peace which is now with the printer.

In a letter to my wife dated May 7th describing the incident I added: 'He' (the President) 'looked so odd with the bed-clothes up to his chin! I was in my blue uniform' (instead of my usual khaki), 'and he said, 'Are you a sailor tonight?' Both he and Lloyd George assented to the new draft as Clemenceau had approved it but, as we shall see anon, it was modified next day on the advice of the Drafting Committee, before the new version had been printed. As I suspected, it was a 'try-on'.

Next day (Tuesday, May 6th), the afternoon of which had been allotted to the Plenary meeting of the Preliminary Peace Conference, the Council of Four met as usual at 11 a.m. and a most remarkable gap in the settlement (though not in the Treaty) was revealed, namely in the guarantee by the British Empire and the United States of America to France, in case of a German breach of the Rhineland settlement. This subject had always been dealt with between Heads of Delegations direct, under very 'hush-hush' conditions—intimate conversations between Prime Ministers and the President without the presence of any official or secretary. Once it was agreed in principle there had been no special need for secrecy about it. For example, it was mentioned in the Fontainebleau memorandum, though not in Tardieu's summary of the Peace Treaty, because, although it was a condition of the French acceptance of the Treaty, it was concluded between the three Powers only, Great Britain, the United States and France. It had also been reported to and approved by the British Empire Delegation. But the letters implementing it had never been exchanged nor even drafted and now, when the Treaty was to be handed to the Germans in two days' time, Clemenceau demanded very strongly that the guarantee should be given in writing immediately. That was at once agreed to, but the drafting was not so simple as one would expect and it was only after considerable discussion that a draft by Wilson was approved in the following terms:

In addition to the securities afforded in the Treaty of Peace, the President of the United States of America has pledged himself to propose to the Senate of the United States and the Prime Minister of Great Britain has pledged himself to propose to the Parliament of Great Britain an engagement subject to the approval of the Council of the League of Nations to come immediately to the assistance of France in the case of unprovoked attack by Germany.

After quoting that formula the Minutes of the meeting record that it was agreed:

(1) That the announcement should be made in the words proposed by President Wilson, and
(2) That President Wilson on behalf of the United States of America and that Mr Lloyd George and Mr Balfour on behalf of Great Britain, should respectively send letters to M. Clemenceau based on Mr Balfour's draft.

The two letters to Clemenceau, one signed by Lloyd George and Balfour, and the other by Wilson and Lansing, were handed to Clemenceau at the end of the Council meeting that followed the meeting of the Plenary Conference on May 6th at 6.30 p.m.[1] That was the first time I had realized the full scope of the guarantee and I confess it made me uneasy. But it was too late for me to propose any modification. I still wonder whether Wilson realized how disastrous this would be for himself and for the cause for which he stood.

There were several other important last-moment changes made that morning, some at the suggestion of the Drafting Committee, others by the French Government, and one by Borden to enable Canada and other Dominions to be represented on the Council of the League of Nations.

The original intention had always been that the draft Treaty as handed to the Germans would not be published at once as it was too long. Indeed it was estimated that to reproduce it in full would require no less than three entire copies of the London *Times*. Consequently it was decided later to publish Tardieu's official summary. But that also proved much too long and, just after the last

---

[1] *Vide infra*, p. 147.

meeting of the Council of Four before the Plenary session the question was raised as one of extreme urgency, regarding the date on which the summary of the Peace Treaty should be published. For the sequel I cannot improve on my own minute[1]:

Sir Maurice Hankey consulted M. Clemenceau who was already in his motor car, and President Wilson and Mr Lloyd George who were in the ante-room, with the result that it was agreed that the summary of the Treaty of Peace should be published in the morning newspapers of Thursday, May 8th; that arrangements should be made to secure publicity simultaneously in all countries concerned; and that no publicity should take place before that date. The question of publicity by wireless telegraphy was left to be decided when the Council of Three met in the afternoon at the Plenary Conference.

That is a good enough example of the hectic conditions in which we were working.

In the afternoon of Tuesday (May 6th), at 3 p.m., the Plenary meeting of the Preliminary Peace Conference was duly held. It differed from other plenaries in the respects that only the members and a very limited number of official advisers were present, and the press were excluded. The only subject on the agenda was 'the Conditions of Peace with Germany', and, as soon as a 'hang-over' from the previous meeting of a comment by the Honduras Delegation on 'Responsibility for the War' had been disposed of, Tardieu, according to plan, read in French his explanatory statement of the conditions to be handed to Germany. Although he did it extremely well, it was inevitably a dreary performance, which covers forty-four pages.[2] This must have had a soporific effect on the English-speaking members of the Conference none of whom spoke French; in fact, it was not repeated in English as that would have taken up too much time.

Consequently the comments were few. They consisted of a strongly worded demand by Portugal for better treatment over reparations, and other matters such as Portuguese rights on former German cables which pass by the Azores; a Chinese protest against the Shantung settlement and a formal reservation by Crespi on any modifications of the clauses of the Treaty made during the absence of the Italian delegates in Rome.

To the general surprise of the whole Conference, however, Foch, who admitted that he had not yet read the Treaty, delivered a

[1] *The Foreign Relations of the United States: The Paris Peace Conference 1919*, vol. v, p. 485.
[2] *Ibid.*, vol. iii.

devastating, and, as coming years were to show, a prophetic criticism of the settlement on the western frontiers of Germany, notably on the temporary nature of the Allied occupation, and military difficulties in defending France on any frontier other than the Rhine. It was a courageous utterance which would have been far more dangerous and damaging if the Council of Four, in order to avoid wholesale leakage of the contents of the Treaty, had not taken the precaution of excluding the press.

I had hoped that after the Plenary meeting we should be free from any more last-moment alterations in the Treaty to be presented next day to the Germans. But I was much too optimistic. The Plenary ended at 5.5 p.m. on May 6th and at 5.30 p.m. we were back at the Quai d'Orsay in Pichon's room. At the outset the oft-considered list of nations to be present at the hand-over of the Treaty on the morrow was superseded by a new decision that 'all *belligerent* Allied and Associated States, should be present . . .'. No reasons for the change are recorded. Next, Hurst, on behalf of the Drafting Committee, came to re-open the question of the French draft on 're-militarization of German territory west of the Rhine', 'purporting to come from Clemenceau' (as he put it), which had been substituted for the original draft.[1] The new draft had then been incorporated in the Treaty by the Drafting Committee but, on examination, it had been found to differ from the original text in several respects, including the omission of the following important passage:

In case Germany violates in any way whatever the provisions of Articles 42 and 43, she shall be regarded as committing an hostile act against the Powers signatory of the present Treaty and as intending to disturb the peace of the world.

Wilson then insisted on the reinstatement of a new draft corresponding more closely to the original draft. That was another example of the attempts made in certain quarters to get behind decisions of the Council of Four.

A long, but inconclusive, discussion on mandates for ex-enemy colonies followed, and at the end of the meeting, as already recorded, the British and United States letters containing the undertaking to come to the assistance of France in the event of an aggression by Germany, were handed to Clemenceau.

Even on the morning of May 7th, the date of the ceremony at

[1] *Vide supra*, p. 144.

Versailles, the Big Four met again at 11 a.m. in Wilson's study and instructed the Secretary-General to issue one copy of the Peace Treaty to each Delegation with a notice that it was strictly confidential—an absurdity in the case of some countries. He was also to prohibit photographs during the meeting, though sketches would be allowed. Next Botha appeared on the scene, as chairman of the Polish-Ukrainian Armistice Commission, with a request for authority to warn the High Command of the Allied Forces in those regions to beware of every provocation of the enemy while the Treaty was under consideration. This was approved, and a general authority was delegated to him to authorize the despatch of such telegrams from time to time as required —but always through the Secretary-General, and I was instructed to notify the Secretary-General accordingly. During the above discussion Orlando and Aldrovandi entered the room, having arrived that very morning from Rome.

The minutes do not record, and I do not remember any interruption in the business, which was concerned at the moment with Russia, but Aldrovandi records in his diary that I had written to Imperiali asking him to warn Orlando that the Big Four would be meeting in President Wilson's study at 11 a.m. and of the meeting with the Germans in the afternoon. He continues:

They rose to salute Orlando who restrained his annoyance (*domina il suo corruccio*). Wilson looked pale, embarrassed, Clemenceau troubled, discourteous, Lloyd George, in offering his hand, staring (*fissa*) and scrutinizing (*scruta*), Orlando and I interrogative, cordial, smiling. Not a word on what had happened, or on the return of the Italian Delegation.

That sums it up well. The business just continued without interruption on Russia, whether Tchaikowski should be heard, and then with Simon, asking more time for the completion of his remit on West African Colonies; a demand by Montenegro to be heard; and the coming arrival of the Austrian and Hungarian Delegations. It was only on the last point that Orlando spoke in reply to a question by Lloyd George and made a rather telling observation that Austria-Hungary had ceased to exist and that the next Treaty could only be with Austria *not* with Austria-Hungary. This led to a slightly acrimonious discussion, quite outside the range of the Treaty with Germany, which we were discussing, but Orlando agreed that the various sections of the settlement could not be discussed simultaneously, and the meeting was adjourned to the offices of the

Supreme War Council at the Grand Hotel Trianon *after* the presentation of the Treaty to the German Delegation at the Palais de Trianon.

Nevertheless, the indefatigable Lloyd George persuaded Wilson and Clemenceau (not to mention myself) to cross the road to his flat, and to discuss there (at 12.15 p.m.) the accumulating evidence of menacing Italian naval and military activities at Smyrna and elsewhere in the Aegean, with Venizelos, the Prime Minister of Greece—but that was the continuation of another story,[1] which has no immediate connection with the Treaty with Germany.

[1] *Vide infra*, p. 162.

CHAPTER XVI

THE PRESENTATION OF THE TREATY

'An immeasurable relief.'[1]

My own notes on the ceremony of handing over the famous Treaty of Versailles are somewhat sketchy. I was not in a good mood to act as a mere observer. My head was full of the varied subjects discussed first in Wilson's study and afterwards in Lloyd George's apartment with Venizelos. I was conscious that I was responsible for setting on foot a good deal of urgent action to implement the decisions as well as for the usual record, and that, immediately after the ceremony and before I had caught up with that business, I should have to render similar services at a further meeting of the Council of Four at the offices of the Supreme War Council at the Hotel Trianon at Versailles. So, in writing this chapter, I had to refresh my memory from other accounts of which my library contains several; these do not differ very much from one another. But I was confronted immediately by one extraordinary difference between them, namely where in Versailles the meeting took place. Lloyd George's excellent account, covering fifty-four large pages of print, which I 'vetted' at an early stage, begins with the words—'The meeting with the German delegates took place at the *Trianon Hotel* at Versailles, where the Allied Supreme Council had held its anxious meetings. . . .'. Riddell's diary says the same thing, describing it as 'a great white building standing in beautiful grounds,' which did not accord with my recollection of the Supreme War Council's offices. Sir Harold Nicolson[2] also mentions '*The Trianon Hotel*', but Count Aldrovandi's usually correct account begins by stating that 'For handing over the Conditions of Peace to Germany a room *on the ground floor of the Trianon Palace at Versailles* had been prepared'. In other respects his account was similar to the other versions.

The official Peace Conference, Protocol No. 1, Plenary Session of May 7, 1919, begins:

'The German Delegates, their credentials having been verified and found to be good and in due form, were invited to go to the

[1] *Vide infra*, p. 155.
[2] Riddell was present and pays me a warm compliment for securing a ticket for him, but Nicolson was not present.

Trianon Palace (*Versailles*), on the 7th May at 15 o'clock (3 p.m.) there to have the conditions of peace communicated to them'. That document[1] was signed by Clemenceau and attested by the Secretary-General (Dutasta) and by the joint secretaries of the five Inviting Powers (*including myself*), and must be accepted as authentic. Any lingering doubt, however, was dispelled by my 'discovery' in Lady Hankey's scrap-book of two incontestable pieces of evidence: (1) a strictly personal card of admission to the 'Trianon Palace' and giving access to it in the streets of Versailles, marked in red 'secretaries', and (2) a car pass for the same purpose and permitting 'circulation' in the streets of Versailles which enabled me to drive from the Palais to the Grand Hotel Trianon.

That leaves no doubt that the meeting with the German representatives took place at the Trianon Palace, but there is no doubt at all that *the meeting of the Council of Four immediately after the short ceremony* of handing over the Treaty took place at the hotel, for the heading to my minutes[2] is 'Notes of a Meeting Held in the Conference Room of the Supreme War Council *at the Grand Hotel Trianon, Versailles*, on Wednesday, May 7, 1919 at 4.15 p.m.'

As explained earlier, I arrived at Versailles preoccupied and moody, but the unique occasion of the ceremony soon gripped me. As an official secretary to the Preliminary Peace Conference I had naturally received a good place just behind Lloyd George. The hall was a very light one, with large windows opening upon a garden, decorated in white, about seventy-five feet square. The numerous tables were arranged in a hollow square, with small tables behind. Clemenceau, as President of the Conference, sat at the central table, with Wilson on his right and Lloyd George on his left, and the other British plenipotentiaries beyond (Balfour, Bonar Law, Barnes and Joseph Ward, Minister of Finance, New Zealand, to whom our fifth seat had been allotted because that Dominion, owing to its smaller population than the others, was only allowed one seat). All the seats on three sides of the square were allotted to the plenipotentiaries of the other delegations, totalling twenty-six nations, exclusive of the Hedjaz (whose seat was unoccupied) and the Germans, for whom a table within the hollow square, opposite Clemenceau but several yards away from him, with five seats, had been provided as well as a separate

---

[1] The document is printed in *The Foreign Relations of the United States: The Paris Peace Conference 1919*, vol. iii, p. 46.   [2] *Ibid.*, vol. v, p. 506.

table on their right for their secretaries and the interpreters. The Secretary-General and the five secretaries of the Inviting Powers, and Mandel, Clemenceau's *chef de cabinet*, were seated immediately behind Clemenceau, Wilson and Lloyd George. I was in the centre of that group. The forty-five journalists were accommodated behind the seats allotted to the Germans and facing the central table, but I had obtained a much better seat for Riddell whose initiative was responsible for the wise, last-moment decision to admit them.

The room was crowded; Riddell records that he counted 205 people. These included sixty-two delegates of twenty-eight countries, of the Dominions and India. Apart from the leading figures of the five Inviting Powers, there were present many distinguished people such as the Prime Ministers of Dominions, Venizelos and Politis (Greece), Paderewski (Poland), Beneš (Czechoslovakia), Bratiano (Roumania), Pachitch (Serbia). Besides the plenipotentiaries and their secretaries there were many admirals and generals in uniform, among them Foch, on whose presence there had been some doubts after his critical speech on the previous day at the Plenary meeting of the Allied and Associated Powers.

The period of gossip was superseded by silence as the hour of 3 p.m. approached. Dutasta then gave the word to telephone. Very shortly after the door opened and an usher announced—'*Les Plenipotentiaires allemands*'. At this point I cannot improve on Riddell's account:

All eyes were turned to the door halfway down the room on the right of the chairman. In they walked, stiff, awkward-looking figures, and, as I thought, comparing badly with the Allied representatives. They all wore morning coats, and were followed by their secretaries and two interpreters, who sat at a separate table on the right of the German delegates. As the Germans walked in, after a moment's hesitation everyone stood up. Count Brockdorff-Rantzau looked ill, drawn and nervous. He walks with a slight limp. His complexion is yellowish and there are dark rings under his eyes which are sunk deep in his head. When he was taking off his coat, I noticed that his face was covered with beads of perspiration. He strikes me as stiff, precise, industrious, mechanical, tactless sort of man. His colleagues looked in better health, and more at their ease. . . .[1]

The chief German delegate bowed to Clemenceau, who returned the bow and declared the *séance* open, and everyone sat down. Then Clemenceau rose again, solid and stalwart, and without a tremor in

---

[1] Riddell, *Intimate Diary of the Peace Conference*, p. 71.

his voice delivered his speech, which by general assent of everyone present was perfect in tone, in delivery and substance. The opening words are sufficient indication of its purport:

This can be neither the time nor the place for superfluous words. You see before you the accredited representatives of the Allied and Associated Powers both small and great, which have waged without intermission for more than four years the pitiless war which was imposed on them. The hour has struck for the weighty settlement of our account. You asked us for peace. We are disposed to grant it to you. The volume, which the Secretary-General of the Conference will shortly hand to you, will tell you the conditions which we have fixed. Every facility which you may require for examining the text will be granted to you, including of course the usages of courtesy commonly practised among civilized peoples.

In order to acquaint you with another aspect of my thought, I am compelled to add that this second Peace of Versailles,[1] which is about to become the subject of our discussion, has been too dearly bought by the peoples represented here for us not to be unanimously resolved to secure by every means in our power all the legitimate satisfactions which are our due.

After that introduction Clemenceau proceeded to a brief description of the contents of the Treaty and of the subsequent procedure of the Conference—*not* by discussion, but in writing, with a maximum of fifteen days for the German reply and questions, after which the Supreme Council would send an answer in writing stating the period within which the German Delegation must hand in its final reply to all questions. The description of the Treaty consisted of a statement of headings. Clemenceau's speech was then translated into English by the admirable Mantoux and by another French interpreter into German. After Clemenceau's speech, Dutasta slipped through an opening that had been left in the top table for the purpose, received from Clemenceau the bulky Treaty and carried it across the room to Brockdorff-Rantzau.

When the interpreters had finished, Clemenceau then asked if anyone else wished to speak and Brockdorff-Rantzau held up his hand, and, after being called on to speak, *without standing up* as Clemenceau had done, proceeded to read his speech seated, in harsh and provocative tones, from a manuscript. Instead of being read as a whole and then translated into French and English as in Clemenceau's case, the Count's speech was read and translated sentence by sentence.

[1] The reference to the *second* Peace of Versailles was no doubt prompted by Clemenceau's recollection that he had been present at the *first* Treaty of Versailles, when the positions of France and Germany were reversed.

This made it very difficult for the two German interpreters, admirable though they were, for, as already mentioned, they were at a separate table on Brockdorff-Rantzau's right, and after each sentence he had to pass his manuscript, of which there was only one specimen available, to each of them in turn to reproduce at sight in French and English respectively, and when both had completed their respective interpretations the manuscript had to be passed back to Brockdorff-Rantzau to continue.

This faulty procedure made it very difficult for his hearers to obtain a correct impression of his speech as a whole, which was in fact by no means a bad one, when read in its entirety later. He said:

We are deeply impressed with the lofty character of the task which has brought us together with you, namely to give the world a speedy and enduring peace. We cherish no illusions as to the extent of our defeat or the degree of our impotence. . . .

After that admission he could hardly be blamed for his refusal 'to admit that we alone are war-guilty', nor for seeking to find deeper reasons for the calamity than the assassination of the heir to the throne of Austria-Hungary. On war crimes his admission that 'Here again, we are ready to acknowledge that wrong has been done' was frank, as was his statement that 'we repeat the declaration which was made in the German Reichstag at the beginning of the war: wrong has been done to Belgium and we wish to redeem it'. The same applies to much of his statement, notably his claim that by accepting Wilson's principles on which peace was to be based 'the Allied and Associated Powers abandoned the idea of a peace of violence and inscribed the words "Peace of Justice" on their banner'. His warning about the dangers of a financial collapse resulting from the imposition of outrageous reparations was not out of place, nor, especially on a long view, was his claim that 'if the slain in this war are not to have died in vain, then the portals of the League of Nations must be thrown open to all people of goodwill'. His final words were unexceptionable: 'We will examine the document submitted to us with all goodwill and in the hope that the final result of our meeting can be subscribed by us all'.

Unfortunately, the intrinsic merits of the speech were spoiled for his hearers, first, from the outset by his failure to stand up to speak as Clemenceau had done, second, by his harsh and almost menacing intonation, third, by the loss of coherence due to the delivery and interpretation in sections, and, fourth, by the defective arrangements for interpretation which suggested lack of prescience and rehearsal. The result was that when Clemenceau, without giving much time for anyone else to speak up declared the session adjourned at 4 p.m., there ensued a buzz of conversation, directed almost entirely against the unfortunate chief German delegate. A few short extracts from Riddell's diary, however, do not entirely confirm my own impressions:

As the Count proceeded it was interesting to watch the effect produced on some of the principal figures. Clemenceau, Wilson and Lloyd George in particular listened most intently. Clemenceau tapped on the table with a pencil in his hand with which he always seems to be about to take notes, but rarely does. When the Count uttered some of his most pungent and tactless remarks, Clemenceau turned to Lloyd George and evidently made biting comments on what was being said. . . . It was interesting to see Marshal Foch marching down the side corridor . . . smoking a cigar, and smiling as much as to say, 'I always told you that these Germans were not repentant, and now what I said has been proved. . . .' As President Wilson said to me as he walked out of the Conference: 'The Germans are really a stupid people. They always do the wrong thing. They always did the wrong thing during the war. That is why they are here. They don't understand human nature. This is the most tactless speech I have ever heard. It will set the whole world against them.'

My own note, made late in the evening, was short but by no means sweet:

I was present today at Versailles when the Treaty of Peace was presented to the Germans. Brockdorff-Rantzau was a sinister-looking rascal, a typical junker. His speech was a strange mixture of cringing and insolence.

That was all I had time for, as I had been obliged to work until late to bring up to date the aftermath of the meetings of the Council of Four before and after the ceremony of presentation. But when my private secretary Sylvester, who had typed the translations of the speeches, showed me an advance copy I was not sure that my judgment was not too hasty, and some considerable time later, when I heard that Brockdorff-Rantzau had at the time been seriously ill and physically incapable of standing to speak, and that his whole attitude had been governed by his infirmities, I was even more doubtful. That accounts for my difference from Riddell's view. Still *it was an immeasurable relief* to all to have broken the back of our first task, and I fell on my knees that night in deep gratitude to the Almighty.

CHAPTER XVII

MANDATES AND THE AUSTRIAN TREATY

'Many a mickle makes a muckle.'

No one could accuse the Council of Four of being dilatory. The emotional ceremony of handing the Treaty to the Germans ended at 4 p.m. and by 4.15 p.m. they were assembled in the conference room of the Supreme War Council at the nearby Hotel Trianon to consider the distribution of mandates for the ex-German colonies, which by Article 119 of the Treaty were to be handed over to the Allied and Associated Powers. On this subject Lloyd George, with his habitual prescience, had circulated a memorandum. The ground had been well prepared, and the following decisions were taken without much difficulty:

Togoland and Cameroons to be passed to Great Britain and France for a joint recommendation, and mandates for the other German Colonies to be allotted as follows:

German East Africa to Great Britain.

German South West Africa to the Union of South Africa.

The German Samoan Islands to New Zealand.

Other German Pacific possessions south of the Equator, excluding the Samoan Islands and Nauru, to Australia.

Nauru to the British Empire.

The German islands north of the Equator to Japan.

In addition it was decided to set up an Inter-Allied Committee representing Great Britain, France and Italy to consider the possible application of Article 13 of the 1915 Treaty of London, i.e. the article relating to equitable compensation to Italy in the event of France and Great Britain increasing their colonial territories in Africa at the expense of Germany. Although these decisions did not touch the mandates in former Turkish territory which were not yet ripe for settlement, they constituted a very useful disposition to ease the way for the discussion on future procedure which followed next day.

On that occasion (May 8th) it became clear at once that the first question to be settled was the boundaries of the new states already arising on the ashes of the former Austrian Empire. This brooked no delay since, until that was settled, no firm decisions could be taken on many other questions; notably, the military terms for Austria, the size of whose army could not be assessed without some relation to the size and strength of her future neighbours. Fortunately the German frontier had already been fixed in the draft Treaty handed to her plenipotentiaries on the previous day, except in the case of Poland and East Germany. Also, new states bordering on Russia, namely Poland, Czechoslovakia and Roumania, would require greater latitude in many respects, notably in the size of their military forces, than ex-enemies like Austria and Hungary, and this was bound to react on them in many matters involving close and detailed study; for example, the boundary between Poland and the Ukraine presented an unsolved problem.

On May 8th the Council of Four[1] therefore, took three important decisions on boundaries:

First: Wherever they can be fixed, this shall be done, but where they cannot be fixed, the High Contracting Parties shall be bound to accept what the principal Allied and Associated Powers decide (Wilson's draft).

Second: That the Council of Foreign Ministers should be asked to consider at once, and to make recommendations in regard to, the territorial boundaries of Austria and Hungary, and of the new states created out of former Austria-Hungarian territory, and states contiguous thereto, as dealt with in the reports of the various commissions set up by the Preliminary Peace Conference (Sonnino's draft).

Third: That the Council of Foreign Ministers should be asked to hold their first meeting on this subject on the afternoon of today, May 8th (the secretary's draft).

After that copies of a number of resolutions, which I had prepared under instructions from Lloyd George, were handed round to members of the Council and passed, setting to work at once the various commissions that had prepared the articles for the German Treaty within the range of their respective limits and for the draft of corresponding articles appropriate to the Austrian and Hungarian Treaties. These applied severally to the groups that had advised the Supreme Council at the final stages on reparations, the financial clauses, breaches of the laws of war, ports, railways and waterways, and the military, naval and air terms. In addition, the military group

[1] Between May 7th and May 15th the proceedings of the Council of Four and Council of Five were given only restricted circulation, for security reasons which no longer apply. That is why they do not appear in the American *Foreign Relations of the United States.*

were asked to advise on certain outstanding inter-Allied questions such as a draft convention on the military occupation of the territories west of the Rhine (Art. 432 of the draft Treaty of Peace), and on the size of the Army of Occupation of these territories, a Belgian representative being added for these subjects.

Besides that, the Supreme Economic Council of the Allied and Associated Powers, which, under the stimulus of its very active and able chairman, Robert Cecil, had already forwarded for consideration various resolutions on immediate questions such as supply of raw materials to Czechoslovakia and Poland, and the lifting of the blockade of Germany and Hungary, and similar matters, was invited to discuss them with the Council on the following morning, when a number of important decisions were taken.

Thus, by the end of May 8th, the first day following the presentation of the Treaty to the Germans, the whole of the machinery of the Peace Conference had been set to work in preparation of the treaties with Austria and Hungary. One key committee was excluded for the moment, namely the Drafting Committee, which, on Wilson's suggestion, was given a rest after its very heavy labours in preparing the German Treaty.

After this excellent start the Council took up the subject of what military, naval and economic action should be taken if the Germans should refuse to sign the Treaty, a subject that had to be reconsidered from time to time, as the forces of the Allied and Associated Powers decreased under the process of demobilization, for which the public pressure was strong in all the countries concerned. As that particular emergency did not arise, it is sufficient to record that Foch outlined what seemed to his hearers an admirable plan and within his capacity to carry out. Before long, however, we shall meet this subject again and find the French marshal in a more pessimistic mood.

The ever-changing situation in Russia was another subject which occupied much time up to the end of the Conference and involved serious controversies that hampered treaty-making. Defects of detail also were brought to light from time to time in the draft Treaty presented to the Germans, and appropriate corrections were passed to the German Delegation.

The first two of the notes on the peace terms were received from the German Delegation on May 9th and discussed on May 10th, when somewhat acid replies drafted by Wilson were approved, and thereafter they poured in in ever increasing numbers. The scheme described earlier[1] was now brought into force and the German letters were handed to selected groups of the appropriate commissions and committees of the Conference, whose answers usually took the form of a draft reply. After preliminary consideration and if necessary discussion, the replies were signed by Clemenceau and sent to Brockdorff-Rantzau. The system worked very well, but, owing to the understandable obstinacy of our friend the enemy who contested every point, it took up a good deal of time. There was, however, no personal discussion between the delegations of the Allied and Associated Powers and the German delegates, as had been announced by Clemenceau at the presentation ceremony. That procedure sounds very stiff, but it is practically certain that, if some more humane method had been adopted, the Germans would have split the Allies and there would have been no Treaty. It was 'cruel only to be kind'.

From the first arrival of the German observations, however, the time of the Council of Four, and of the whole machinery of the Conference, had to be divided between the Austrian and Hungarian treaties, the replies to the German notes, and extraneous but vitally important ancillary questions such as the Italian claims, the Greek adventures, the development of the situation in Russia, etc. As at this stage we are concerned here primarily with the Treaty of Versailles, the two latter groups will be handled as lightly as possible, except so far as they bear on the German Treaty. The work now proceeded very much on the same lines as before, as the material came in from the commissions and committees which were dealing with the German comments and the Austrian Treaty respectively, and as the subsidiary points (Russia and the like) cropped up and had to be dealt with.

The Austrian delegates, though allowed a little more freedom than was accorded to the Germans, were kept waiting a long time by the Council of Four. It will be recalled that originally they were summoned much too early, namely for May 12th, a date at which there was not the slightest prospect of a draft Treaty being ready for them. They actually arrived at St Germain-en-Laye on May 14th, and the usual process of dilly and dally began. Their full powers were submitted only on May 19th to the president of the Committee on Credentials,

[1] *Vide supra*, p. 137.

but not approved until May 22nd, more than a week after their arrival. On May 25th the Austrian Chancellor (Karl Renner) sent a dignified letter to Clemenceau protesting against the delays and demanding the immediate opening of peace negotiations. On May 26th the letter was considered by the Council of Four, who found that the very controversial southern boundary of Austria was still unsettled, and the Council of Four was in an awkward fix. Lloyd George, who had had a good deal of responsibility for the premature invitation to the Austrians, then paved the way to a solution by suggesting that it was not necessary or desirable to treat Austrians on exactly the same lines as the Germans, and that a new procedure might be adopted. That plan was approved, and the Austrian Delegation was invited to meet the Allied and Associated Powers at the château at St Germain-en-Laye to receive the terms of peace a week later, i.e. on June 2nd.

By a tremendous effort a simulacrum of a Treaty was produced for presentation to the Austrian Delegation with exactly the same ceremony and procedure as in the case of the Germans. But in his speech Clemenceau had to explain that, while sixteen main subjects were included, the following sections would be handed to them later, and as soon as possible:

1. Political clauses (Italy).
2. Financial clauses.
3. Reparation clauses.
4. Military clauses.
5. Clauses in regard to the Serb-Croat-Slovene Treaty.

Renner made a dignified and very conciliatory reply in French and the whole function occupied exactly forty minutes (12.30 to 1.10 p.m.)

Not unnaturally, with so many loose ends the later stages of the Treaty with Austria took time to clear up, and the Treaty was not signed until September 10th. Lloyd George was not present, and Balfour was the principal signatory for the British Empire. I notice that I was present and countersigned the protocol covering the Treaty as British representative on the Secretariat-General, as I had done at Versailles. From now on, however, we need not concern ourselves much more here with the Austrian Treaty except so far as it bears on the concluding phases of the German Treaty. That applies also to the Hungarian, Bulgarian and Turkish Treaties, so far as they bore on the German Treaty, but none of them was even presented before the signature of the German Treaty with which this book ends.

Among the extraneous subjects which had to be cleared up in part before the German Treaty could be signed, by far the most important was the Italian claims but, as these claims had become complicated by an invitation by the Big Three (an hour or two before the presentation of the Treaty to the Germans) to Venizelos to send troops to Smyrna, it will be convenient to turn first to the Greek episode.

CHAPTER XVIII

THE GREEK EPISODE AND ITALIAN CLAIMS

'By a divine instinct men's minds mistrust
Ensuing danger.'

(SHAKESPEARE, *Richard III*, act II, sc. 3.)

IT will be recalled that on May 2nd the Big Four gave consideration to discussing some disturbing rumours of Italian naval and military activities in the region of Smyrna that had been current for some days. Lloyd George had sprung a suggestion that Venizelos should be allowed to send Greek forces from the Allied army in Macedonia to Turkey for the protection of the Greek inhabitants of Smyrna and other places along the coast and in the hinterland. In the pressure of urgent business on that day the Big Three were unable to follow up the suggestion.

On the morning of May 7th, however, after the arrival at the Council of Four from Italy of Orlando and Sonnino and the adjournment for the purpose of proceeding to Versailles for the presentation of the Treaty to the Germans, Lloyd George invited Clemenceau and the President to cross the road to his apartment for a few minutes. There they found Venizelos with Admiral Hope and Henry Wilson, who had already prepared a report recommending that Hope should leave at once for London to arrange for sea transport and ascertain the time required to assemble it, while Venizelos should collect as much sea transport as he could at Kavalla, where the troops were to be concentrated. To my great surprise this plan was adopted by the Big Three after a short discussion. Perhaps at this point I may be allowed to record what happened eventually in connexion with this decision.

During the whole of that varied and crowded day of the presentation of the Treaty to the German Delegation, and throughout a sleepless night that followed, my mind had been obsessed by the decision to support Venizelos's plan to send Greek troops to Smyrna. I rose at 5 a.m. on the following day (May 8th) and wrote a letter to Lloyd George, which I afterwards took personally to his apartment, where I instructed his valet to put it on the top of the pile of letters and newspapers with which the Prime Minister was accustomed to open the day. The letter, of which I had not time to take a copy, expressed the gravest doubts about the decision to encourage Venizelos to send Greek troops to Smyrna, or indeed anywhere in Turkey, as it would be very difficult ever to withdraw them. Looking to a distant future, I foresaw that, whatever the immediate result on the Turkish peace settlement, the time would come when Turkey would seek to recover Smyrna and the whole of the territory south and east of the Sea of Marmara and the Dardanelles. Turkey was intrinsically a stronger fighting nation, and who could foresee whether the present combination of powers now backing Greece, or even the League of Nations, would be able to come to her aid.

At 10 a.m. I was surprised to receive a telephone call from Philip Kerr who told me that Lloyd George had read my letter and had passed it to him with instructions to take it at once to Venizelos. This he had done. Venizelos had read it and put it in his pocket without comment. I tried to recover it from Venizelos, with whom I was always on friendly terms, but never succeeded in getting the original or a copy from him. Soon the episode was forgotten for the time being. I lived, however, to witness the sequel. In H. A. L. Fisher's words:[1] 'The Greek landing (April 15, 1919), disgraced by crime, roused all that was fiercest and most determined in the Turkish temper and offered to Mustapha Kemal, "the Saviour of the Dardanelles" and the most brilliant officer in the Turkish army, the chance of creating out of the shattered fragments of the vanquished empire a new and independent Turkish State'.

It so happened that the consequence of the Greek episode brought the Council of Four face to face with the Italian claims in the Turkish theatre of war, which hitherto had not attracted much attention, as under the 1915 Treaty of London they were to come into force only if, or when, the war should spread to the Turkish theatre. At the Peace Conference the subject actually arose at a meeting of the Council of Four on May 12th when Clemenceau informed Orlando frankly of the decision to bring Greek troops to Smyrna for the protection of the large Greek population in the city and district and invited Italian co-operation. When Orlando and Sonnino accepted this invitation I was frankly astonished.

Already rumours had started—notably a telegram received by Riddell on May 11th—that the Italians were sending troops to the

Turkish coast, and these were confirmed day after day by official reports of Italian troops landing at Scala Nuova, Marmaris, Makri and Bodrum, which aroused the suspicions of Clemenceau, Lloyd George and Wilson. The President, however, as he explained a little · later, was less concerned than his colleagues because these could not lead to any obligation on him to use force, as the laws of the United States did not permit the use of the country's armed forces in a country against which they had not declared war; thus he was able to take a more detached attitude. Nevertheless, on May 17th he joined in a formidable memorandum to Orlando signed by all three.

On the afternoon of Sunday (May 18th), when there was no official meeting of the Council of Four, Orlando called on Lloyd George, and, after the latter had rejected an absurdly extravagant proposal, the Italian Prime Minister made it clear that he no longer was interested in Italy's colonial claims and that the only claim on which he must insist was for Fiume, as the vital necessity for Italy. In this attitude he claimed to express the view of the Italian people.

On the following morning (May 19th) at 11.30 a.m. Lloyd George described this attitude to Clemenceau and President Wilson. On the afternoon of that day, therefore, there was no surprise when Orlando did not appear, but Sonnino put up a pretty good case for the Italian ship movements on the coast of Asia, in the course of which, after referring to the fact that Italy had been in occupation of Rhodes since the war with Turkey in 1910 (a fact which, I suspected, that his colleagues had forgotten), he pointed out that the Italian flag was well known in that region and that it was probably a normal occurrence for ships to call in for coal at the Turkish ports. Late in the afternoon however, almost as an afterthought, Sonnino asked his colleagues quietly to agree to leave things as they were, and not to insist on the withdrawal of the Italian troops. Wilson replied that, as far as he was concerned, the Italian Government must take the whole responsibility. Lloyd George said that was his view and Clemenceau said it was his view also.

The main result of Orlando's change of attitude on the Italian colonial claims was to direct the attention of the Council of Four more closely to the Adriatic. There was of course no prospect of achieving a settlement based on the 1915 Treaty of London because neither Wilson nor Lloyd George and Clemenceau were willing to yield on the question of principle, but there was a tendency, not only on the level of the Supreme Control, but among the experts of their respective delegations, who were working together on territorial commissions and the like, to discover a way out and avoid a break-down. Thus, as early as May 13th, at a meeting of the Big Three without Orlando, Wilson stated that he had set his experts to make a further study of the Italian claims. After mentioning a proposal put to him 'which he thought would, at any rate, prove acceptable to the Jugoslavs and which was based on the idea of a plebiscite all down the Dalmatian Coast', he produced some proposals which had emanated from the British Delegation for the solution of Adriatic problems. He also explained on a map the proposals of the American experts for the northern frontier which for Italy were an improve-ment on the Italian proposals.[1] This is only one example of a very important effort by American and British experts to get together spontaneously to help their chiefs. On this occasion, at any rate, their action met with high appreciation.

Another example of the unconventional method was about a fortnight later on May 29th when, at the outset of a meeting fixed for 11 a.m., Wilson announced that 'the Heads of Government had reached a decision regarding the southern frontier of Austria'. He went on to say that it was (*mirabile dictu*) 'the frontier laid down in the Pact of London with the addition that the Sesten Valley and Tarvis should be Italian and that the railway junction of Villach should be Italian'. I could hardly believe my ears, but the mystery was partly explained there and then when he produced a map showing the boundaries, which he said had been 'attached to No. 2 Report of the Committee on Roumanian and Jugoslav Affairs'. It was decided there and then 'that the experts on Jugoslav affairs should meet promptly and draw up a text in accordance with the above decision, to be sent to the Drafting Committee'.

The President next outlined the whole plan in detail to 'the Allied experts on Jugoslav affairs', who had been waiting and to whom he there and then explained the scheme in detail and answered their questions. The record was as follows:

It was decided that the experts on Jugoslav affairs should meet promptly and draw up a text in accordance with the above decisions, to be sent to the Drafting Committee.

The acceptance of this decision on the southern frontier of Austria, constituting the northern frontier of Italy, was a great relief

[1] *The Foreign Relations of the United States: The Paris Peace Conference 1919*, vol. v, pp. 581 *sq.*

to the members of the Council of Four (and their secretary) and revived hopes that the southern frontiers along the coast of the Adriatic (including Fiume and Dalmatia) might be settled in the same way. So a great and continuous effort was made to find a solution. Ingenious plans were submitted one after another. There was a Tardieu plan, which found some favour with Orlando; several plans prepared to meet the changes that arose in a fluctuating situation; a Lloyd George plan; a Wilson plan, and a joint Lloyd George-Wilson plan, handed to Orlando on June 7th. Orlando did not like it but promised to give it consideration. On June 9th he was ready to discuss it, but was asked to circulate his views in writing, which he agreed to do. Strange to say, though the subject was on the agenda paper for June 10th copies had not been circulated, and all that happened was that Clemenceau took Wilson and Lloyd George into a corner of the room and, after a whispered conversation, the subject was dropped.

Perhaps the explanation is to be found in what happened two days later (June 12th) when Orlando quietly informed his colleagues that, owing to the resignation of two of his ministers and economic troubles in Italy, he might have to leave Paris that evening. A short, friendly and sympathetic talk followed. But leave he did, never to return to the Paris Peace Conference, and on June 21st, just a week before the signature of the Peace Treaty with Germany, his colleagues heard that Nitti and Tittoni were forming a new government. Thus it befell that Sonnino, for the remainder of the Conference, took the place of Orlando at the Council of Four and became the principal signatory for Italy of the Treaty of Peace with Germany; he proved a helpful colleague on all matters relating to the German Treaty. It will be necessary, however, to refer occasionally to the Italian claims and to show how they dogged the Conference literally until the signature of the German Treaty.

CHAPTER XIX

CHANGES IN PROCEDURE

'All things change, words and philosophies and awkward systems, but God remains.'

(MRS HUMPHRY WARD.)

IT was found necessary to interpolate the previous chapter on the Italian claims in Asia Minor and the effect thereon of the Greek diversion in order to explain the harassing conditions in which the Council of Four, often reduced to a Council of Three, had to complete the German and Austrian Treaties. But that was not by any means their sole embarrassment, for, like the Council of Ten before them, they were constantly diverted from their main themes by troubles elsewhere—in Poland, Roumania, Hungary (especially the Banat), and to some extent Czechoslovakia.

In Poland, for example, Haller's army had eventually arrived, but during the continued unrest and fighting and the confused situation in the Lemberg region, it had, at one point, been sent into that district, and notwithstanding a remonstrance telegraphed by the Council to Paderewski, that this should not be done, it had been in action with Ukrainian forces. Botha, chairman of the Polish Commission, had reported that the Allied and Associated Powers were being held up to contempt, and had been summoned to account for it.

In Hungary, the Bela Kun Government was still in office, and was reported to be anxious to restore order, but apparently without the power to do so, and proposals were made for a joint Franco-Roumanian occupation (May 19th).

In Russia, too, the ups and downs of the various anti-Bolshevist forces under Kolchak in Siberia, Denikin in the south, and in the far north had to be carefully watched. Valuable information was received at first hand on May 20th from Tchaikowski, the head of the Archangel Government who was in Paris, and made an enlightening statement to the Big Four. The trend of his advice was to suggest the possibility that these movements might be combined to resist and overcome the Bolshevists. But such hopes proved illusory, and no boundaries with Russia could be fixed in the continuing state of chaos. Still, it provided one more inconvenient distraction from the main tasks of the Council of Four, i.e. the completion for signature of the

German Treaty and the compilation of the Austrian Treaty for presentation.

In spite of these inescapable distractions, however, meeting almost continuously the Supreme Council never ceased to pursue its plans and programme for these two main objectives with persistence and determination.

As we have said,[1] plans of action had been worked out at an early stage to meet the contingency of a refusal by the Germans to sign the Treaty. Consequently the Council of Four were able to deal with the comments of the German plenipotentiaries in full confidence that, in case of default, they had ready the means to enforce it. It will be recalled that, although the German reply as a whole was due on May 22nd, permission had been given for them to forward instalments earlier if ready. This they did, the first section being received as early as May 10th—three days after they received the Treaty. It consisted of an attack on the adoption of the League of Nations Covenant as the basis of the Peace Treaty, and President Wilson drafted a somewhat acid reply which was approved the same afternoon, but was afterwards modified by Robert Cecil.

After that the comments continued to pour in in an endless stream every day, and were dealt with in accordance with the plan decided on before the Treaty was handed to the Germans, i.e. their receipt and purport were reported by Clemenceau as chairman to the Supreme Council, and then forwarded by me to the Secretary-General of the Conference, who passed them on to the appropriate small groups selected from the members of each commission or committee of the conference, who prepared replies on their respective subjects. Their drafts then came back to me to submit to the members of the Council of Four, and, when approved, to forward to the Secretary-General to pass to the Germans.

That plan worked out surprisingly well, and the majority of the draft replies were approved by the Council of Four. Occasionally, however, the Council would form a different opinion, and other methods were resorted to. For example, on one occasion (May 20th) a draft reply to Brockdorff-Rantzau's comments on the economic effects of the German Treaty was referred, for strengthening, to Curzon in London. On the same day the draft replies to two notes from Brockdorff-Rantzau on the subject of Alsace and prisoners of

[1] *Vide supra*, p. *158*.

war respectively proved unsatisfactory, and another expedient was adopted. Philip Kerr was brought into the room and given his instructions by the Council (just as used to happen to me in early days when the meetings were held without a secretary) and then permitted to leave the room to produce a draft, which he completed before the end of the meeting, as he was an exceptionally quick and able draftsman.

I had been working for this procedure for some time, for I was finding it impossible, at the rate decisions were being taken, simultaneously to keep the record and to draft documents to give effect to the decisions. One or other was bound to suffer. After that the precedent was followed with increasing frequency.

About this time another decision was taken (May 17th) affecting my own functions and responsibility, namely that the Drafting Committee should accept no decision for incorporation of any article in the Peace Treaty unless initialled by the Big Four. The object of this change was to protect the Drafting Committee from being 'bounced' by plenipotentiaries or officials, however eminent, into making changes in the drafts without proper authority, of which there had been more than one example since the night of May 5th when I had had to wake Wilson and Lloyd George from their 'beauty-sleep'.[1] At first I apprehended that this might involve delays, particularly at a time when Orlando was not attending very regularly, but I avoided that by sending advance copies to the Secretary-General and to the British member of the Drafting Committee as an intimation of what to expect—a course to which I had had to resort in the early days of the London War Committee. In practice, however, the Big Four proved very amenable, and Wilson sometimes helped by typing short conclusions on his private typewriter during long passages of interpretation into French.

Perhaps, however, the most important procedural change made in mid-May was an alteration in the title of the Supreme Council. As mentioned above, Orlando did not attend so regularly as before, and it was often more convenient that he should stay away in order not to give his colleagues an opportunity to discuss together the various phases of the Italian claims, complicated as they were by the Greek episode. Fairly often, therefore, they met as a Council of Three. Also, undertakings had been given to Japan, the fifth Inviting Power, that her representatives should be present whenever their special interests were concerned, which included a good deal of the German

---

[1] *Vide supra*, p. *144*.

Treaty, and some of Brockdorff-Rantzau's comments thereon. On some occasions the number would rise to five. That made great complications for my small office in the distribution of papers, and for the Secretary-General and myself in drafting formal letters.

I met the former difficulty by a dodge of my own adopted, unnoticed, by recording each of the various subjects discussed at a long sitting as though it were a separate meeting, in which the list of those present was given at the head of the record, so as to simplify the question of distribution of minutes and other papers. For example, for the morning of May 10th (selected at random), I find records of no less than three separate meetings, the first at 11 a.m. including, besides the Big Four, only Foch; the second at 11.45 a.m., only the Big Four; the third at noon, including, besides the Big Four, Tchaikowski, head of the Archangel Government. In the afternoon the Big Three met at 3 p.m. to discuss the Smyrna episode with Venizelos, but without any Italian being present. Again, at 4 p.m., a separate meeting is recorded including Orlando to discuss some of Brockdorff-Rantzau's replies and a letter from Lord Cunliffe, chairman of the reparations group for drafting replies. On that day, therefore, two long meetings with varying personnel were recorded as five short ones, each having its own distribution list to avoid risk of communication of decisions taken to anyone not concerned.

Another difficulty was the designation to be used by the Secretary-General, myself and others in communications in connexion with meetings, which would normally open with some such phrase as 'I am directed to inform you that the Council of X decided this morning that . . .'. Was X to vary according as the meeting had been attended by Three, Four or Five? On May 17th I raised the difficulty at the Council of Four, when I informed them that I had for some time been using the term 'Supreme Council of the Principal Allied and Associated Powers'. It was decided to drop the word 'Supreme', but that no public announcement should be made. In view of that latter decision, I thought it best not to change the heading in the minutes, which was simply 'Notes of a Meeting held at . . . on . . . (date) at . . . (time)' followed by the list of those present, but I notice that the American editor of the published version of these minutes uses the page-heading 'Council of Four' throughout. I think he was wise, as to change the title after May 17th would have caused great confusion in editing and indexing. So I follow his example in this story.

A useful procedural decision taken on May 13th (4 p.m.) was the postponement of work on the Turkish settlements. That was a relief to the whole Conference and especially to the Drafting Committee. One more important procedural decision, taken in May by the Council of Four almost without discussion, was that the official languages for the Austrian Treaty should be French, English and Italian—a sop to the *amour propre* of the Italian delegation.

These procedural details may seem out of place in this account of how the Big Four, a 'Summit Conference', handled the world problems with which they were confronted. Yet they are an essential part of the story, for only by the adoption of such methods and their adaptation to fluctuating conditions can the secrecy, which is as essential at some stages to success as publicity is at other stages, be preserved. Without a highly trained and tested staff specializing in the top secret work of the Council of Four, the Council of Five, and incidentally the British Empire Delegation, the Paris Peace Conference would probably have failed as completely as have so many of the conferences since World War I which were, for the most part, run on totally different and hastily improvised lines.

CHAPTER XX

WILL THE GERMANS SIGN?

'They shall work for an age at a sitting and never grow
tired at all.' (RUDYARD KIPLING, *L'Envoi.*)

WHEN the Treaty of Peace was handed to the German Delegation
(May 7th), Brockdorff-Rantzau had been given fifteen days in which
to formulate his reply. A few days later detailed comments on the
various points had been received in what seemed an endless stream
by the Council of Four who, after their consideration by the expert
bodies set up to advise on them, had forwarded appropriate replies.
By May 22nd, the date on which the final reply was due, the majority
of the detailed replies had been received and answered, but the correspondence continued owing to German rejoinders. On Thursday,
May 29th, the President of the German Delegation sent a long global
despatch covering a memorandum of observations on the conditions
of peace as a whole, which between them cover nearly 200 pages of
the large volume of *The Foreign Relations of the United States* in which
it is published.

Up to the end of the previous week the Council of Four had already
been engaged on rejoinders to some of the lengthy and contentious
German replies on details of the Treaty and other urgent matters, and
it was only on Monday, June 2nd (4 p.m.), that they got to grips with
the German global observations which still required translation. In
the meantime Lloyd George had consulted as many British Cabinet
ministers as possible, who had come at his invitation to Paris, and
with whom he had held four meetings, two of them attended also by
the members of the British Empire Delegation. I was present at all
these meetings. He began by giving the results of these consultations.
They were by no means palatable to his colleagues, nor perhaps to
himself. On certain points those consulted had been unanimous. For
example, they were not prepared to continue the war and march on
Germany, or to join in the reimposition of the blockade unless certain
points in the Peace Treaty were put right. The Labour member of
the Cabinet, George Barnes, as well as Botha and the South African
Delegation were refusing to sign the present Treaty without certain
alterations. The whole of them had unanimously agreed that, unless
certain defects in the Treaty were put right, they would not advise

that the British Army should be allowed to march, or that the British Navy should take part in the blockade. Those consulted were a very fair representation of all sections of the Cabinet, Conservatives and Unionists, Labour and a moderate Liberal, H. A. L. Fisher, who carried great weight. They had read all the documents, and several had expressed surprise that the German counter-proposals had gone so far in concessions to the Allies. Lloyd George added that in particular Austen Chamberlain and Robert Cecil were strongly of the opinion that certain changes were necessary—as well as both the Archbishops, who had written to our Prime Minister. Lloyd George gave the Council of Four full details of the various criticisms and proposals, at great length, under each constructive heading, and concluded as follows: 'To sum up, the main points on which his colleagues pressed for a change referred to the eastern front, reparations, the army of occupation, the League of Nations and the pin-pricks.' He might have added the Anglo-American guarantee to France, which was not popular.

This statement to the Council of Four at once provoked an extemporized outburst from Clemenceau. He thanked Lloyd George for his frankness, but it had produced a very grave position. For he too had to consider public opinion, and the insistence of his own colleagues, which differed totally from British public opinion as presented by Lloyd George. It included subjects vital to France, such as the Army of Occupation of the Rhineland, reparations, and the eastern front, where the creation of a strong Poland was vital to the future security. Already he was constantly subjected to accusations of weakness, which might bring him down, in which case his friends would have to deal with people of a very different type. Wilson, who, at that stage, was subjected to less personal pressure than his colleagues, adopted a conciliatory and understanding rôle which led to an adjournment for further study and reflection, and paved the way to a further discussion on June 2nd, when Lloyd George made the suggestion that, as the German global document had made a certain impression in the Allied and Associated countries, a general letter answering Brockdorff-Rantzau's global reply should be prepared. He added that he had already set Philip Kerr to work on it. Wilson agreed. It was essential to controvert the argument that the bases had been ignored. If they had been, 'he, for one, would be ready to make the necessary changes. The real case was that justice had shown itself overwhelmingly against Germany'.

Clemenceau added that in the last lines of the letter the Germans should be given a final period within which to say whether they would sign or not—which Lloyd George suggested should not be longer than seven days. All these suggestions were agreed to, as well as a suggestion by Wilson that in the meantime no further separate answers should be sent to the outstanding German notes, as their subjects would be included in the general comment; in fact only three were still outstanding.

Thus on June 3rd Philip Kerr had a lead on the line he was to follow, and the Council of Four were able to turn to a series of difficult problems arising over the Austrian Treaty and other subjects. It was not until Thursday (June 12th) that the Council of Five (for Orlando and Makino were both present, the former for the last time) received Philip Kerr's draft reply to Brockdorff-Rantzau's letter. After careful examination and discussion it was approved, subject to some drafting and verbal alterations. At the same meeting a proposal by Tardieu to appoint a committee to edit the detailed reply to be covered by Philip Kerr's despatch, was adopted. The task was remitted to Tardieu for France, Hudson for the United States, Philip Kerr for the British Empire, Vanutelli for Italy and Nogaoka for Japan. Most of the various portions of the reply had already reached the Secretariat-General, but the final editing proved an exacting job, and it was only very late on June 16th, after many last-moment additions had been approved, and some rejected by the Council of Four, that the documents were signed and despatched to Brockdorff-Rantzau. We shall meet it again before long, when it will be referred to as 'the note of June 16th'.

For the moment, however, we must turn to another aspect of the problem which Clemenceau had wisely decided, notwithstanding the immense pressure of work, would brook no delay, and must now be taken up again that very day (June 16th) namely what was to be done before 7 p.m. on Monday (June 23rd) when the Armistice expired, if the German delegates had not agreed to sign the Treaty. The reason for this urgency was the following passage at the end of Clemenceau's long covering note, as drafted by Philip Kerr:

As such the Treaty in its present form must be accepted or rejected. The Allied and Associated Powers therefore require a declaration from the German Delegation within five days from the date of this communication that they are prepared to sign the Treaty as it stands today. If they declare within this period that they are prepared to sign the Treaty as it stands, arrangements will be made for the immediate signature of the Peace at Versailles. In default of such a declaration, this communication constitutes the notification provided for in Article 12 of the Convention of February 16, 1919, prolonging the Armistice which was signed on November 11, 1918, and January 16, 1919. The said Armistice will then terminate, and the Allied and Associated Powers will then take such steps as they think needful to enforce their terms.

The object of the meeting, therefore, was to ascertain the present state of Foch's preparations for an emergency that might arise in exactly one week's time, i.e. on Monday (July 23rd). The Marshal first insisted that he must be told clearly what was the political object that the Government had in mind, and what was the political result that the Allied and Associated Governments required as the result of military action.

Clemenceau replied that 'they did not seek an economic but a military conquest. What they sought was a political result, namely that the Treaty should be signed as soon as possible. . . . For his part he could think of nothing but a march on Berlin to secure this object'. Wilson, Lloyd George and Sonnino agreed. Foch then proceeded to elaborate his plan for achieving that object. There was no serious enemy force in front of the Allied army, but there was an enemy government, which had to be destroyed and replaced by one willing to sign. He emphasized that his forces had been reduced by demobilization from 198 divisions at the time of the Armistice on November 11th, to 39 (18 French, 10 British, 5 American and 6 Belgian). The enemy would make no organized resistance to his 39 divisions and he could certainly advance to Weimar, the present seat of the German Government and beyond. But he had to operate through very populous districts, teeming with German ex-soldiers, and the further he advanced, the more troops he would have to leave behind to guard his lines of communication against sabotage, and for the protection of supply depots and the like. He also had to make special arrangements for guarding his southern flank against attack from Baden, Wuerttemberg and Bavaria, for which he envisaged enforcement of separate armistices by these states. In this he hoped for some co-operation by Italian forces from the Brenner. He could probably advance as far as the Weser, but he did not know whether that would be sufficient to secure the political objects desired, and he was less confident about the further advance to Berlin, for which he envisaged co-operation from Poland and Czechoslovakia where forces were available.

Foch's attitude came in for heavy criticism from the Council of Four and was compared adversely with his confidence a month ago (May 10th–11th) and Lloyd George went so far as to read a passage from my minutes on those dates, which I was able to produce from my 'black box'. But Foch discounted this owing to the new factors he had brought to light, and stuck to his guns. He was asked to send his views in writing.

After Foch had left, Clemenceau asked that no major decision should be taken because he wanted to discuss the matter further with Pétain, and perhaps with Foch himself, but some misgiving was expressed about the latter's change of attitude, and on the following day (June 17th, 3 p.m.) Lloyd George showed the President and Clemenceau a copy of a memorandum by Henry Wilson describing his talk with Pétain. Afterwards Foch's memorandum, which was a short military appreciation on the lines of his previous statement, was read aloud and discussed. The Council then passed to other business.

On Thursday (June 19th) Lloyd George paid a long desired visit to the battlefields of the southern Champagne front (not to mention a champagne factory *en route*) and to Verdun, on which he was accompanied by his daughter Megan, Riddell, Lady Hankey and myself among others. It was a notable trip, much publicized in the British press but extremely exhausting owing to our great speed on war-worn roads, lavish hospitality, and, in the Prime Minister's case, many improvised speeches. The weather was very hot, and after a long tramp over the Verdun battlefields, Lloyd George caught a chill and returned by train from Châlons on the Thursday evening, and was laid up until Sunday evening (June 22nd). My wife and I arrived in Paris much later, having returned by motor.

The sequel to the meeting with Foch on June 16th–17th was a final discussion on Friday (June 20th), at 5 p.m.—a kind of council of war—at which Foch, Pétain, Weygand, Henry Wilson, Sir William Robertson (now C. in C. of the British Armies on the Rhine), Bliss and Cavallero were called on to express their views, and gave general support from their respective standpoints to the commander-in-chief of the Allied Army. On this occasion, Balfour represented Lloyd George, who as a result of his chill was still indisposed.

The result was that Foch stuck to his plan, and the Council of Four accepted it, including certain arrangements for securing cooperation from Poland and Czechoslovakia at the appropriate moment and—most important of all—Foch was authorized to commence his advance immediately on the expiration of the Armistice. Corresponding instructions were approved for the naval authorities. These prudent precautions gave some relief to those who were aware of them, but the last thing anyone wished was the end of the Armistice and the reopening of hostilities; and the long delay of the Germans to answer whether they would sign the Treaty of Peace continued to cause anxiety.

It was only at 7 p.m. on Sunday (June 22nd) that a rift appeared in the sky. The Council of Three was immediately summoned and met at Lloyd George's residence at 7.15 p.m. where they found the British Prime Minister 'seedy, with a bad cold'. Three notes had been brought up to the meeting by Colonel Henri, the French liaison officer. They were all in German, a language with which none of the three Heads of Delegations was familiar, but Henri and the French interpreter, Mantoux, read a rough translation of the third note (no. 70) which, after beginning with a long, powerfully reasoned protest against the Treaty, ended with the following declaration:

The Government of the German Republic accordingly gives the declaration of its consent, as required by the Note of June 16, 1919, in the following form: 'The Government of the German Republic is ready to sign the Treaty of Peace without, however, recognizing thereby that the German people was the author of the War, and without undertaking any responsibility for delivering persons in accordance with Articles 227 to 250 of the Treaty of Peace.'

The Council of Three at once fastened on that passage, and all agreed that an immediate answer should be sent refusing any alteration in the Treaty. President Wilson there and then drafted the text of a short reply to this effect.

Another item of news that came on that momentous day was the sinking by the Germans of the German ships in the Orkneys, which was not only a technical breach of the Armistice, but was agreed to be unquestionably a breach of faith for which the German Government must now be held responsible. I was instructed to ask Balfour to take the matter up at once, and a meeting was fixed for 9 p.m.

M

Mantoux records that at the end of the meeting (after I had left to warn Sonnino and Makino of the 9 o'clock meeting) Lloyd George reopened the question of Foch's plans to meet the case of a German refusal to sign the Treaty. He was still anxious about the possible stalemate on the river Weser. On the previous day he had seen Winston Churchill (now Secretary of State for War and Air) who had told him that he could muster three additional divisions in case of need within a fortnight. Possibly President Wilson could do something also—which the President did not refuse to consider with General Pershing. No decision was taken, however, on Lloyd George's proposal. In spite of my preoccupation with the 9 o'clock meeting, my diary records that 'Adeline[1] and I had a hasty meal, between the meetings, with the Prime Minister, Churchill and Henry Wilson'.

The 9 p.m. meeting was commendably brief. Sonnino and Makino, after reading the German document and the draft reply, at once accepted the draft. Clemenceau then signed it and the letter was despatched by the hand of Colonel Henri to Versailles. It was decided also to publish it in the newspapers of the following day, Monday (June 23rd). Here is the text:

The Allied and Associated Powers have considered the Note of the German Delegation of even date and in view of the shortness of the time available feel it their duty to reply at once. Of the time within which the German Government must make their final decision on the signing of the Treaty less than twenty-four hours remain. The Allied and Associated Governments have given their fullest consideration to all of the representations hitherto made by the German Government with regard to the Treaty, have replied with complete frankness and have made such concessions as they thought it just to make; and the present Note of the German Delegation presents no considerations not already examined. The Allied and Associated Powers therefore feel constrained to say that the time for discussion is past. They can accept . . . no qualification or reservation and must require of the German representatives an unequivocal decision as to their purpose to sign and accept as a whole or not to sign and accept the Treaty as finally formulated. After the signature the Allied and Associated Powers must hold Germany responsible for the execution of every stipulation of the Treaty.[2]

After that no more work was done that night, as Balfour was not quite ready with his draft letter to the Germans on the sinking of the

[1] My wife.
[2] The Foreign Relations of the United States: The Paris Peace Conference 1919, vol. vi, p. 612.

German ships in the Orkneys, and had sent it to Hurst on a point of law. Consideration of this and other questions, including the other two communications from the German Delegation, which had only arrived two hours before, was left for the morning.

When I studied these outstanding documents later, they cleared up several points which had puzzled me, for example, who was Herr von Haniel who had signed all three notes? Up to now the German Delegation's communications had been signed by Brockdorff-Rantzau—what had happened to him? That was explained by the first of Haniel's communications which covered two telegrams (both dated June 21st), which he had received from the President of the German Republic, Herr Ebert, informing him that, in alteration of the full powers of April 27th, he was now empowered 'to hand in the answer to the note of the President of the Peace Conference of the 16th instant, to afford explanations, to receive counter-explanations and to conduct negotiations'.[1] In a sentence, he had relieved Brockdorff-Rantzau, who now disappears from our story.

The third communication from Haniel (No. 67) stated that he had been instructed by 'the President of the Reich Ministry' (Herr Bauer) to inform the Allied and Assocated Powers that the previous Cabinet had resigned and to send a list of the (eleven) members of the new Cabinet, which was to appear on June 22nd before the National Assembly in order to demand of it the vote of confidence prescribed by the Constitution.

After dictating my minutes and giving instructions on the office preparations for the next day's business, I went to bed that Sunday night, exhausted but happy. But within a few hours my complacency was shaken by a loud knock on the door in circumstances which can best be described by an extract from my diary, written a few days later:

At 6.30 a.m. (Monday, June 23rd) I was awoken by the Secretary-General with a fresh note from the Germans, again trying to gain time. I put on my uniform over my pyjamas, and went to Lloyd George's flat, but could not wake anyone up. I crossed the road to President Wilson's house, had him awakened and Dutasta and Arnavon (Dutasta's admirable private-secretary) and I went in. He was in his dressing gown, very sleepy, and as it was cold, took us into his bathroom. While waiting, I had drafted a reply—a categorical refusal. The President would not assent very readily, but said he would accept it if Lloyd George pressed the matter. So back

[1] The written full powers were on their way.

we went, and after much hammering Lloyd George's valet Newnham opened the door in his pyjamas. I found Ll. G. reading a novel by a reading lamp, and very sleepy. He agreed with me that we had better have a meeting at 9 a.m. So off I went to organize it, and then back to breakfast alone with Lloyd George.

My draft reply had been based on the mood of the night before, and in view of the fact that only twelve hours were left before the expiration of the armistice, no other answer seemed to me possible. At the 9 o'clock meeting the pros and cons were carefully weighed. As President Wilson put it, if he was dealing with honourable men he could give, not forty-eight hours as asked for, but twenty-four hours. However, he shared to the full Lloyd George's suspicions, which had been strengthened by the sinking of the German ships at Scapa Flow. The President also pointed out that Haniel had been given authority to hand over the German Government's note to the Allies, to afford explanations, to receive counter-explanations, and to conduct negotiations, but he had no power to sign, although the German Government had been formed to sign the Treaty. Makino added to this that the German National Assembly had passed a vote of confidence in the new Ministry by 256 votes to 89, with 68 abstentions and had made no reserves. Lloyd George reported that Balfour was in favour of refusal, and what influenced him was that the Germans could not be trusted. On the whole it was thought better not to complicate the reply by any reference to the Scapa Flow incident, which could better be dealt with separately. Lloyd George added a word in favour of politeness in the reply. My draft was then discussed and superseded by a letter to Haniel:

The Allied and Associated Governments beg to acknowledge the receipt of your communication of June 23rd. After full consideration of your request they regret that it is not possible to extend the time already granted to your Excellency to make known your decision relative to the signature of the Treaty without any reservation.

The letter was signed by Clemenceau and dispatched at once to Versailles by the hand of Colonel Henri.

After a short adjournment the Council (now a Council of Five) met again to consider first the action to be taken on the sinking of the German ships, which was found to involve important questions of international jurisprudence which had to be referred to lawyers and experts; after which a variety of outstanding points had to be considered all the morning, and much of the afternoon, in an atmosphere of considerable tension. They returned to the Scapa Flow incident at 5 p.m. and, while they were discussing a long and learned report from the legal advisers, Dutasta, followed by Colonel Henri and Captain Portier, burst into the room with a note from the German Delegation signed by Haniel expressing willingness on behalf of the German Republic to sign under compulsion a dishonourable peace. The terms of the undertaking were not very gracious, as indicated by the last sentence:

Yielding to overwhelming force, but without on that account abandoning its view in regard to the unheard-of injustice of the conditions of peace, the Government of the German Republic therefore declare that it is ready to accept and sign the conditions of peace imposed by the Allied and Associated Powers.

The Minutes close with these words—'ORDERS WERE GIVEN FOR GUNS TO BE FIRED'. No further discussion took place.

That must have been at about 5.30 p.m., only an hour and a half before the expiration of the Armistice, and my diary adds that:

we had to hurry up to stop Marshal Foch and our Admiralty from carrying out the plans. There was no more work that afternoon. Clemenceau had been pacing the room like a Tiger, but there was universal joy at the great news. But I had to go off and work as usual, though I got my dinner at a reasonable hour.

CHAPTER XXI

THE SIGNING

'Something attempted, something done.'
(LONGFELLOW, *The Village Blacksmith*.)

I SUPPOSE most of my readers will imagine that with the acceptance of the German Government to sign the Treaty the work of the Council of Four was done; that nothing remained but to fix the date and announce the procedure for the final ceremony of signature amid the roar of guns, the blare of brass bands and bugles, and processions of troops of all the Allies through streets lined with French soldiers, culminating in an orgy of oratory by the famous leaders of the many nations that had taken part in the Conference headed by the members of the Supreme Council. It may be that, for a few minutes, such thoughts lingered in my own mind. If so, when I opened my 'black box' to study and bring up to date the list of questions still awaiting settlement, I had no more illusions, and, if a trace of them had survived, it would have vanished when the Big Four got down to the job.

As no news had yet been received about who would sign the Treaty for Germany or how soon they would be available, the Council settled down in a businesslike mood to tackle urgent outstanding details. After a Belgian claim for priority reparation, came the urgent question of the sinking of the German ships at Scapa Flow, on offence which had now been aggravated by the burning in Berlin of French flags which, under the Peace Treaty, were to have been restored, and a report of German fomentation of insurrection in Silesia, which, indeed, Haniel had warned us would happen when the Polish clauses became known. The second of these questions was disposed of on the evening of Wednesday (June 25th), when a letter based on a legal report by the Drafting Committee was signed by Balfour and Loucheur, denouncing the sinking as a breach of the Armistice and warning the Germans that, when the investigation of this and other acts mentioned above had been completed, 'the necessary reparation would be extorted'.

Meanwhile, at the end of the morning meeting, it had been reported to the Council that great hilarity had been caused in the German Delegation by a rumour that Germans of minor importance were to be sent to sign the Treaty—as had happened in the case of the Armistice—and there and then Dutasta was sent off to the German Delegation to make an immediate enquiry who the delegates would be. At the afternoon meeting (4 p.m. on the 25th) Dutasta reported that Haniel had telegraphed twice to Berlin asking who the German representatives would be, without getting an answer. But the German Government had removed from Weimar to Berlin that day, and their first Cabinet Council would be held in Berlin next day, when an answer might be expected. According to Haniel, the German Government was encountering great difficulty in finding anyone willing to sign the Treaty. Dutasta was told to proceed to Versailles next morning at 9 a.m. and the Council passed to a lot of urgent business including a discussion on the date of ratifying the Treaty, during which Wilson and Lloyd George announced their intention to return home immediately after the signature and to send the Treaty, the former to Congress, the latter to Parliament. Clemenceau also intended to hand the Treaty to his Parliament as soon as possible, and there was a tendency to time the British and French speeches to follow close on the President's.

A little later, after an exchange of information about food shortage in Germany, a decision was taken that the blockade should cease on the same date as the ratification of the Treaty, as provided for in it. On the next morning (June 27th) I reported that the Supreme Blockade Council had been informed, but it was decided not to inform the German delegates until after the signature of the Peace Treaty.

Then, on Lloyd George's suggestion, it was decided in principle to set up a special committee to consider the working out of the various measures for putting the German Treaty into effect. The membership was to be decided on the following day. The arrangements for ensuring the food supply, etc., of the Baltic Provinces on the evacuation of the Germans was also taken up, and the proposals of the Commission on Baltic Affairs were approved and sent to Foch to demand German co-operation in railway transport and other aspects, including financial assistance. Next, a note to the German Delegation submitted by Lloyd George protesting against German intrigues on the eastern frontier was approved, with slight amendments, signed by Clemenceau and dispatched. It was also decided to publish it.

Lloyd George then reported a disastrous defeat by the Bolshevists of Kolchak's thrust directed at Moscow, but better news was reported from Denikin in the south, where the Don Cossacks also had risen. He also mentioned a proposal he had received from Winston Churchill for co-operation of the Czechoslovak troops in Siberia with the right wing of Kolchak's army, which was referred as a matter of extreme urgency to the military representatives of the Supreme War Council, a Japanese and a Czechoslovak military representative being added *ad hoc*.

After that a Chinese threat to sign the Treaty only with reservations about Shantung was brought up. This led to a dispute about whether a signature with reservations was legitimate, during which Makino said that Japan, although critical about some parts of the Treaty, had decided to sign without reservations. It was then decided that Pichon should there and then be asked to take the matter up with the Chinese. The message was telephoned at once by Captain Portier.[1]

Presently, President Wilson raised the question of a demand on Holland for the surrender of the Kaiser, and it was decided to ask Lansing, as chairman of the Commission on Responsibilities, to draft a despatch to the Dutch Government. The draft was approved in an amended form on the same afternoon, and dispatched by telegram on June 27th.

Then an important decision was taken to authorize the Polish Government to pursue their operations in Galicia up to the river Zbruch, but without affecting the decision to be taken by the Supreme Council about the political status of Galicia.

The Council then returned to the Turkish question; an Ottoman delegation was still in Paris asking to be heard again (it had already been heard on May 17th). On Lloyd George's suggestion a full discussion with a Turkish delegation with a view to 'a short, sharp peace' with Turkey was agreed to, somewhat reluctantly, by his colleagues.

It was only on the morning of Thursday (June 26th) that the full Council, including Sonnino and Makino, learned from the Secretary-General, Dutasta, that the Germans had nominated two plenipotentiaries, Herr Müller (the new Minister of Foreign Affairs) and Herr Giesberts (the new Postmaster-General), of whom only the former and a Dr Bell actually signed. They had arranged to arrive on

---

[1] From June 24th onwards Captain Portier of the Versailles Secretariat frequently accompanied Clemenceau to the Council of Four and was very helpful.

Saturday morning early by the ordinary train, to which a special carriage would be attached. The first remark was by Lloyd George, who recalled that a global list of amendments (mostly advantageous to the Germans) had been sent to Haniel, and it was important that the Germans should realize that they were included; Clemenceau undertook responsibility for this. *Only then, at about 11.30 on June 26th, was the decision taken without discussion that the signature of the Treaty of Peace should take place on Saturday, June 28th at 3 p.m.*

Next it was arranged that the exchange of credentials should take place at 10 a.m. on the same date, and that the *seals of the signatories of the Allied and Associated Powers should be affixed to the Treaty of Peace at the office of the Quai d'Orsay on Friday, June 27th, at 2 p.m., and that the secretaries of the various delegations were to bring the seals at that hour.* The seals of the German delegations should be affixed on Saturday morning at the ceremony of verifying credentials. At the mention of the word 'seals' I shuddered. It was my first official association with the signature of a great international treaty. Several questions sprang to my mind at once: 'How many of the British signatories have seals?' 'What about the Dominions?' Was I, at long last, to be caught napping? Did my 'black box' and my list of outstanding questions contain nothing on the subject? Not a word! My office had to be informed at once, to pass the 'glad' news to all concerned immediately. Clement Jones tackled it with his usual efficiency. According to Riddell, Lloyd George himself had no seal but got one made with 'D.Ll.G.' on it. A few possessed seals and had brought them to Paris; others possessed them but had not brought them—but there were telephones and an aeroplane service. A few, especially from the Dominions, were stymied at first but great ingenuity was brought to bear. The Paris curio shops were scoured, and in at least one case a metal brass uniform button of a Dominion soldier was mounted on a holder and used on the Treaty. My reputation was saved! That evening I had the honour of being a guest at a magnificent banquet at the Elysée given by the President of the French Republic, M. Poincaré. I was overwhelmed with congratulations on my work at the Conference.

The penultimate day, June 27th, differed in no respect from the previous days, and long hours were spent, mostly on dreary subjects requiring completion or correction. Only a few call for mention. Among these was a last-moment attempt by the popular Polish

Prime Minister, Paderewski, to obtain modifications in the treaty between Poland and the Principal Allied and Associated Powers, which had to be signed on the same day as the Treaty with Germany. But it was now too late for alterations, and in one matter Paderewski was reminded that he could have recourse to the League of Nations as soon as it was established. Paderewski took the adverse decisions very well, and was rewarded by a promise that the Principal Allied and Associated Powers would do their best to complete the very deficient equipment of the Polish military forces—a question which was referred for urgent consideration to the military representatives of the Supreme War Council.

Towards the end of that meeting the Council discussed its future work after the departure, immediately following the signature, of Lloyd George and Wilson, and the important decision was made that the Council of Ten should take charge, the Prime Minister being replaced by Balfour and the President by Lansing or House. Another important decision was that consideration of the Treaty of Peace with Turkey should be suspended until the United States Government had decided whether they could accept a mandate for a partition of the territory of the former Turkish Empire (Constantinople and Armenia had both been hinted at in previous discussions). Arrangements were also made for breaking the news gently to the Turkish Delegation that was, so to speak, waiting on the doorstep. As usual, Balfour was selected for this delicate task. Yet another important decision was that the Polish Government should be authorized to utilize any of its military forces, including Haller's army in eastern Galicia. This was a sequel to the decision on the previous day to sanction the use of the Polish forces up to the river Zbruch.

At a meeting in the afternoon—still on June 27th—Wilson, Lloyd George, Clemenceau and I adjourned to another room, where we were joined by Hurst, and approval was given to a re-draft of the agreement on the guarantee to France by Great Britain and America. The original American draft had made it subject to the League of Nations, in which case a single member of the Council would have been able to interfere with its validity. The new British version was agreed to, Lloyd George giving a reminder that he could not bind the self-governing Dominions.

We come at last to the final day, June 28th, and the final act of the Paris Peace Conference, namely the signature of the German Treaty.

Nothing could be more normal than the start in Wilson's familiar study in the Place des États-Unis, except that the Big Three held an advance meeting at 10.30 a.m. to discuss their last will and testament to Tittoni, the new Italian Foreign Minister. I appeared in my best khaki uniform with sword-belt and sword smartened up by one of the faithful Royal Marines who were so useful in my office at the Villa Majestic.

After referring Balfour's draft back to him for some changes, the Big Three were joined at 11 a.m. by Sonnino and Makino. First the two treaties for assistance by the United States and Great Britain respectively to France in case of agression by Germany were signed. Next the representatives of the five Principal Allied and Associated Powers initialled the reparations clause and the financial clauses of the Austrian Treaty. Then a new proposal by Hoover for the appointment of a resident commission in Armenia with full authority from the United States, Great Britain, France and Italy was accepted, and immediately afterwards Balfour's tactful draft inviting the Turkish Delegation to leave Paris (whither they had come uninvited) was approved subject to minor alterations. Terms of reference to a new commission to draft model mandates and hear statements from several interested countries, as well as the Aborigines Societies, were at my request approved.

After that Robert Cecil was introduced and made a powerful plea for the establishment of some form of international consultation in economic matters to cover the gap between the end of the Peace Conference and of its Supreme Economic Council and the establishment of the Council of the League of Nations. The Supreme Economic Council was asked to suggest proposals to the several Governments concerned. That was followed by approval to a draft telegram to Kolchak about the Czechs, subject to the agreement of the military advisers of the Supreme War Council who were working on the subject. And finally a heroic last-moment effort was made by Crespi (the Italian chairman of the Commission on Roads, Railways and Waterways) to get a decision on the long-lived dispute about the railroads of the former Austro-Hungarian Empire, but the matter had to be adjourned at about 12.30 p.m. without a decision.

That was not a bad beginning to the day, when it was remembered that in one hour's time we had, all of us, to be assembled for the grand finale at Versailles. For my part, it was particularly difficult because they had left me a good deal of urgent business to clear up before I picked my wife up and motored as fast as possible to the Galeries des Glaces at the Château de Versailles, including arrangements for meetings which these indefatigable people had decided to hold *after* the ceremony of the signing of the Treaty. Lady Hankey and I had just time to peep in at the famous chapel before taking our seats. I had, of course, managed to obtain a good seat for her among the wives of the leading delegates, but I had to warn her that, when the ceremony was over, I should have to follow the Big Four to the foyer of the theatre of the Palace at the other end of the building where they had arranged to meet. I told her to make her way to our car after the signature, and to expect a very long wait.

Of the actual ceremony I have only a hazy recollection. By previous arrangement there were no speeches beyond a few short and dignified words by Clemenceau to explain the procedure. As usual he rose to the occasion. What could be more appropriate than the following?:

The text has been drawn up; the President has certified in writing to the identity of the text to be signed with that of the two hundred copies which were handed to the German delegates. The signatures are about to be appended; they will signify an irrevocable undertaking to observe and carry out legally and faithfully and integrally all the conditions that have been laid down. I therefore have the honour to request the German plenipotentiaries to be good enough to come and place their signatures to the Treaty which is before me.

Accordingly, after the translation of the speech into English and German, the German plenipotentiaries were the first to sign, Hermann Müller and Dr Bell, and after them the plenipotentiaries of the Allied and Associated Powers, who successively signed both the Treaty of Peace and a Protocol indicating precisely the conditions in which certain provisions of the Treaty were to be carried out. All the above, as well as the plenipotentiaries of Belgium, then signed the agreement with regard to the military occupation of the Rhine. Then the plenipotentiaries of the five Allied and Associated Powers and of Poland signed the Polish Treaty. Meanwhile, Dutasta's staff had formed a queue of the other signatories, namely the Dominions and the other nations whose belligerency was brought to an end thereby. The whole business was completed in fifty minutes, thanks to the admirable organization of Dutasta and his French and foreign associates. They had been forced to find sixty seats apiece to be put at the disposal of each of the five Principal Powers, and great numbers for other delegates, to say nothing of the horde of journalists, and it was extremely difficult to organize the ceremony in such novel and overcrowded surroundings as the Galerie des Glaces. They deserve more credit than they have ever received. Riddell, that wonderful diarist, admits that 'the signing of the Peace was a great sight' but adds that 'from a spectacular point of view very badly arranged' before he proceeds to condemn 'the unsatisfactory arrangements for the journalists'.

I fancy that most of the central figures of this story were too engrossed in their thoughts to do justice to the great ceremony at which they were assisting, for example, what they had already accomplished and what still remained to be done before peace could be brought once more to mankind. For a more detached description of the ceremony in all its aspects both spectacular and human, I commend the wonderful account by Harold Nicolson in the last seven pages of his diary with which he closes his book *Peace Making*, *1919*. While I shared at the time, and still share, the sympathy he extends to the lonely German signatories of the Treaty, I cannot say the same for the note of pessimism, which he shared with his colleague, Headlam-Morley, and which is well illustrated by the last words of his book: 'To bed, sick of life'.

It was in a spirit of optimism, then, that immediately after the ceremony, without an opportunity for a word with my wife, I seized my heavy black despatch case, which I had had to bring with me for the final meeting in the foyer of the theatre, and closed up to the Big Four. To my horror, they had already decided to go out to the terrace below 'to look at the fountains'. As I expected, a vast, though not a rowdy, crowd had assembled there, who passed round me so closely that I had the utmost difficulty in keeping up with them, impeded as I was by the huge black box and my sword, as, preceded by a solitary police officer, they toiled their way towards the far end of the Palace. Harold Nicolson who, from a window above, watched the four top hats struggling through the crowd, records that we were rescued by a platoon of troops who arrived at the double; but I, being of low stature, missed that.

On arrival at the foyer, Clemenceau first took us into the theatre and sat down in the seat he had occupied, or one just like it, in 1870, when the Germans had been the victors and France the vanquished, and told us something of his feelings at that time. This mood, however, did not last long, for at 5 p.m. the five members of the Supreme Council of the Allied and Associated Powers were assembled in the rather primitive surroundings of the foyer for their final meeting. They began with an unexpected letter from Herr von Bethmann-Hollweg, insisting that he himself, and not the Kaiser, was alone responsible on behalf of the German Government for the events that precipitated the war, since he had been Imperial Chancellor of the German Empire. He urged that it was he and not the Kaiser who ought to be called to account. I confess that I chuckled, for I had always insisted that the proposal to try the Kaiser was an outrage. The decision taken was a wise one, namely, that the Commission on Responsibilities, of which Lansing was chairman, should be asked to reply to Bethmann-Hollweg, but that a general indication should be given to the Commission of the Council's view, put forward without an opportunity for close examination of facts, namely that the Allied and Associated Powers recognized the spirit in which the offer was made but could not accept Bethmann-Hollweg's interpretation of the German constitution.

Then I reported that I was being pressed by various officials to supply copies of my notes of the meetings of the Council of the Principal Allied and Associated Powers, and asked for instructions. There was a long and very interesting discussion during which all the important points were raised. It was recalled that originally the Council of Four had begun to sit without a secretary and that the meetings had taken the form of private conversations. Then they got into difficulties through having no record of decisions taken and the reasons for them. A secretary (myself) had been called in to meet the difficulty and ensure that the decisions reached those who had to act on them. But there had been no distribution of the actual notes beyond the members of the Council and an extremely limited number of very trusted colleagues. The crucial question was raised whether copies ought to be passed on to their individual successors or to Governments succeeding them, and soon it was realized that this was indispensable to sound administration, and continuation of the work of the Peace Conference.

No formal decision was reached but the gist is clear from the following passage at the end of my notes on the subject:

President Wilson said that the net result seemed to be that each Government must take the course traditional in his own country with the clear and distinct understanding that no one should, under any circumstances, make the *procès-verbal* public.

Mr Lloyd George said that if an attack were made on the political heads, he might feel bound, in particular cases, to refer to these notes. He gave fair warning that he might have to do this unless someone protested now.

M. Clemenceau said it would not be possible to refuse extracts from the *procès-verbal* to prove particular facts.

For the future I adopted those statements as the basis of my action, and in practice I limited the circulation of the complete dossier to the successors of the Council of Four, i.e. Lansing (United States), Balfour (British Empire), Pichon (France), Sonnino (Italy; he, I understand, passed it on at once to his or Orlando's successor), and those designated by them. I also kept a copy for myself and my successor in the office of the War Cabinet, with a few spare copies for use as required. Lansing, Balfour, Pichon, Orlando and Sonnino eventually bequeathed their copies to their respective Foreign Offices, which all observed the utmost discretion until the time came, many years later—and presumably by agreement—for the American publication in 1948, long after my own retirement from official life.

Long before that, however, the first serious leakage, so far as my information goes, was in the United States. During the Washington Conference on Naval Armaments 1921–22, where, strange to say, I was filling a rôle almost identical with that at Paris, I was astounded to find in my newspaper, day after day, extracts from a book on the Paris Peace Conference by Ray Stannard Baker, reproducing long verbatim quotations from my own notes of the Council of Four, including sometimes *photographs* of the original roneoed copy, occasionally showing corrections I had made in my own crabbed handwriting. Personal enquiry from various high authorities revealed that (as I knew at the time) the President, on leaving Paris, packed all his papers, including the minutes of the Council of Four, in a large metal strong box. There they remained until later he authorized Ray Stannard Baker, his director of the Press Bureau at the time of the Peace Conference (occupying a position rather similar to that of Lord Riddell), to write an account of his work at the Conference, and he had handed over his strong box with keys, without refreshing his memory on its contents. Now it so happens that the strong box, which was sent away with the heavy luggage on the evening of June 28th did not contain my notes for the last day, including those of the meetings after the signing of the Peace Treaty, which were in my presence popped into the President's despatch case just before his departure. There is reason to believe therefore that Baker never saw the notes of these final meetings at Versailles and was not aware of the limitations on publicity. In these circumstances I think he was justified in quoting the minutes. In addition, when a few years later Lloyd George published his own memoirs of the Conference, he was unquestionably justified (particularly in view of his own statement at the time and quoted above) in making free use of the minutes.

After the discussion on the distribution of my minutes only a few questions remained for settlement. Balfour's admirable explanation to the Turkish Delegation of the reasons for the unavoidable postponement of their Treaty was approved for Clemenceau's signature. That was followed by a desultory and inconclusive discussion on responsibilities and penalties, matters which were not yet ripe for final discussion. It was also decided that a suggestion by Haniel that there might now be some conversations with German representatives on the execution of the Treaty should be referred to the new Committee on the Execution of the Treaty. The previous decision in favour of the appointment of a resident commissioner responsible for Armenia, on which I reported that difficulties had been encountered, was bequeathed to the Council of Ten, as was a joint note by the Allied Admirals on the disposal of the remaining German warships.

The meeting of the five was then adjourned, and after a short interval the Big Three, without the Italians, met to settle the terms of their last will and testament to the new Italian Government. While President Wilson was reading aloud the revised version of the Balfour note, the Three were somewhat embarrassed by the arrival of Sonnino and Makino, but Lloyd George went to the door and explained to them that the subject under consideration was declarations by France and Great Britain on the one hand, and by the United States on the other hand, to the new Italian Delegation, and they withdrew. The document was then approved by the British and French Prime Ministers with the omission of a reference to the Dodecanese which it was considered might be interpreted as a repudiation of the 1915 Treaty of London. I collected their signatures before Lloyd George left Paris, but Wilson, who was not bound by the Treaty, decided to reshape it in his version. Thus, the Italian claims, which had so terribly dogged the work of the Council of Four through the Conference, remained unsettled at their final meeting.

To quote my diary:

June 28th: The final parting then came. It was unceremonious. They all spoke the kindest words to me. President Wilson told me that I had completely won his confidence. Clemenceau also said something nice. Later in the evening I had to give President Wilson (who was leaving for America that night) the final corrected minutes of the Council of Four, which I had had bound and beautifully indexed. He also gave me a signed photograph with the following manuscript inscription: 'Sir Maurice Hankey who so abundantly earned the confidence, admiration and affectionate regard of his friend, Woodrow Wilson.' Shortly after, a beautiful basket of flowers arrived for Adeline from him. And that was the last I saw of him in Paris. While all Paris was rejoicing I and my office were working at minutes until 10 p.m. The dining room was being cleared for a dance, and Adeline and Sylvester and I had a dismal meal in a corner of an empty coffee room! That was our joy night.

Next day, however, my diary strikes a more cheerful note:

This morning I saw the Prime Minister off (to London). . . . I have had many congratulations and some presents—a signed photo from Clemenceau, some beautiful birds of paradise feathers for Adeline from Makino, a lovely bouquet for Adeline from the Secretary-General, and some Japanese candies from Saburi, the Japanese Secretary, one of the salt of the earth. . . .

This is only the roughest summary and outline of the most memorable episode of my life, for had I not been the Secretary of the Cabinet of the World?

N

EPILOGUE

PRESIDENT WILSON left Paris on June 28th, on the evening of the signature of the German Treaty. I saw Lloyd George off next morning. Balfour was left in charge of the British Delegation and as our chief representative on the Council of Ten, whose first function was to clear up and complete the Austrian, and as soon as possible, the Hungarian and Bulgarian Treaties. I myself stayed behind for a few days to wind up my responsibilities to the Council of Four, to give what help I could to Balfour in taking over his new duties as chief British delegate, to reorganize my office and to reduce personnel, if possible, following the completion of the German Treaty. But I was under orders to curtail my stay as much as possible, as the Prime Minister 'insisted on my coming home to help him in tackling the problems of national reconstruction'. I was not sorry to miss the Prime Minister's homecoming, the ovations, the huge crowds and the many public ceremonies, which never had much attraction for me.

During those days I found time to write in my neglected diary, which now swelled temporarily to the size of a journal, a fairly full survey of the Peace Conference as a whole, on which I have drawn in this story, and I pondered much over those tempestuous events in which I had been privileged to play a responsible, but deliberately inconspicuous, part. Those diary notes and a few shorter ones, and snatches of correspondence with my family, have been invaluable in refreshing my memory, but as already mentioned, my own minutes, as published by the United States Government, supplemented occasionally by Mantoux's notes published many years later by the French Government, have provided my main sources.

To draw up a political balance sheet of the gains and losses resulting from the Paris Conference is no easy task. On a long view, among the disappointing features must be put first the comparative failure of the League of Nations. Its positive achievements were few. The long years devoted to disarmament produced next to nothing except bitter controversy and were perhaps one factor in enabling Hitler to re-arm, and to secure the support of Fascist Italy and Japan. It was during the earlier stages of the disarmament controversy also that Germany started to re-arm under the noses of the Allied Commissions of Control set up under Section IV (Inter Allied Commission of Control) of Part V, Military and Air Clauses of the Treaty. The failure of the

reparations plans, included in the treaty, also caused great disappointment in many quarters, and provided a running sore to the political
well-being of Europe and brought France and Germany to the verge
of war during the French occupation of the Ruhr in 1924. To quote
H. A. L. Fisher: 'The occupation of the Ruhr, against which every
British party protested, was one of those extreme historical misfortunes
which, when suffering has reached an intolerable point, supply their
own correction'.

The section of the Treaty entitled 'Penalties' (Part VII) was also
one of the worst items on the debit side of the Treaty, especially when
the Government of the Netherlands, wisely as I thought at the time,
after remaining neutral all through the war, *refused to admit* (January 23,
1920) the claim of the Allied and Associated Powers that 'it was an
international duty to associate itself with the act of high international
policy of the Allied Powers'. The latter never recovered from this
well-deserved snub, and the whole of the penalties clauses had almost
negligible results. To that list can be added the shaky character of the
eastern frontiers of Germany, which, however, is accounted for by
the chaos in Russia during the whole period of treaty-making.

In mitigation of that formidable list of failures, the following
adverse factors, which no one could have been expected to foresee,
must be taken into acount.

First, there was the failure of the American people to ratify the
signature of their former President. Among the disastrous results which
followed that astonishing event was their refusal to take part in the
League of Nations, the Covenant of which had to a considerable
extent been forced down the throats of many delegates. Throughout
its existence the absence of the United States exercised a paralysing
influence on the League's prestige and influence which was not
compensated by American participation later in discussions on
disarmament.

The second point in mitigation of the failure of the Treaty of
Versailles was the chaos that prevailed in Russia throughout the
whole of the Conference up to the signature of the Treaty of Versailles,
and the uncertainty this created about the possible spread of the con-
tagion westward and eastward.

A third point where mitigation is to be found is the violent contrast
between the principles on which the United States entered the war,
typified by Wilson's 'fourteen points', as accepted by the Allies, and
the commitments of the latter under their own treaties, of which the

Anglo-Franco-Russo-Italian Treaty of April 1915 was the outstanding example. The difficulties this caused are well illustrated by the clash in the Council of Four which led to the disappearance of the amiable Orlando from the international scene. Something of the same kind threatened over the Japanese claims, and was only avoided by the reasonable attitude of both parties, but much of the ground had to be gone over again two years later at the Washington Naval Conference of 1921–22.

A fourth point of mitigation is to be found in the unavoidable pre-occupation over the 'side shows'. The Italian intervention without warning in Anatolia and the clashing ambitions of Venizelos in the Smyrna area were too dangerous to be ignored, and time and energy had to be found for them. The same applies to numerous big ideas of French generals, sometimes with support from Foch, for using Roumanian forces—with or without support from French forces—withdrawn from south Russia or in the Banat area, to combine with Polish forces to drive the Ukrainians out of the Lemberg region, and generally to oppose by force the spread of Bolshevism. The adventures of Haller's army alone took up a lot of time, as did some of the big ideas for combining and supporting with supplies and other aid from Archangel the armies of Denikin in south Russia and those of Kolchak in Siberia. All that was very interesting, but diverted time and energy from the main task of completing the German and Austrian Treaties.

So far we have discussed at some length the disappointments of the Paris settlement and the various points in mitigation, and we must now turn to the positive advantages to set against the admitted weaknesses of this great international effort.

The first advantage was that it brought the war to an end, which after all is the first object of a peace treaty.

The second was that it was followed rapidly by the demobilization of the various armies, and the disappearance of the long-sustained tension and strain in the countries of all the belligerents and some of the neutrals.

The third was that the Paris Conference set going the machinery for bringing relief to many starving populations scattered over Europe, and for starting up the economic life of the former belligerent and neutral countries. That was aided by the work of the Commission on Ports, Waterways and Railways, which was being carried into the Austrian, Hungarian and Bulgarian Treaties at the time of the signature of the Treaty of Versailles.

Fourth, the International Labour Office was destined to do a great work within an important sphere.

And, finally, the Conference had built up a machinery for later international conferences, and especially for the Supreme Control, which was destined to produce, very shortly after, treaties drawn up on the same pattern with Austria, Bulgaria and Hungary, and three years later with Turkey. These things redress, I think, some of the gloomier aspects of the Treaty of Peace.

My personal career was affected considerably by my work at the Paris Peace Conference. It left me a legacy of a long sequence of international conferences. They took me from London to places as far distant as Washington, San Remo and Genoa, as well as often to Paris, to The Hague more than once and at last to Lausanne where, mercifully, Ramsay MacDonald succeeded in bringing to an end the interminable subject of reparations by Germany, which had threatened the peace of Europe for years, especially during the occupation of the Ruhr. At all these conferences I made many friends, but never did I serve a more friendly, genial and efficient team than: Clemenceau, Lloyd George, Woodrow Wilson and Orlando.

INDEX

Abraham, Maj. Edgar, British secretary, 24, 25–6

Albi, Gen., French CGS, 69

Aldrovandi-Marescotti, Count L., Italian secretary: duties with Council of Four, 105–6, 115; his diary, 112, 119, 124–5, 148; and the author, 127–8; returns to Rome, 131

Alsace-Lorraine, 102

Amery, Leo, 15

Armenia, 186, 187, 192

Armistice Enforcement Commission, Spa, 78, 93

Arnavon, Dutasta's private secretary, 179

Asquith, H. H. (later Earl of Oxford), Prime Minister, 10, 20

Auchincloss, Gordon, 115

Australia: and German colonies, 15, 156; representation at the Conference, 34–7; and see Hughes, W. M.

Austria: treaty with, 79–80, 117–19, 137, 139–40, 158, 159–60, 187, 194; as bulwark against Bolshevism, 98; boundaries of, 125, 156–7, 165–6

Baker, Ray Stannard, 191–2

Balfour, A. J. (later Earl of): and war crime trials, 13, 114; on German colonies, 15; in London talks with President Wilson, 15, 17; 20; 39; on Prinkipo Conference, 70, 72; deputizes for Ll. George, 74–7; plan to speed up Conference, 78–80; on military terms of peace, 84–5, 91; and Japanese/Chinese claims, 132–3; at Versailles ceremony, 151; and the Foch plan, 177; 182; serves on revived Council of Ten, 186, 191, 192

Barnes, G. N., British Labour minister, 114, 151, 172

Bartholomy, Gen., 95

Baruch, Bernard, 115

Bauer, President of the Reich Ministry, 179

Belgian Congo, 62

Belgium: representation at the Conference, 33–5, 37, 38, 45, and on Council of Ten, 85; territorial claims of, 114

Bell, Dr, German delegate, 184, 188

Benes, Eduard, Czechoslovak delegate, later President, 64, 152

Berthelot, Philippe, 141

Bethmann-Hollweg, Theobald von, 190

'Big Five', precedence, 38

'Big Four', 74; and see Council of Four

'Big Three', 192

Bliss, US General Tasker, 24, 67, 90, 91, 176

Bolivia, 33, 37

Bolshevism see Russia

Borden Robert (later Sir), Prime Minister of Canada, 13; and German colonies, 15, 57–8; on good relations with US, 19; challenges Big Five leadership, 45–6; suggestion for speeding up Council proceedings, 75–6

Botha, Gen. Louis, Prime Minister of South Africa, 13; and German colonies, 15, 56–7, 59, 61–3; chairman of Polish Commission, 167; dissatisfied with the treaty, 172

Boundaries Co-ordinating Committee, 80–1, 82

Bourgeois, Léon, Special Delegate, 44–5

Bratiano, Ion I. C., Roumanian statesman, 64, 152

Brazil, 33–4, 37, 45

Brebner, Botha's private secretary, 27

Brest-Litovsk, Treaty of, 49

British Delegation, composition of, 19

British Empire Delegation: derived from Imperial War Cabinet, 26; staff, 27; rôle of, 63

Brockdorff-Rantzau, Count, German delegate, 139, 152–5, 179

Bulgaria, 79–80, 194

Burke, Edmund, quoted, 11

Caccia, Maj. Anthony, British secretary, 24, 25–6

Cambon, Jules, French diplomat, 47, 95, 136, 138–9

Canada, 34, 36–7; *and see* Borden

Carew, W. J., Newfoundland delegate, 27

Cavallero, Italian General, 67, 90–1, 176

Cecil, Lord Robert (later Viscount), 10; and League of Nations, 16, 45; on good relations with US, 19; Spa negotiations, 89; author's letter to, 104–5; chairman of Supreme Economic Council, 158, 187; criticizes Versailles Treaty, 173

Chamberlain, Sir Austen, 18, 173

Charles I, Emperor of Austria, 94

China: representation at the Conference, 33, 37; disputes Japanese claims, 60, 102, 131–3; protest at treaty terms, 146, 184

Chinda, Viscount, 131

Christie, Loring, Canadian delegate, 27

Churchill, Winston (later Sir): on American debt, 18–19; intervention regarding Prinkipo Conference, 67–72; as Secretary for War and Air, 178, 184

Clemenceau, Georges, French Prime Minister, 12, 13; inaugurates Council of Ten, 24; President of the Conference, 32, 42; answers challenge to Big Five, 46–7; on Russian representation, 52–3; on Prinkipo Conference, 52–3, 70–1; on mandates, 60; attempted assassination of, 72, 76; and the author, 74; on Anglo-American guarantee to France, 100, 102; on Dalmatian claims, 121–2; at

handing over of Versailles Treaty, 152–5; answers British criticisms of treaty, 173; at signing of treaty, 188–9

Costa Rica, 33, 37

Council of Five (Foreign Ministers), 103, 108–9; subjects dealt with, 109–10; last meeting, 174

Council of Four, 96, 103, 107–8; author becomes secretary of, 105, 111–16; informality of meetings, 110–11; discusses reparations, 113–14, and war crimes, 114; becomes the Council of the Principal Allied and Associated Powers, 169–70; leakages, 191–2

Council of Ten: christening of, 24; staff, 24, 25–6; organization, 25; as steering committee to Preliminary Peace Conference, 29; publicity, 38; precedence, 38; order of Conference agenda, 39; replaced by Council of Four, 96, 103, 108; leakages to French press, 99, 102–3; takes over after signature of treaty, 186; agenda for, 194

Council of the Principal Allied and Associated Powers, 170; publication of *procès-verbal*, 190–1

Council of Three, 128, 169

Cowans, Lieut.-Gen. Sir John, 10

Crespi, Chairman of Commission on Roads, etc., 140, 187

Croatia, 83, 122

Crowe, Sir Eyre, 81

Cuba, 33, 37

Cunliffe, Lord, Governor of Bank of England, 18n, 170

Curzon of Kedleston, Marquess, 10, 13, 18, 20

Czechoslovakia: representation at Conference, 33–4, 37; and Poland, 64, 96; military forces, 157; supplies for, 158

Dalmatia, 120–2, 126–9; plebiscite suggested, 165–6

Danzig, 102

Davies, J. T., 129

Davis, Norman, 115

Degoutte, Gen., 87, 90–1

Demobilization, 158, 175

Denikin, Gen., anti-Bolshevist leader, 49, 167, 184

Derby, Earl of, Ambassador to Paris, 28

De Wiart, Gen. Carton, 95

Disarmament, 98, 194

Dmowski, Roman, President of Polish National Committee, 44, 64, 99

Doherty, C. J., Canadian Minister of Justice, 44

Dominions; rôle at Conference, 13, 15; representation at Conference, 19, 33–7; on mandates issue, 63; *and see* British Empire Delegation; German colonies; War Cabinet, Imperial; and individual entries for each Dominion

Dutasta, Secretary-General to the Conference, 24, 42, 179, 181, 183, 184, 188

Duval, French General, 90

Ebert, Friedrich, President of German Republic, 179

Ecuador, 33, 37

Esher, Viscount, 10

Feisal, Emir, 64

Fisher, H. A. L.: quoted, 49, 163, 195; criticizes Versailles Treaty, 173

Fiume, 120–3, 126–30, 164–6

Foch, Marshal Ferdinand, 13, 23–4; on intervention in Russia, 73; suggests relief of Lemberg, 73; report on military etc. terms to Germany, 77, 84–5, 87–90, 135–6; redrafts this, 91–3; Polish proposals, 94–5; on Anglo-American guarantee to France, 100, 102; attacks Franco-German frontier proposals, 146–7; at Ver-

sailles ceremony, 152, 155; plan for action if Germany rejects treaty, 158, 175–8

Fontainebleau Conference, 98–102

Foster, Sir G. E., Canadian Minister of Finance, 18n

Fourteen Points, President Wilson's, 17, 40, 124, 195

France: representation at Conference, 33–4, 37; Anglo-American military guarantee to, 100, 102, 144–5, 173, 186–7; restitution of frontiers, 102; *and see* Alsace-Lorraine; Clemenceau; Foch; London, Treaty of; Rhineland; Saar

Frazier, A. H., us secretary, 24, 26

Freedom of the Seas, 16

Galicia, 184, 186

Garran, Sir Robert, Australian Solicitor-General, 27

George V, King, 10, 20

German colonies, 15, 17; Council of Ten discusses, 55–63; Article 22 of Peace Treaty, 65–6; distribution of mandates, 156; *and see* League of Nations mandates

Germany: military etc. terms of peace, 16, 84–5, 87–93, 135–6; capacity to resume war, 64, 158, 175–8; lifting of blockade of, 87, 158, 183; surrender of ships, 87, 136; as bulwark against Bolshevism, 97–8; membership of the League, 98; boundaries, 102, 195; attitude to peace terms, 154–5; scuttling of fleet, 177, 180–1, 182; Cabinet resigns, 179–80; Government moves to Berlin, 183; *and see* Rhineland; Versailles Treaty

Gibbs, Herbert (of Antony Gibbs & Son), 18n

Giesberts, German P.M.G., 184

Gompers, Samuel, us Labour leader, 115

Gout, Jean, 133

Grant, Col., us secretary, 26

Great Britain: representation at Con-
ference, 33, 37; *and see* Balfour;
Lloyd George; Wilson, Sir Henry
Greece: representation at Conference,
33-4, 37; *and see* Venizelos
Guatemala, 33, 37

Haiti, 33, 37
Haller's Polish army, 73, 80, 83, 95,
115, 167, 186
Haniel, von, German plenipotentiary,
179-81, 182, 183, 192
Hankey, Adeline, Lady, 9, 74, 188, 193
Hardinge of Penshurst, Viscount: heads
British Delegation, 11, 22; appointed
'Organizing Ambassador', 27-8, 29,
78, 138
Harrison, US secretary, 26
Headlam-Morley, 136, 141, 189
Hedjaz, 37, 64, 151
Heligoland, 137
Henri, Col., French liaison officer, 177,
178, 180-1
Hewins, W. A. S., 18n
Holland: asked to hand over Kaiser,
13, 116, 184, 195; to facilitate passage
of Allied troops, 67, 75
Honduras, 33, 37
Hoover, Herbert, later US President,
89, 187
Hope, Admiral: Spa negotiations, 89;
and Greek crisis, 162
House, Col. Edward M., 12, 69, 70, 72,
75; on Council of Ten, 186
Hughes, William M., Australian Prime
Minister: on German colonies, 15,
18, 56, 59, 60-2; attacks President
Wilson's views, 18; chairman of
Reparations Committee, 18n; on the
League, 45
Hungary: treaty with, 79-80, 137-8,
139-40, 158, 194; Bela Kun Govern-
ment, 139n, 167; boundaries of,
156-7; lifting of blockade of, 158
Hurst, Cecil, 103-4, 135, 140, 179, 186
Hymans, Paul, 45

Ijuin, H., 81
Imperiali, Marquis, Italian Ambassador
to London, 141-3
Indemnities, *see* Reparations
India, 19, 34-5, 36-7
Inter-Allied Conferences, 12, 17-18
International Labour Organization, 39,
114-15, 197
Inviting Powers, 22
Ironside, Gen. (later Lord), 50
Italy: President Wilson on, 17; repre-
sentation at Conference, 33-4, 37;
Tyrol, 125; naval and military moves
in Aegean etc., 140, 149, 162, 164;
Orlando's Government falls, 166;
and see Dalmatia; Orlando; Sonnino;
London, Treaty of

Japan: claims against Germany, 17, 60,
102, 131-3, 156; representation at
Conference, 33-4, 37, and on Council of Ten, 43, 58, and Council of
Four, 169-70; 'Twenty-one Points',
132; *and see* Makino
Jones, Clement (later Sir), British
secretary, 27, 78, 185
Jones, Maggiore, Italian secretary, 24,
26
Jugoslavia, 17; relief for, 89; recognition of, 136; *and see* Dalmatia;
London, Treaty of

Kemal, Mustapha (Atatürk), 163
Kerr, Philip (later Marquess of Lothian),
20, 28, 71-2, 97, 140; at Fontainebleau
Conference, 100-1; drafts 'note of
June 16th', 173-5, 178
Kiauchau, 60, 102, 131-3
Kiel Canal, 88
Kimura, Japanese representative, 138
Kisch, C. H., of British Empire Dele-
gation, 27
Klotz, chairman of Reparations Com-
mittee, 115, 116, 140
Kolchak, Admiral, anti-Bolshevist
leader, 49, 167; defeat of, 183-4, 187
Koo, Dr Wellington, 132

Lane, Capt. E. F. C., private secretary to Smuts, 27

Lansing, Robert, US Secretary of State, 69, 75, 91; on Committee on Breaches of the Laws of War, 94; opposed to war crimes trials, 114, 116, 184; on Council of Ten, 186, 190, 191

Latham, Lieut.-Com. J. (later Chief Justice of Australia), 27

Law, A. Bonar, 14, 20, 44; at Versailles, 151

Lawrence, Col. T. E., 64

League of Nations: President Wilson on, 16; Commission for, set up, 44–5; membership, 102; secretary-generalship, author decides not to apply for, 103–5; US unlikely to join, 103–4; German objection to Covenant as basis for Peace Treaty, 168; paralysed by absence of USA, 195

League of Nations mandates: principles and features of, 58–9; Turkish territories, 61, 156; and see German colonies

Lebanon, 75

Lemburg (Lvov), 73, 83, 95, 167

Leygues, French Minister of Marine, 88

Liberia, 33, 37

Lloyd George, David (later Earl): and author, 9, 103–4, 143, 194; appoints him British Secretary to the Conference, 11, 27–8; electoral victory, 12, 20; on Kaiser's trial, 13; Buckingham Palace talks with Wilson, 15–18; organizes Council of Ten's secretariat, 25; on Dominion representation, 34–6; on Russian representation, 50–1; on intervention in Russia, 51, 53–4, 71, 73, 95; on mandates, 55, 60–1; attacks Foch proposals for German army, 87–9, and makes counter-proposals, 89–93; criticizes Foch's Polish proposals, 95; on leakages from Council of Ten, 99, 102–3; Fontainebleau Conference, 99–102; meets Commons critics, 116–17; on Italian claims, 122, 124, 125; and Austrian delegation, 160; and Greek crisis, 162; advances British criticisms of Versailles Treaty, 173; visits Verdun, 176; his memoirs, 192

London, Treaty of (1915), 120–5, 156, 163–5, 192, 196

Long, Walter (later Viscount), Colonial Secretary, 13, 18

Loraine, Sir Percy, 29

Lothian, Lord, see Kerr

Loucheur, 115, 182

Luxemburg, 114

Lvov, Prince, 50

Maclean, Ronald, 133

Makino, Baron, Japanese delegate, 43, 44, 54, 75, 131–2, 174, 178, 184

Mandated territories, see German colonies; League of Nations mandates

Mandel, Clemenceau's chef de cabinet, 152

Mantoux, Prof. Paul, interpreter, 92, 105, 107, 177; posthumously published notes, 111–12, 124–5, 194; at Versailles, 153

Massey, W. F., New Zealand Prime Minister: on German colonies, 15, 57, 59, 60–2; on representation at Conference, 36, 44

Matsui, Japanese Ambassador to Paris, 43, 75

Mezes, Dr. S E., 81

Milner, Viscount, 10, 26, 67, 69, 75

Montagu, Edwin, 84

Montenegro, 37, 86

Müller, Hermann, German Minister of Foreign Affairs, 184, 188

Newfoundland, 35–6

New Zealand: and German colonies, 15, 156; representation, 34–7

Nicaragua, 33, 37

Nicolson, Sir Harold, 189

Nogaoka, Japanese delegate, 174

Norman, H., 29, 109, 134

Noullens, French Ambassador to Russia, 52

Oliver, F. S., Editor of *Round Table*, 10
Orlando, V. E., Italian Prime Minister, 13, 43; on intervention in Russia, 53–4, 69; presses for Italian Treaty, 117–19; puts Italy's claims, 120–30; returns to Rome, 131; back in Paris, 140–3, 148; and Greek crisis, 163–5; again demands Fiume, 164–6; final departure, 166, 174
Oxford and Asquith, Earl of, *see* Asquith

Pachitch, Nicholas, Serbian Prime Minister, 75, 152
Paderewski, Ignacy, Polish Prime Minister, 44, 83, 152, 167, 186
Pago, 127–9
Panama Republic, 33, 37
Peace Conference, Paris: delay in inaugurating, 11–13, 39–41; language problem, 18, 30–1, 38, 44; author appointed British secretary to, 28; first Plenary session, 29, 42–3; nations represented at, 33–7; order of agenda, 43; commissions set up by, 43–5, 47, 77–8, 82, 83–4; Great Power leadership challenged, 43, 45–7; third Plenary, 67; criticism of slow progress, 78, 83; Balfour's plan to speed up, 78–80; results of, 194–6; *and see* Council of Ten; Versailles Treaty
Pershing, Gen. John J., 178
Peru, 33, 37
Pétain, Gen. Philippe, later Marshal of France, 176
Petlyura, Gen., anti-Bolshevist leader, 49–50, 51
Phipps, Eric, 29, 109
Pichon, French Foreign Minister, 50, 72, 75, 76, 78, 95, 184, 191
Place des États-Unis, Paris (President Wilson's house in), 20

Poincaré, Raymond, President of France, 42, 185
Poland: representation, 33–4, 37; boundaries, 80, 83, 157; and Czechoslovakia, 64, 96; Danzig corridor, 102; supplies for, 158; Galicia question, 184, 186; treaty with, 186, 188; *and see* Haller's Polish army; Paderewski
Portier, Capt., French secretary, 24, 26, 181, 184
Portugal, 33–4, 37; protests at treaty terms, 146
Powers with General or Special Interests, 45, 47
Prinkipo Conference, proposed, 52–4, 67–71
Prisoners of war, return of, 102

Rawlins, Lieut.-Col., author's superintending clerk, 22, 24, 77
Reading, Marquess of, 20
Renner, Karl, Austrian Chancellor, 160
Reparations: President Wilson on, 17; Hughes Committee on, 18n; Commission on, 82; for shipping losses, 88; Fontainebleau proposal, 102; delegation to Reparations Commission, 113–14; failure of plans for, 194–5, 197
Responsibilities (war crimes trials), 13, 39, 190; Lansing's report, 94; divided views on, 114, 116, 184; negligible results of deliberations, 195
Rhineland demilitarization, 17, 102, 147, 158, 188
Riddell, Sir George (later Lord): his diary, 107, 111, 125, 152, 155; and the press, 143, 189
Robertson, Gen. (later F.-M.) Sir William, 176
Roumania: representation, 33–5, 37; and Poland, 95; military forces, 157
Rue Nitot, Paris (Lloyd George's flat in), 20
Ruhr, occupation of, 195

Russia: support for anti-Bolshevist forces, 16, 37, 49–54, 67–73, 95, 167, 183–4, 187; problem of representation, 37, 50–1; 'Allied Council for Russian Affairs', 70–1; Germany and Austria as bulwarks against, 97–8; *and see* Tchaikowski

Saar, 17, 114, 136
Saburi, Japanese secretary, 26, 43, 133, 193
Saionji, Marquis, head of Japanese Delegation, 44
Savinkov, Russian leader, 50
Scavenius, Danish Ambassador to Petrograd, 52
Schleswig, 85, 102
Sebenico, 127–9
Secretariat-General to the Conference, 25, 30
Serbia: representation, 33–5, 37, 38; claims of, 75
Shantung Province, 131–3, 146, 184
Siam, 33, 37
Silesia, 182
Simon, François, French Colonial Minister, 60
Smith, F. E. (later Earl of Birkenhead), 13
Smuts, F.-M. Jan: and League, 16; on South West Africa, 56–7; at Fontainebleau Conference, 100
Smyrna, 140, 149, 161, 162–3
Sokolow, Zionist delegate, 81
Sonnino, Baron, Italian Foreign Minister, 17, 30, 40–1; urges reinforcement of anti-Bolshevists, 53, 69; on Prinkipo Conference, 70–1; raises Austrian question, 79–80; on war crimes, 13, 114; on Dalmatia, 121, 126–7; returns to Rome, 131; and Greek crisis, 163; replaces Orlando, 166, 178, 191
South Africa, Union of: and German colonies, 15; representation, 34, 36–7; *and see* Botha; Smuts

South West Africa, 15, 56–7, 58–9, 156
Spring-Rice, Hon. T.A., 29, 109
Stevenson, Miss (later Lady Lloyd George), 129
Suffrage Association, 96
Supreme Control: assumed by Council of Ten, 29; passes to Council of Four, 103
Supreme Economic Council, 77, 158; future of, 187
Supreme War Council, 22–4; considers Foch report, 87–91
Sykes, Sir Mark, 64
Sylvester, A. J., author's private secretary, 22

Tardieu, André, French politician, 75, 81, 100, 102, 174
Tchaikowski, head of Archangel Government, 138, 167, 170
Teschen, 64, 77, 96
Thomson, F. D., Massey's private secretary, 27
Tittoni, Italian Foreign Minister, 166, 187
Turkey: President Wilson on, 16–17; Turkish territories, 61–2; treaty preparations, 79–80, 184, 187, 192; Greek and Italian landings in Anatolia, 163–4

Ukraine: separatist movement, 49–51; and Poland, 95, 157; *and see* Lemberg
United States of America: representation, 33–4, 37; and League membership, 103–4; 195; *and see* Wilson, Woodrow
Uruguay, 33, 37

Vannutelli, Count, 81, 174
Venizelos, Eleutherios, 44, 149, 152; asked to send troops to Smyrna, 161, 162–3
Versailles Treaty: author's views on, 97–8; Fontainebleau Memorandum, 98–102; date of presentation, 117–19, 135, 139; publication of text, 117

134, 145–6; demand for plenipotentiaries from Germany, 126, 134–5; reception of German delegates, 134–5; Tardieu's summary of, 134, 146; last-minute amendments, 135 ff., 169; nations invited to ceremony, 136, 140; Credentials Committee, 136, 138–9; handling of German observations on, 137–8, 153, 158–9, 168–9, 172–4; admission of press, 143, 152; venue of ceremony, 150–1; presentation of, 150–5; plan for action if signature refused, 158, 168, 175–8; British criticisms of, 172–3; Note of June 16th, 173–5; German reply, 177, and its rejection, 178; further German note, 179–80; Germany acquiesces, 181; status of German Delegation, 182–3; arrangements for formal signature, 184 ff.; the ceremony, 188–9

Villa Majestic, Paris (author's office), 21–2, 25

War Cabinet, British, 9–10
War Cabinet, Imperial, 12, 19; secretaryship of, 22; becomes British Empire Delegation in Paris, 26; *and see* British Empire Delegation; Dominions
War crimes trials, *see* Responsibilities
Ward, Sir Joseph G., New Zealand Minister of Finance, 36, 44, 151

Washington Naval Conference (1921–2), 191, 196
Weizmann, Dr Chaim, 81
Wemyss, Admiral Sir Rosslyn, First Sea Lord, 16, 87, 90
Weygand, Gen. Maxime, 24, 91, 176
Wilhelm 11, Kaiser, proposed trial of, 13, 114, 116, 184, 190
Williams, B. T., 133
Wilson, Gen. Sir Henry, CIGS, 16, 24, 87, 89–91; on Bolshevist danger, 97–8; at Fontainebleau Conference, 100–1; on Council of Four, 111; and Greek crisis, 162; and the Foch plan, 176
Wilson, Woodrow, US President, 12, 13; Buckingham Palace conversations, 15–18; Royal Banquet to, 19–20; on Dominion representation, 34–6, and Russian representation, 52; on intervention in Russia, 68–9, 72n; on military etc. terms of peace, 92; on Anglo-American guarantee to France, 100, 102; on Italian claims, 121–4; on Japanese/Chinese claims, 131–2; at Versailles ceremony, 155; and Greek crisis, 164; on British criticisms of Peace Treaty, 173; authorizes Baker's account of Conference, 191–2; and the author, 193

Zara, 127–9
Zionism, 81

GEORGE ALLEN & UNWIN LTD
London: 40 Museum Street, W.C.1

Auckland: 24 Wyndham Street
Bombay: 15 Graham Road, Ballard Estate, Bombay 1
Buenos Aires: Escritorio 454–459, Florida 165
Calcutta: 17 Chittaranjan Avenue, Calcutta 13
Cape Town: 109 Long Street
Hong Kong: F1/12 Mirador Mansions, Kowloon
Ibadan: P.O. Box 62
Karachi: Karachi Chambers, McLeod Road
Madras: Mohan Mansions, 38c Mount Road, Madras 6
Mexico: Villalongin 32–10, Piso, Mexico 5, D.F.
Nairobi: P.O. Box 12446
New Delhi: 13–14 Asaf Ali Road, New Delhi 1
São Paulo: Avenida 9 de Julho 1138-Ap. 51
Singapore: 36c Prinsep Street, Singapore 7
Sydney, N.S.W.: Bradbury House, 55 York Street
Tokyo: 3 Kanda-Ogawamachi, 3-Chome
Toronto: 91 Wellington Street West

A YANKEE MARLBOROUGH

AN INTERPRETATION OF WINSTON CHURCHILL

R. W. THOMSON

According to B. H. Liddell Hart this is 'the most penetrating analytical study of Churchill, and also the most vividly life-like portrait, that anyone has yet produced'.

It is a book of interpretation and not biography, an endeavour to understand the man and his activities and not merely to record them. To the author Winston Churchill is an enigma which cannot be explained away simply by classifying him as a genius. The answer is to be found, he believes, in Churchill's mixed Anglo-American blood, to both branches of which his extreme 'egocentricity' is due. The book is a search for an explanation of the basic Churchill and its origins.

'By far the most discerning and penetrating study of Churchill's character that I have ever read. . . .'   LORD BOOTHBY

'Immensely readable, tingling with excitement.'–*The Listener*

'I found "The Yankee Marlborough" fascinating reading. The writing is very good. The psychological penetration almost uncanny. . . . As an admirer of the wartime leader, who understands Winston's little ways and faults, I thoroughly enjoyed Mr. R. W. Thompson's book and thought it pretty true to life. Well worth reading.'   LORD MORRISON

Demy 8vo.   35s. net

ECONOMIC PLANNING IN FRANCE

J. W. and A. M. HACKETT

This may claim to be the first full study in English of French planning as it is now and of the way it has developed. It appears at a time when the United Kingdom is beginning a similar experiment.

The book describes the entire administrative machinery of planning but the authors are selective and critical. They have excluded inessentials and are aware that actual decisions may not be made by the man formally responsible for them. Their intimate and accurate knowledge enables them to concentrate on the vital issues.

A final section summarizes the great position of the 4th Plan and the problems associated with drafting the 5th Plan—for example economic democracy, a policy for incomes and relations with the Common Market.

John Hackett is an economist working with the Organization for Economic Co-operation and Development in Paris and his wife is Conseiller Référendaire at the French Cour des Comptes.

Demy 8vo.   424 *pages.*   40s. net

GEORGE ALLEN & UNWIN LTD